The Climate General

Other titles available from Éditions La Butineuse:

Land and Climate. Insights from the IPCC Special report, Patrick Love

Energy chronicles. Keys to understanding the importance of energy, Greg de Temmerman

Feeding the Earth. A Manifesto for Regenerative Agriculture, Daniel Baertschi

Hydrate the Earth. The forgotten role of water in the climate crisis, Ananda Fitzsimmons

Farmers have the Earth in Their Hands, Paul Luu, with Marie-Christine Bidault

Revised and updated edition of:

Klimaatgeneraal. Bouwen aan weerbaarheid

© Uitgeverij Podium, Amsterdam, February 2022

Cover and interior design: © Agence Coam

ISBN : 978-2-493291-55-4

© 2023 Éditions La Butineuse
Atelier des Entreprises
Place de l'Europe – Porte Océane 3
56400 Auray – France
www.editions-labutineuse.com/en

Tom Middendorp
with Antonie van Campen

The Climate General

Stepping up the fight

Translated from Dutch by Kate Walsarie Wolff

Foreword by Ban Ki-moon and Feike Sijbesma

ÉDITIONS la Butineuse

Table of contents

Part Two – From words to actions

For my children, Joris and Renee.

For their generation.

And all the generations that follow.

Foreword

At a time when the consequences of climate change are manifesting more pronouncedly around the globe, and as the intricate interplay between environmental changes and the lives of many vulnerable people and so the global security becomes clearer, this book emerges as an important publication and asks attention for one of most complicated topics of our time. *The Climate General* presents a well thought through analysis of how climate-driven crises impact people and so endanger global safety, and provides a comprehensive exploration into the complex relationship between our changing climate, the need for adaptation and even the multifaceted realm of global security.

What sets this work apart is Middendorp's background as the former Chief of Defence of the Dutch Armed Forces. His blend of hands-on military experience, coupled with an understanding of geopolitical dynamics, affords readers a holistic approach. Middendorp also outlines a path filled with hope and feasible solutions. He doesn't just warn us, he indicates the direction of solutions as well. He demonstrates the power of technological advancements, stresses the importance of well-considered strategies, and highlights the vital role of collaboration in addressing climate security challenges. A combination of mitigation, meaning prevention and adaptation, meaning resilience against climate change, is needed.

Thus, *The Climate General* serves not just as an informing resource but also as a compelling motivation for commitment and action, aimed at a more sustainable and stable future for people today and upcoming generations. In essence, this book is a relevant guide for policymakers, academics, security specialists, and anyone interested in the future of our global society and planet.

We therefore recommend *The Climate General* to anyone keen on understanding the multifaceted challenges posed by climate change, and more importantly, the solutions and strategies that can lead us to a better tomorrow.

Ban Ki-moon and Feike Sijbesma,

Co-Chairs of the Supervisory Board of the Global Center on Adaptation

Introduction

"There is little scientific dispute that if we do nothing, we will face more drought, famine, and mass displacement that will fuel more conflict for decades.

For this reason, it is not merely scientists and activists who call for swift and forceful action – it is military leaders in my country and others who understand that our common security hangs in the balance."

President Barack Obama at the 2009 Nobel Peace Prize awards ceremony

Monday 5 December 2016. An email pops up on my phone screen from my spokesperson with a Twitter message from the Netherlands Broadcasting Foundation, the NOS. "General Middendorp claims that climate change threatens world peace," I read. Shortly beforehand, I was speaking at the Planetary Security Initiative at the Peace Palace in The Hague. Although my statements at the climate conference organised by the Ministry of Foreign Affairs were somewhat more nuanced than this tweet, it did set the tone. Various local officials, council members and MPs retweet the statement attributed to me. "Now you're hearing it from someone else", *GroenLinks* MEP Bas Eickhout responds. Well-known Dutch cabaret performer Claudia de Breij also seems to be enthusiastic and shares my tweet. Another writes: "How can Middendorp say something so stupid? The climate is always changing, we can't do anything about it, so is it always war?" Some activists respond indignantly that I should not make a security issue out of their topic. An angry gentleman forwards the news tweet to Jeanine Hennis-Plasschaert, the then Dutch Defence Minister, with the text: "Maybe climate propagandist Middendorp can join the KNMI [the Royal Dutch Meteorological Institute] to work on 'world peace' there."

The commotion surprised me. In Afghanistan, I experienced how water scarcity led to tensions among farmers and how the Taliban exploited it. In Iraq, I saw how water was used as an instrument of power by ISIS occupying the Mosul Dam. In Somalia, Sudan and Mali, the ever-increasing drought drove people to despair and into the hands of extremists. I saw how climate change in itself may not directly lead to conflict, but how in combination with other factors, it can become a driving force.

I gained that insight during my second deployment to Afghanistan in 2009, and it developed further during my tenure as Director of Operations at the Ministry of Defence in The Hague, from late 2009 to early 2012. In this capacity, I was responsible for more than 20 Dutch military operations worldwide and for the deployment of thousands of Dutch military personnel. These men and women perform their remarkable and often perilous work in harsh climatic conditions, particularly in regions specifically affected by the consequences of climate change. This insight into the connection between all those actors and factors has made me increasingly aware over the years that climatic conditions, and particularly the changes resulting from them, are a major source of local tensions and conflicts and have the potential to impact significantly on the security of populations in Europe and worldwide.

Wilful blindness

When I made the link between climate change and security in that speech in the Netherlands in 2016 and stressed the urgency, many people were nevertheless surprised. So I was ready for the inevitable criticism when I arrived back at the ministry. Surprisingly, however, absolutely no one took me to task for my remarks, even though I knew that in the ministry's halls of power, many people were wondering why the Chief of Defence would say something like that, without their prior knowledge and on his own initiative.

On the one hand, this silence was understandable. At the time, the Dutch armed forces were in the process of trying in some way to repair the damage inflicted by years of budget cuts. Some policymakers felt that it was not sensible to focus urgent attention on such a major topic as climate change and security, which was for some still a somewhat vague issue, certainly not at election time. That is precisely the time when the defence organisation needs to present a clear and unambiguous narrative based on one logical line of reasoning that would give the organisation the financial scope to work on the much-needed recovery under the next government.

In contrast, some MPs responded to my statements quite quickly. Minister of Defence Jeanine Hennis-Plasschaert was presented with parliamentary questions the very next day. "Is Middendorp speaking on behalf of the government? Do you support this? How does this fit in with Defence policy?" Within a week, however, the uproar was over. My story was somewhat more nuanced than the news media would suggest, and this was later confirmed by the fact checkers of Dutch newspaper *NRC Handelsblad*.[1] This spurred me on to continue stressing the link between climate and security and to emphasise that climate change did indeed pose a major threat to our security. As former South Miami mayor Philip Stoddard once asked a reporter: "What would we do if Martians come to Earth and said "We are going to destroy your planet by injecting carbon dioxide into your atmosphere and cooking you out." We would fight back with everything we had. And we would start that fight tomorrow. All of us. Like it was World War III." He adds: "And that's what we're facing. Except the Martians are us. We're cooking ourselves."[2]

I still find that a very apt analogy. I find myself sharing the same sentiment to an ever increasing extent, that we ourselves have become the Martians who are destroying life on earth and killing humanity. Nature is making this painfully clear to us on a growing scale. Average temperatures are rising, heatwaves have become hotter and evaporation is increasing. As a result, dry periods become longer, more extreme and even hotter, and rainy seasons become shorter and more intense, making ever larger regions of the world virtually uninhabitable and infertile.

We saw evidence of this in the terrible images in the news in 2023. Unprecedented droughts and heatwaves in western Canada, the US, India, the Middle East and southern and eastern Europe. Devastating floods in China, Africa, Pakistan, and closer to home in Slovenia, Italy, Germany and Belgium. The relentless forest fires in places as diverse as Siberia, parts of the US, Hawaii, Canada, Australia, Greece and Turkey. Drought-struck valleys in Spain, a tornado in the Czech Republic, a cyclone in India, unprecedented thunderstorms and hailstorms in Europe and severe hurricanes and tropical storms in the US, South and Southeast Asia and Central America. Twice as many summer downpours in the Netherlands, and water scarcity growing at an alarming rate in large parts of the Middle East and North Africa. Anyone who would dare to suggest that there is no such thing as climate change is guilty of wilful blindness.

Stranglehold

For me, climate change is not a stand-alone issue, but should be seen in the context of three other dominant trends: population growth, resource scarcity and geopolitical polarisation. The global population reached 8 billion in 2022 and is expected to reach 10-11 billion by the end of this century, according to the UN. Such an increase poses major problems for humanity, especially in the world's developing countries that are also hardest hit by climate change. This population growth is accompanied by an even sharper growth in the need for water, food and goods, a need which is more and more difficult to meet due to the increasing scarcity of a widening range of raw materials. This creates a global gap between supply and demand. Climate change makes it harder to bridge that gap because it reduces the cultivable and habitable part of our planet.

Another complicating factor is the shift from a globalised to a more fragmented and polarised world. The war in Ukraine illustrates how energy and climate change are linked to security and how this affects international relations. The world is changing from one that is increasingly connected and collaborative to one of sharp contrasts and opposing blocs. Dependencies are seen as vulnerabilities and calls for autonomy are growing louder in different parts of the world, all of which leads to intensifying geopolitical competition for access to resources.

This disunity paralyses the work of multilateral UN institutions, for example, which can only take decisions by consensus. It makes a global approach difficult in a world with growing divisions and geopolitical conflicts. We need each other more and more to reach global solutions, but we are finding it harder than ever to connect with each other.

Security

I was becoming increasingly aware that climate change in this broader context was probably the greatest challenge of this century, even when viewed from a security perspective. It was for that reason that I became chairman of the International Military Council on Climate and Security (the IMCCS Expert Group) in February 2019, when I officially stepped down from my military role. This is an independent and global network of senior military officers, security experts and research institutes who want to raise awareness of the threat posed to our security by climate change and to contribute to actual measures and possible courses of action. For all participants in the network, including myself, the key issue is that climate change is turning into a determining factor for our national security, that the armed forces must be part of the solution and that we need to speed things up.

I find that by approaching climate change from a security perspective, there is a wider understanding and recognition of the issue. Climate and security are two sides of the same coin. They are inextricably linked. Climate change cannot be addressed without security, but neither can security be achieved without global, robust action to combat climate change. And that is precisely why climate change should be a unifying factor for all of us, a common enemy that we need to confront, regardless of the differences and tensions between us.

Spaceship Earth

That is why I wanted to write this book. What does the complexity of climate change look like? What impact does it have on our physical, economic and societal security? And above all, how do we solve the problem and how can we as individuals contribute? These are some of the questions I want to address in this book with the help of numerous examples.

I am and will always be optimistic, because I have great faith in our ability to survive and innovate. I cannot recall any other crisis in which we had so much detailed research and such a unified view of what lies ahead. That gives us the opportunity and responsibility to tackle this climate and biodiversity crisis as a priority, to prepare for what is to come and to do all we can to limit the damage. The more we recognise this need and the better we understand this common issue, the greater the likelihood that climate change will become a cause that unites us and one in which we can join forces.

I also have great faith in the difference individuals can make, so this book provides many examples of pioneering inventions by ordinary people who dare to venture from the beaten track, who dare to think big and who just get started. There is a good reason why my motto is "*Think big, act small, start somewhere*". After all, we have no alternative to our spaceship Earth. We have to make do with that special little sphere in space. It is the only home we humans have.

So let us start focusing all our creativity and energy on stepping up the fight and forming a united front against global warming. For us, our children and the generations to come.

Notes

1. Luttikhuis, P. (2016, 27 December), "Climate change contributes to war". NRC Handelsblad, https://www.nrc.nl/nieuws/2016/12/27/klimaatverandering-draagt-bij-aan-oorlog-5937347-a1538593

2. Video by Jeannette den Boer and Stefan Coppers for *Algemeen Dagblad*, 11 Feb 2019, "Rising water turns Miami into a ghost town", https://www.ad.nl/wetenschap/opkomend-water-maakt-van-miami-een-spookstad-a9208b49/

Part One

How climate change is making the
world a more dangerous place

Chapter One
Afghanistan, the start of my mission

"There can be no peace or development without water."

Jan Eliasson, former president of the UN General Assembly

"Sir, I need help."

Major Matt Coburn, a US Special Forces company commander, calls me. He has an unusual request, he says. I am the commander of Task Force Uruzgan, and Coburn tells me that a young Afghan mother has killed her husband in self-defence. She had been mistreated and abused by him for years. She is now relatively safe in a police cell, courtesy of the local police chief. But everyone knows that sooner or later the Taliban in-laws will come to claim the woman to take revenge and kill her. So the Afghan police chief has turned to the Americans for help. They, however, have few resources at their disposal in Uruzgan at the time. Without hesitation, I immediately arrange for a helicopter. In the dead of night, the woman is taken to a safehouse in the capital Kabul.

It is not normal practice to launch an operation like this for a civilian, but I simply cannot refuse. We are, after all, in Afghanistan to make the country safer and more stable, so that Afghans can build their future themselves and with outside help. That is the ultimate goal and I act accordingly. Moreover, the Afghan police chief has stuck his neck out by asking the Americans for help, and I have no desire to betray that trust.

This is not just one of the better memories I have of Afghanistan. It also shows how we enable security on the ground. As a soldier, you are in the area for over six months – in some cases for a year. I am therefore well and truly immersed in the military mission. First as NATO's Senior Political Advisor in Kabul in 2006 and 2007 and two years later as the commander of Task Force Uruzgan. We have a mandate from the Dutch government, as part of the NATO mission, which is being conducted under the UN flag at the request of the Afghans. Our mandate is to work towards security and stability to enable rebuilding in Afghanistan. In practice, however, that means I am in charge of both rebuilding activities and combat operations, because the situation is far from safe and stable in Afghanistan at the time.

The phone call from the US commander is also a reminder of a time when I was not really aware of the effects of climate change on security. As a soldier on deployment, climate is nothing more than a given, just as it is for the local population. You feel the constraints imposed by the climate on a daily basis and take that on board as a factor influencing the plans you make to keep the country safe and stable while keeping fatalities and injuries to a minimum. The idea that climate conditions will continue to deteriorate in the longer term is something you don't really worry about.

Suicide bombings and attacks

My first working day as Task Force commander on 1 February 2009 is actually indicative of how everything can suddenly change in Afghanistan. You cannot let your guard down for a moment. The evening before my change of command, we intercept radio traffic from the Taliban and their henchmen. We hear that they are planning a suicide attack the next day in Deh Rawod, a small village in another valley 30 kilometres from our camp in Uruzgan. As other sources confirm this information, we set up an operation the same evening. The aim is to have the bomber picked up by the Afghans even before he can put on the suicide vest, and to give the Afghans a prominent role in the action. That way, the Afghan people gain more confidence in their own police force. This does make our mission complex at the time, because it means that a Dutch captain in his mid-20s has to work with an Afghan army unit mentored by French military personnel. It also requires cooperation between Afghan police officers, who are accompanied by a US team. In addition, we provide the young officer with various specialists in medical support, explosives, Apache helicopters and air support with F-16s for emergencies. All of this is done under enormous time pressure.

So in a situation like this, you have to find answers to a great many questions very quickly. What does the terrain look like at the operation site? Is it flat or hilly? Overgrown or not? Are there many buildings? Can you move safely to where you need to be? What is the weather like and will it affect us? What could go wrong and how can we prevent it? These are all things you need to think about and plan for to make sure you eliminate the threat without incurring casualties. And you have to do all that with a multinational team and only a few hours of preparation time. Fortunately, we have great young military leaders in the Task Force who prepare this operation down to the finest detail within a few hours. In the middle of the night, we give the green light for the operation. It will be carried out that same night, before sunrise. And so it is. The suicide bomber is taken totally by surprise and handed over to the Afghans. A great success and an auspicious start to my command, I think to myself at the time.

The sense of euphoria is short-lived. The next day, everything is different. It starts with a dull thud in the distance, shortly after the start of the change of command ceremony. Reports start coming in immediately and we see police pick-ups driving towards our camp at great speed. The vehicles appear to be full of dead and wounded Afghan police officers. There was apparently a second suicide bomber, who did manage to blow himself up. It happened near a local police training centre in the capital Tarin Kowt, about 2 kilometres from our camp. It is one of the heaviest attacks at the time in Afghanistan and the deadliest since the beginning of that year. The Taliban soon claim responsibility, and Taliban spokesman Qari Yousuf Ahmadi threatens to continue committing attacks against Afghan government personnel and foreign troops. Welcome to Afghanistan, I'm already thinking at that point.

Three steps forward, two steps back, or more in some cases. That realisation will never go away.

We are regularly bombarded by missiles. Not long after my change of command, a missile strikes our camp near Tarin Kowt in Uruzgan. It happens less than 20 metres from me. I hear a huge bang, the earth shakes. I remain unharmed because I am behind a wall, but others are not so lucky. The missile struck near the shower containers. Someone was showering at the time, but manages to escape with minor injuries. The missile went through the shower container and landed on the path next to it where a group of young men just happen to be walking; they take a direct hit. One of them dies on the spot: Private 1st Class Azdin Chadli, 20 years old. It has a profound effect on all of us, a missile attack on the camp where we feel relatively safe. But there is no time for emotion. I must ensure that the right actions are taken to care for the wounded, secure the camp and take measures against any further threats. Helicopters and drones are immediately deployed to find the perpetrators. Meanwhile, the wounded are treated and the ministry in The Hague is notified so that the relatives can be informed of this horrific news. We also need to focus on Azdin's unit. It is a huge blow for them to deal with, literally and figuratively.

At times like this, everyone is there for each other, everyone supports each other. Within a few days, we say our goodbyes to Azdin in a moving ceremony. Together with all the international units, we form a guard of honour around his body, all the way to the airstrip. It is really important to come to terms with the loss, because the mission goes on and the unit has to get back to work. They do so with admirable resilience and without any feelings of revenge. Indeed, Azdin's platoon goes on to become one of the best units in the Task Force. Determined to ensure that Azdin did not die in vain, they led the way in the operation that ended the shelling at the time. To this day, his comrades commemorate Azdin's death annually, along with the family. And I am still in touch with them every year.

Almost daily, I am confronted with the climate in Afghanistan, even just the searing heat and flooding in the spring. And yet I am not concerned at the time with the effects of climate on security. I just don't have time to worry about what I then called "other issues".

Tensions over water shortages

My predecessors also saw the vast sandy plains, as well as fields full of red poppies and even valleys full of blossom trees and streams. Yet even in their time, there was too little or no water for growing crops, air pollution was a major health problem, and Afghan farmers were citing irrigation systems destroyed by years of drought and war as the main reason for increasing opium cultivation. Even then, there was little awareness of the impact of climate change.

That changed in 2007. In the village of Chora, it is about 40 degrees Celsius in the shade. Heavy fighting continued for days when the Taliban controlled the village. After a long and intense battle, our people were able to drive the Taliban away, but the problems did not disappear. It took several months to find out that tensions had existed in the village for some time, and the Taliban had been exploiting them: it was all about the shortage of water and a growing disagreement over its distribution. Only when we succeeded in negotiating an agreement about the distribution of water for drinking and especially for irrigation, tensions started to ease. This also removed one of the breeding grounds for the Taliban, who were using that same water shortage to turn people against each other, to blackmail and recruit them. To me, it was a striking example of the simple fact that military solutions alone are not enough. There is no security without development, and no development without security. Better distribution of the limited amount of water available took the sting out of the problem and stabilised the situation in Chora. As a result, later, in 2009 when I was the commander in Uruzgan, I could walk down the main street with our king, then the crown prince. That's how safe it was then.

Later, when I have had more time to really reflect on the mission in Afghanistan, I realise just how much climate and security impact on each other and how water shortages cause local conflicts all over the place. They are a breeding ground for extremism. For the military, climate, weather and geographical conditions and the terrain are always a given that you have to take into account when preparing and executing missions and operations. Any operational analysis starts with an assessment of these aspects and, of course, of the enemy. But it is only when you zoom out and look at trends over the years that you see the strategic and existential significance of the changing climate. Looking back, I realise that we could have done more as an international community if we had been more aware of what was happening.

The crucial role of agriculture

A significant and complicating factor in establishing security and stability is the lack of a sustainable and robust agricultural economy in Afghanistan. As early as 2007, a US military report by an advisory group of former senior military officers suggested that climate change had a direct impact on terrorism in many countries, and particularly on the war in Afghanistan. The advisory group was set up by the then First Deputy Undersecretary of Defense, Sherri Goodman, tasked with examining the impact of climate change on US national security.[1] In this report, unknown to me during my preparations for the mission, US retired general Gordon R. Sullivan describes how terrorists were aided by the effects of global warming and increasing drought. "[It's in] the conflict over water and crops", he later said on the subject in an interview with ABC News. "Afghanistan… has an agricultural economy, but it is not robust and a lack of water would be devastating."[2]

We now know much more about this issue. It is now common knowledge that global warming increases the severity of drought. When you consider that more than three-quarters of Afghanistan's population depends on agriculture, you realise how crucial it is to work on food security.

Food security cannot be seen in isolation from water security, especially in view of the fact that agriculture accounts for the vast majority of total water consumption.[3] Efficient water distribution across the country is crucial in this regard, and this is no easy task; as well as poor infrastructure, inhospitable Afghanistan has a poorly functioning government, partly because of years of conflict and war. It is more like an anarchic system of small farmers doing their own thing. For example, we see groups of Afghans, affiliated with local leaders, tapping the groundwater in higher ground and using old kareshes, ancient underground canals still in place, or other means to divert the water to the fields. Elsewhere, farmers draw off a disproportionate amount of surface water. This leaves less water for people in the areas downstream. Rules and agreements on water distribution are therefore badly needed, as are supervision and enforcement of those rules. In effect, there needs to be a transition from irrigation management *via* water management to water governance. Afghans have always known that water and its distribution are crucial for livelihoods and development.

Partnerships are thus indispensable here, in much the same way as cooperatives, water boards and polder administrations used to work in the Netherlands. The former Dutch water envoy Henk Ovink concluded in 2019, after a working visit to Afghanistan, that there was much to be gained in terms of efficiency in water distribution. Agriculture is Afghanistan's largest employment sector and economic engine, but it is mostly practised by small farmers in traditional ways. For them, more water means higher yield and they eagerly use solar-powered water pumps that can water their fields all day "for free". In 2011, Wageningen University, with support from the Dutch embassy, set up an agriculture education college to train teachers in agricultural colleges. They then take this knowledge to rural areas and train small farmers. Irrigation is currently a small part of the curriculum, but this can be expanded further if there is cooperation with Dutch knowledge institutions, such as Wageningen University and the IHE Delft Institute for Water Education. Teachers can then be trained in new, accessible water efficiency techniques and greater awareness can be fostered about water use in agriculture.

Afghans must then recognise the need for cooperation to achieve more efficient use of increasingly scarce water. It is therefore important to encourage willingness and trust in cooperation and Afghan farmers must be persuaded that collective regulation of the water supply is to everyone's advantage. Also necessary in this regard is the use of drip irrigation, as well as joint procurement and marketing. In any case, the local development of such agricultural plans must come from the Afghans themselves, so that they can also implement them themselves. From experience, I know that people are certainly open to this if they are in control and find that it helps them move forward; in other words, if they can market their products and earn money to support their families. In short, it is about forging partnerships and distribution mechanisms for dealing with scarce resources. Without these efforts that focus more on societal development, stability operations and peace missions will have no long-term effects.

Drinking water supply and the export market

Another important consequence of climate change presented itself during my time in Afghanistan. The glacial ice from the Hindu Kush in the Himalayan region, located in northeastern Afghanistan and northern Pakistan, is melting at an increasing rate. The mountain range in this region is also referred to as the world's third "pole" because of the vast quantities of ice. The rapidly melting ice, on which huge numbers of people in Afghanistan depend, not only reduces the amount of water available to sustain life and grow crops in the long run, but also contributes to dangerous situations in the short term, especially for riverside populations. The natural dams there could burst due to the overflowing glacial lakes; large areas could flood as a result, with dire consequences for the safety of the population and for the fertility of the land.

The accelerated melting of glacial ice is therefore dangerous. However, capturing excess water from the glaciers, ideally in the mountains themselves, will require huge investments. This is not an option in Afghanistan. In addition, the ancient subterranean irrigation systems, the highly ingenious *kareshes*, were largely destroyed by the Russians during the occupation to prevent Afghans from using them for hiding and storing weapons and ammunition, or they have just fallen into disrepair. As a result, water distribution is simply no longer possible.

An additional problem is that Afghans no longer have anywhere to store and dry fruit: all the drying sheds – whose draught holes once provided cover for snipers – have been destroyed by the Russians. It is these very sheds that were so important for trade and exports, as apricots, grapes and mulberries of the highest quality could be dried there in the shade. In 2009, when I was in Afghanistan, this left fruit farmers unable to sell the famous Afghan export produce, such as dried fruit, to countries like the Gulf states. Other foreign producers have now taken their place. So besides establishing an efficient water distribution system and setting up cooperatives, it is vital that Afghans regain access to drying sheds and that *kareshes* be restored or other ways found to irrigate the fields. Crops can then once again be grown, processed, stored and distributed, and people can get their lives back.

Sale of opium

There are also the many poppy fields of Afghanistan, with the colourful poppies that are used to produce opium. When I was in Afghanistan, many farmers were so poor that they were up to their eyes in debt to the Taliban or their affiliates. Their crops had failed because of flooding or drought, or they were unable to grow anything because they had been living in a war zone for so long and it was not safe. There was simply no food on the table. If a farmer is then offered money to grow poppy, he is not going to refuse. In Afghanistan, poppy is one of the few crops that allow farmers to support their families. It is drought-tolerant and easy to harvest. Moreover, it requires little land, can be stored for years and has a guaranteed outlet at a high price. What more could you want as a farmer? The fact that you are also funding the Taliban is something many people are prepared to accept. Meanwhile, this has provided the Taliban with a huge source of income. Cultivation in

Afghanistan accounted for about 90% of global opium production in 2008; in that year, the Taliban earned about 75 million euros from the opium trade, according to US NATO commander General Craddock.[4]

According to journalist Gretchen Peters, who travelled through Pakistan and Afghanistan for more than a decade, that is putting it mildly. In her book *Seeds of Terror*, she shows how heroin actually helped put the Taliban and al-Qaida in power. Peters calculates that the sale of opium and the "taxes" levied on it by the Taliban earn them over $500 million a year.[5] She talks to Afghan farmers who tell International Security Assistance Force (ISAF) soldiers: "If you protect us and restore our irrigation systems, we will stop growing opium and work with you instead of the Taliban."[6] I believe this is what these locals really want, because opium is haram, or impure, and therefore forbidden. A good Muslim must not harm himself or others. But the trade-off is understandable when there is no other way to feed your children. The situation did not improve after the international community left in 2021 and Afghanistan is still the largest producer of opium in the world, according to the United Nations Office on Drugs and Crime (UNODC). In fact, 95% of the European market is dominated by Afghan opium.[7]

So we know that in Afghanistan water is scarce and poorly distributed, glaciers are melting faster, there are no outlet markets, farmers are in debt to the Taliban and, partly because of this, they grow poppies "en masse" to keep their families alive and the Taliban earn big money from this; a downward spiral that can only be broken if, in addition to a degree of security and good governance, the interdependencies and underlying issues, including the major influence of climate, are properly understood. The intelligence agencies have so far paid little attention to this in their analyses. It is also clear that there is no purely military answer to this or future conflicts. Besides minimal security, many other aspects need to be in place. To start with, an effective and more equitable water distribution method supported by robust agreements and investments to improve water storage, drip irrigation to reduce waste, a credit system for farmers still in debt to the Taliban (and people who risk their lives going to rural areas to sell those credits), other crops on the market that can tolerate drought, a market to sell products, and a place to process and store produce.

The comprehensive plan that never came to pass

While I was in Afghanistan, I did not have the time or the expertise to develop a comprehensive agricultural plan, let alone implement it. However, many small and well-meaning initiatives did emerge. In 2007, for instance, the Netherlands sent a reservist with an agricultural background to Afghanistan together with a few other experts, including engineers from *Rijkswaterstaat,* the executive agency of the Ministry of Infrastructure and Water Management. They were part of the Provincial Reconstruction Team (PRT), consisting of military and civilian specialists. The reservist, in the rank of captain, was tasked with creating a strategic agriculture plan to determine what needed to be done in Uruzgan province. Implementing the plan depended partly on the cooperation of the embassy, and that proved difficult. Any project costing more than 5,000 euros requires embassy approval.

A strategic agriculture plan fully supported by the Afghan provincial agriculture department for Uruzgan eventually disappeared in a forgotten drawer at the embassy. It was a plan by the PRT to switch Afghan farmers in Uruzgan to other long-term and lucrative crops, such as saffron, wheat and almonds, which could be used to build the entire production chain. Almonds, according to our information, could produce a high yield for Afghans. But it takes three years before the trees start bearing fruit. Then you have to make sure it is safe, so that farmers are willing and able to cultivate their fields. And you have to make sure there is enough water to irrigate the fields, bridging that period of non-productivity.

Irrigation works therefore needed to be identified in order to repair and improve them. This could be co-financed through food-for-work programmes, so with the help of the Afghans themselves, by paying farmers without prospects to repair the underground irrigation systems. The same farmers who were once paid by the Taliban to shoot at us and grow poppies. Those Afghans would once again be able to take care of their families and grow the almond trees. When the trees are fully mature, there would also be enough water to irrigate the fields because the irrigation systems would have been restored by then. According to the plan, markets for the new crops could be sought in the meantime, for instance in the Gulf states. So the whole system would be up and running again, because if there is one thing Afghans know about, it is how to grow crops and make use of those irrigation systems. It seemed to be a foolproof plan.

But as we know, the plan unfortunately never came to pass. The PRT was told by the Dutch development cooperation representative that a major water management plan first had to be drawn up for the river basins that supplied Uruzgan with water. A plan, therefore, whose drafting would take years, because complex factors had to be identified and everything had to be measured: rainfall, water flows, and so on. In the end, there was no time for that. Dutch politicians decided three years later that the mission in Uruzgan would be terminated.

No water, no life

Much has been said and written about ending the ISAF deployment in Afghanistan. It is pure speculation as to whether it would have been better to stay any longer. Especially in view of what we know today; the Taliban's takeover of power in 2021, which resulted in the country's massive decline. For many military personnel, it felt like unfinished business.

When I became the commander of the Dutch mission in Uruzgan in 2009, the mission was in its third year. We felt that the tide was turning. Fighting the Taliban in the first years provided more security in the populated areas, creating scope for development efforts and investments, also by Afghans themselves. Dozens of non-governmental organisations (NGOs) were able to get back to work in Uruzgan and the UN opened a regional office there. We were also able to focus more on training and guiding the Afghan services that were going to take over from us. This 3D approach – defence, diplomacy and development – began to bear fruit. With some surprise and admiration, partners and international media watched the change taking place in Uruzgan, which was, after all, one of the least developed and "darkest" provinces in southern Afghanistan.

For instance, I received weekly delegations from Kabul, and the US commander of ISAF, General Stan McChrystal, also came on a familiarisation visit in Uruzgan after taking office, seeking a more population-centric approach. In the end, we only managed to capitalise on this 3D approach to a limited extent, mainly because the Netherlands terminated the mission in Uruzgan after a relatively short time. Our Australian partners stayed on and our work was taken over by the American units, resulting in the loss of much local knowledge and experience, and a different approach. Each country participating in ISAF interprets the required cooperation between military and civil agencies in its own way, but if we wish to achieve our goals and bring stability to a country or province, it is truly a matter of long-term commitment.

The UN Environment Programme (UNEP) estimates that 80% of Afghanistan's population depends on land, water and other natural resources.[8] Many people are still fleeing the country, including those who previously survived the violence of the Russian invasion, then the terror of the Taliban regime and the years of the ISAF campaign, but who are now forced to seek refuge elsewhere due to water and food shortages. Without water, life is simply not possible. Or as one Afghan refugee back home told a *National Geographic* reporter: "No fertile soil. No water. No life."[9] This despair represents a breeding ground for the Taliban and causes more and more people to migrate to cities. In 2018, 25% of people in Afghanistan lived in urban areas, and this is expected to reach 40% by 2050. The capital Kabul in particular is expected to see significant growth in the coming years: from 4.3 million inhabitants in 2021 to over 8 million in 2050.[10]

People in Kabul are already struggling to survive. In 2017, researchers estimated that 68% of Kabul residents had no access to piped water and only

10% had access to drinking water. Moreover, a large majority of residents have too little water, averaging about 20 litres per capita per day, compared to the recommended level of at least 80 litres.[11] Now that the Taliban have seized power, it remains to be seen whether they are capable of proper water management, but the first signs are far from hopeful. That is why Kabul residents are digging large numbers of wells or buying relatively expensive plastic bottles of drinking water, which, like other plastics, end up in the environment and clog waterways and sewers. In addition, Afghans burn a great deal of waste, causing many people to fall ill or die because of air pollution.[12] I cannot get the image of the crying mother in a dilapidated hospital next to a simple metal cot where a child lies on a makeshift ventilator out of my head. It is a picture from 2020 on news channel Al Jazeera's website accompanying an article on the massive pollution in the city of Kabul.[13]

As elsewhere, anyone with money prefers not to flee to the big city but abroad; to Pakistan, for example, to which many Afghan farming families fled because of the lack of prospects in agriculture. We hear from people in Afghanistan that their children often go into the madrassas, where they are introduced to jihadist ideology. Other Afghans desperately try to reach Iran or, even better, safe and prosperous Europe. Not infrequently, they try to get to Europe *via* Iran. In 2015, for instance, around 45,000 unaccompanied underage Afghans came to Europe, according to the European statistics office Eurostat.[14] That is almost 125 children a day, in other words, the equivalent of about five school classes put together, or an entire primary school in a week. Many of these children will have travelled some 5,000 kilometres, on foot across mountains, in smuggling boats across rivers and seas. After the peak year of 2015, the numbers went down considerably, but they remain significant. In 2020, about 5,500 underage migrants came to Europe from Afghanistan.[15]

Many thousands of Afghan men, women and children have fled in recent years, all in search of a safe haven and a dignified existence. Even today, many are still fleeing. "We fled from poverty", 21-year-old Afghan Said Karam tells *The Diplomat* magazine in a 2020 phone interview: "We had nothing to eat, so we decided to go to Iran after the coronavirus outbreak. We knew they might shoot us at the border, but we had no choice."[16] This may not be a direct security problem, but it is certainly a problem resulting from land degradation due to drought and a changing climate and it shows how climate change is leading to rapidly increasing migration flows.

Takeover of power

The Taliban's seizure of power in August 2021, which followed decades of conflict, natural disasters and poverty, only brought further economic decline, food insecurity and hardship to the people of Afghanistan. In addition, the actions and decisions of the Taliban – contrary to their commitments – led to a dramatic deterioration of the political, economic, humanitarian and human rights situation in the country. For instance, the Taliban issued broad decrees with numerous restrictions or prohibitions regarding girls' attendance at secondary schools, dress codes, segregation in the workplace, free movement of women without a male relative (mahram) and women's access to public spaces.

In late December 2022, the Taliban decided that women would no longer be permitted to attend university or work for non-governmental organisations. These decrees are not only discriminatory, according to the EU, but also have major and in some cases life-threatening repercussions, because without female humanitarian workers, providing aid to the most vulnerable is much more difficult.[17] In the summer of 2023, when all beauty salons also had to close their doors and some 60,000 women lost their jobs and income, the UN declared a state of gender apartheid in Afghanistan.[18] Afghanistan is slipping further into decline and becoming extremely impoverished. The country is also having to deal with huge climate challenges, which will be difficult without outside help, but will in part determine the fate of the Afghan people.

Notes

1. CNA Military Advisory Board (2007), *National Security and the threat of Climate Change.* The CNA Corporation, https://www.cna.org/cna_files/pdf/National%20Security%20and%20the%20Threat%20 of%20Climate%20Change.pdf

2. Blakemore, B. (2009, 9 October), "Taliban, al Qaeda Helped by Warming". *ABC News*, https:// abcnews.go.com/Technology/JustOneThing/taliban-al-qaeda-helped-global-warming-us-intel/ story?id=8786346

3. Food and Agriculture Organization, AQUASTAT data (2017), *Annual freshwater withdrawals, agriculture (% of total freshwater withdrawal)*

4. "NATO tackles opium trade" (2008, 11 October). *Het Parool*, https://www.parool.nl/nieuws/navo-pakt-opiumhandel-aan-be728afc/

5. Peters, G. (2009), *Seeds of Terror: How Heroin is Bankrolling the Taliban and al-Qaeda.* Oxford: One World Publications

6. Blakemore, B. (2009, 9 October), "Taliban, al Qaeda helped by warming". *ABC News.* https://abcnews. go.com/Technology/JustOneThing/taliban-al-qaeda-helped-global-warming-us-intel/story?id=8786346

7. André, A. (2021, 19 November). "Afghan farmers continue to supply the world with opium". *NOS*, https://nos.nl/artikel/2406270-afghaanse-boeren-blijven-de-wereld-van-opium-voorzien

8. "Natural Resource Management and Peacebuilding in Afghanistan". UNEP

9. Jones, S. (2020, 3 February), "In Afghanistan, climate change complicates future prospects for peace", *National Geographic, Science*, https://www.nationalgeographic.com/science/2020/02/afghan-struggles-to-rebuild-climate-change-complicates/

10. United Nations (2018), "World Urbanization Prospects 2018 - United Nations population estimates and projections of major urban agglomerations", *Department of Economics and Social Affairs*, https:// population.un.org/wup/Country-Profiles/

11. Amin, M. & Hassanpour Adeh, E. (2017, Aug 22), "Water Crisis in Kabul could be severe if not addressed", *SAIS Review of International Affairs*, https://saisreview.sais.jhu.edu/water-crisis-in-kabul-could-be-severe-if-not-addressed/

12. "Afghan capital's air pollution may be even deadlier than war", 13 November 2019, Associated Press. https://apnews.com/1e566a9f6cd647d2998ec9c2582a6176

13. "In Pictures: Coronavirus exposes the impact of air pollution", Al Jazeera, https://www.aljazeera.com/ indepth/inpictures/pictures-coronavirus-exposes-impact-air-pollution-200422132607593.html

14. Eurostat (2016, 2 May), "Almost 90 000 unaccompanied minors among asylum seekers registered in the EU in 2015". Eurostat Press Release 87/2016, https://ec.europa.eu/eurostat/ documents/2995521/7244677/3-02052016-AP-EN.pdf/

15. Eurostat (2021, 23 April), "13 600 unaccompanied minors seeking asylum in the EU in 2020." Eurostat News, https://ec.europa.eu/eurostat/web/products-eurostat-news/-/ddn-20210423-1

16. Pikulicka-Wilcewska, A. (2020, 27 May), "The Ceaseless Struggle of Afghan Migration", *The Diplomat*, https://thediplomat.com/2020/05/the-ceaseless-struggle-of-afghan-migrants/

17. European Council (2023, 11 April). "Afghanistan: the EU response to the crisis". EU, https://www.consilium.europa.eu/nl/policies/afghanistan-eu-response/

18. NOS (2023, July 25). "Afghan beauty salons close: 'it's about more than hair and nails'". NOS, https://nos.nl/artikel/2484225-afghaanse-schoonheidssalons-sluiten-gaat-over-meer-dan-haar-en-nagels

Chapter Two
Symptom control off the coast of Somalia

"Warlords understand a lot about youth engagement. If there are no other offers of engagement for young people, what do we expect?"

Anna Barrett, researcher at War Child

"Task Force Barracuda's mission accomplished". It is autumn 2011. During the daily morning briefing, I look at Peter van Uhm, the then Chief of Defence (CDS). At the time, I am the Director of Operations in The Hague and responsible for the planning and execution of more than 20 military missions. Every morning, I brief the top military boss on those missions, as well as on the progress of covert missions, including that of Task Force Barracuda, which is part of the anti-piracy missions. Shipping and thus international trade, especially in the Gulf of Aden, has to contend with increasingly audacious and violent pirates operating out of the fragile state of Somalia. The country is not only characterised by its extremely weak political situation, but also by the increasing suffering of millions of people as a result of drought and rising food prices. Here, too, we see how a changing climate is having a serious impact on international security. However, our engagement based on the political mandate focuses not on the root causes, but on their effects.

Just before the final part of that morning briefing in 2011, a number of people are asked to leave the room. This is because the actions I am talking about have a high risk profile, and the personnel carrying out the actions will be in considerable danger. Attendance at these talks is therefore on a strictly need-to-know basis. I look at the printed maps and photos on the table in front of us. That morning, we study the map of the Horn of Africa with a table of figures next to it. It is clear, the figures tell us, that the number of hijackings off the coast of Somalia is still high. This is one of the busiest shipping lanes in the world, and we have been contributing to anti-piracy missions in that area since 2008.[1]

In my opinion, our people have done a good job. I am referring to the marines of the Special Forces Underwater Operations unit, which we sent to the coast of Somalia a while ago to covertly sabotage pirate ships. The frogmen are superbly trained and are also well prepared for this particular deployment. They not only look at the features of the area, such as water depths, currents, shipping routes and which ports and airfields are nearby, but also at ways to prevent pirate attacks. That starts with a knowledge of how Somali pirates operate.

Lucrative business model

We know that Somali pirates often use skiffs for their attacks off the Somali coast where the shipping lanes are located: fast, open boats with one or more powerful outboard engines, which can be deployed directly from the beach. They take with them ladders and boarding hooks, as well as grenade launchers and Kalashnikovs. But further offshore, in the Indian Ocean, shipping is more dispersed, and naval vessels as well as maritime patrol aircraft patrol the area. To hijack merchant ships there, pirates have to sail further and spend longer at sea. That is why pirates in the ocean use mother ships known as dhows. These are larger vessels with several skiffs and supplies on board. In some cases, they are local fishing vessels that have been hijacked with the hostage crew still on board.

When a hijacking begins, pirates usually first open fire on the bridge of the ship they want to overpower. They then try to climb on board using boarding hooks and ladders. Once the pirates are on deck, the crew still have a chance if they have managed to lock themselves in a safe room inside the ship. As long as the pirates have not taken the crew members hostage, naval vessels can still rush to the rescue and use armed teams to overpower the pirates. However, most ships are usually hijacked within 15 minutes. Once the crew and ship are under the control of the pirates, a course is set for the Somali coast, where the ship anchors. The captured crew remains on board or is sometimes taken ashore and held captive there. From then on, ransom negotiations begin; these can last from a few weeks to many months.

Every effort is being made to prevent such hijackings. Methods include sailing through the Gulf of Aden in convoy with other ships, placing lookouts on board merchant ships, attaching barbed wire along the railings and deploying security teams on board. Yet pirates are not easily stopped. In 2009, Somali boys – aged only between 17 and 19 – hijacked a US cargo ship, the Maersk Alabama, for the first time. The hostage situation lasted for five days. Eventually, three of the four hijackers were killed by US Navy Seal snipers and the fourth was later executed in the US. The Somali pirates involved in this incident made the front pages of newspapers worldwide for the first time, and the hijacking was made into a movie (*Captain Phillips*, starring Tom Hanks).

In this instance, things end relatively well for the crew, but this is by no means always the case. If an attack cannot be repelled and the ship is hijacked, a hostage situation can last for months. Besides, a pirate attack is always a traumatic experience for the crew, especially if it ends in a prolonged hostage situation with all the fear and hardship that entails. In such cases, the crew can only hope that an agreement is reached on the ransom. That ransom, often a huge sum of cash, is usually dropped by parachute from a plane, after which the pirates release the ship and release the crew. Each time a ransom is promised, it drives up the ransom to be paid in future hijackings, so we were seeing a rapidly rising trend in ransom demands at that time.

Disrupting piracy activities

That, in a nutshell, is the overall modus operandi of Somali pirates. In military terms: their standard operating procedure (SOP). The task of our military is to secretly sabotage those dhows, in other words, the mother ships, without sinking them *and* without causing casualties, with the aim of preventing future hijackings.

Frogmen Dennis and Alex carry out one of these secret actions the night before the morning briefing. Their mission is to sabotage a pirate mother ship anchored off the Somali coast near a pirate camp. On board that mother ship are about 20 pirates holding 12 Iranian fishermen hostage. We know this from intelligence gathered by the coalition; intel, as we call it. The mother ship also recently had a confrontation on the high seas with a German frigate. This involved heavy fire and the pirates threatened to kill the hostages. So we know that the pirates are on high alert and are likely to call for reinforcements at the slightest suspicion of danger, probably from another mother ship nearby. This is the heart of one of the Somali "pirate nests", exactly where Dennis and Alex need to be. On that very night, there is also a full moon and there is not a cloud in the sky. "You could read a book, it was that bright", Dennis would later say. That also means that you are highly visible under water.

The risks involved in the mission are high, but so are the stakes; after a thorough risk assessment, the decision is made to proceed. At a considerable distance from the pirate ship, on the high seas, Dennis and Alex enter the water wearing special diving suits, gloves and a full-face mask that shields the face. Because they are so far away from the ship, they use a kind of underwater scooter. They know they have to beware of sharks, and there is a pretty strong current. Once they reach the pirate ship, they do not immediately manage to latch themselves on due to the current. Alex is pushed away from the ship only to be slammed back against it with full force.

Dennis has attached a shark shield around his leg, which gives off a small electric shock to deter any sharks, but with every pounding against the ship, Alex now gets a power surge. You would seriously consider turning the device off, but given the danger of sharks, that is not advisable. So he keeps the device on, but in the meantime is dazzled by luminous plankton. As a result, Dennis cannot see what he is doing or how much air he has left. Then they hear rumbling on the deck of the pirate ship and are afraid of being discovered. Despite this, they manage to fix the homemade explosives, which they have brought in a laundry net, to the underside of the pirate ship.

But the current causes one explosive to slip out of Dennis's hands and disappear into the depths. The second explosive will not attach properly to the underside of the ship. The two marines have to make a decision. Carry on or stop? They carry on. After a lengthy attempt, Dennis manages to attach the remaining explosive together with the delay device (a kind of kitchen timer) to the pirate ship. Alex checks the detonation time. With very little air left in their bottles, they set off again under water for the pick-up point, only to surface 15 minutes later, gasping for fresh air. Quickly, Dennis transmits a GPS signal to colleagues on HNLMS *Zuiderkruis*, who then quickly pick them up. When they are finally safely on board the Dutch naval vessel, they exchange only a few words: "Went well, didn't it? Fancy a smoke?"

Then they see flashes of light near the pirate ship. An explosion? Whether the mission was successful, Alex and Dennis do not know at that moment. They hope to find out tomorrow. First some sleep, although that might not be easy when you have just carried out such an extraordinary mission. All sorts of questions are going around in your head. Did you use enough explosive? Too much means the whole ship goes down. Too little means you have risked danger for nothing. But when Dennis and Alex fly a helicopter over the area the next day and see that the pirate ship has been towed to the shore, they breathe a huge sigh of relief. The ship clearly can no longer serve as a base for hijackings. In short, the mission was accomplished and Alex and Dennis subsequently received a well-deserved medal for this action.

Root causes of piracy

My morning briefing to the CDS, however, is not the time to go into the precise details of the operation by Dennis and Alex. Suffice it to say: "Task Force Barracuda's mission accomplished", with a brief explanation of the outcome. We continue with an analysis of developments in the seas around lawless and violent Somalia, where navies from just about every major international player are still patrolling intensively at this time.[2] Somalia's coastline is almost 4,000 kilometres long, and Somali pirates are operating in the Gulf of Aden in the north to the Seychelles in the east and the coast of Kenya in the south. That is a sea area the size of Western Europe. Pirates can sail from anywhere into the Indian Ocean using mother ships and fast skiffs, so it is a hopeless task for any one country to act alone against these pirates without broader international military engagement.

At the same time, there is a growing awareness that we are just treating the symptoms. Right from the start of the mission, we have been aware that Somalia has been known for decades as poverty-stricken and violent. It is a country that has actually been divided along tribal lines since Italian and British rule, between 1856 and 1960: Somaliland (northwest), Puntland (northeast) and Central Somalia (central and southern regions).[3] Somalia's legal system is highly diverse and complex. There are different legal cultures, which also differ by region. These include traditional tribal law (also known as "Xeer"), Sharia (Islamic) law and legislation based on nomadic pastoralism.[4]

When dictator Siad Barre was ousted in 1991, the situation worsened. A whirlwind of violence erupted. Clashes broke out between warlords who saw their opportunity and wanted to fill the power vacuum. As a result, huge refugee flows emerged and the population faced widespread famine. For many people in the West, the image of US soldiers being dragged through the streets of Mogadishu in particular is etched in the memory after widespread media coverage and the 2002 film *Black Hawk Down*.

The UN tried to help the country with emergency aid for a few years in the early 1990s, but left in 1995 due to the lack of security.[5] Somalia was then effectively left to its own devices. The lack of a functioning government means that there is no-one to stand up for the interests of the country or its people. Persistent rumours abound – unsubstantiated by facts, incidentally – about toxic waste from foreign companies being dumped off the coast of Somalia. What is known is that large fishing vessels from other countries are catching huge quantities of fish off the Somali coast. This is easy to do, because there is no functioning coastguard to enforce laws and agreements any more than there is a government. Fishing there is lucrative, because as a result of a highly nutrient-rich upwelling from the depths of the northern Indian Ocean, Somali waters are among the richest fishing grounds in the world.

In addition, the Somali people have always been pastoralists. Major fishing towns never developed on the coast. During the period when the dictator Barre was in power, the 1970s did see some investment in the development of the fishing industry. But this cooperation with Denmark, the UK, Japan, Germany and Sweden ended when civil war broke out in 1991. However, the investors from those countries never stopped the fishing afterwards. In fact, the number of large, modern, foreign trawlers (fishing vessels that use a funnel-shaped net) in the fish-rich Somali waters and on the high seas has actually increased sharply since the break-up of the Somali state, resulting in overfishing.[6] The High Seas Task Force of the International Union for the Conservation of Nature (IUCN) estimates that around $450 million worth of seafood is fished from these waters each year.[7]

A simple, lone Somali fisherman cannot compete with that. And partly because of this, Somalia is turning into an ideal haven for piracy and extremism. Climate change is exacerbating this problem, as coastal waters are also warming and this adversely affects the stocks of certain species of fish, which migrate to other areas.

I remember the story told by a colleague who, during the mission, spoke to Somali fathers whose whildren had become pirates at the time. They recount how their sons once had a fish factory that they were able to keep running successfully because of the plentiful supply. Shark fins, grey mullet, tuna and many other types of fish were sold to countries in Asia or the Middle East. This is similar to the situation in the Netherlands, where oysters are not generally eaten by the local population. Most of those we harvest here go to France. This is also how it worked initially for the simple Somali fishermen. They themselves eat mainly meat (fish is regarded as food for the poor), but they can sell the fish for a good price to other countries. So those revenues drop significantly from the moment foreign fishermen start to operate in their waters. The first Somali "pirates" were therefore local warlords and clan leaders trying to defend Somali waters against these invaders, in what was in effect a violent survival strategy. Foreign fishermen unwilling to buy fishing licences from these "pirates" are intimidated and extorted by local fishermen hired to do so.[8] This is an alternative form of taxation, in a country with extremely weak governance.

As for what the pirates do with all the ransom money, it is divided among themselves; some buy a house, others an expensive car. Some divide the money among family members, invest it in resources for new hijackings or use it to emigrate to, for instance, the US, Western Europe, Canada, Dubai or Kenya. The trade in qat, a stimulant drug, also benefits. But most of the money is used for corruption. In 2013, for instance, the World Bank estimated that pirate gangs spent more than 79% of their income on bribes to local politicians, clan leaders, clerics and businessmen[9] as protection money for keeping areas safe from rival clans or money for regional election campaigns in Somalia.

Drought and floods

We know that besides illegal fishing by foreign companies off the coast of Somalia and the lack of good governance in the country, other disasters have occurred: two years before maritime military operations began, in 2006, some 11 million people were affected by drought in East Africa. And two years later, in 2008, the year the European anti-piracy mission Atalanta[10] was launched, some 20 million people were facing a devastating drought and skyrocketing food prices. That crisis affected Kenya, Eritrea, Djibouti and especially Ethiopia and Somalia, where rain is crucial for people who depend on or work in the agricultural sector. This was a worrying situation in a country that had been without a functioning government since 1991.

The drought in Somalia also lowered groundwater levels and allowed seawater to enter the parched land, resulting in salinisation and even more infertile farmland. And drought persisted in subsequent years. The extreme drought in 2016 and early 2017, for example, had a huge impact on the country and created a domino effect of problems. Millions of Somalis faced acute food insecurity.[11] Estimates were that more than 700,000 people were displaced.[12] According to the UN, nearly 40% of the entire population needed humanitarian assistance, including many children. People became disillusioned and utterly exhausted from the continuous struggle for survival.

"I was a rich man in Balli Ahmed, in eastern Somaliland", 26-year-old nomadic herder and farmer Saeed Ibrahim told a *Trouw* correspondent in 2017. He had been born there, got married and led a good life. Saeed had over 300 cows, more than 250 sheep and just under 200 goats. He also grew grain on a piece of land. But then came the drought. It started back in 2015. Last May, there was a shower of rain, but nothing after that. They kept hoping, but in October it became clear that they had to leave, as there was no more grass and no more water. Some of the animals died. Saeed hired a few trucks and loaded the remaining cattle, his wife and seven children onto them and left for a fertile place in Somalia – or so he thought. A long journey of 100 kilometres. Saeed thought it was always green there, a good agricultural area, so he hoped to find grass and water too. But there was barely any to be found, as drought had struck there as well. Many people had come from the east and soon everything was stripped bare. The animals died in rapid succession. "Now I have basically nothing left except my family, six goats and a donkey. I am deeply ashamed. I used to be able to provide everything my family needed and now we don't even have enough to eat. I have failed as a nomad, as a husband and as a father," Saeed said.[13]

Two years later, in 2019, Somalia was again hit by extreme drought and refugee camps continued to fill up. "The water in the river rose when it rained, water flowed and we could survive", 53-year-old Somali Shalle Hassan Abdirahman told the UNHCR refugee organisation in 2019.[14] He was in a refugee camp in Ethiopia at the time. "We used to grow maize, tomatoes, sesame and other crops along the river" he said. "Then it didn't rain and the river ran dry." This does not mean that it never rains in Somalia. On the contrary; on the few occasions when it does rain, it is usually torrential. As was the case in 2020, when the rainfall was so heavy that rivers burst their banks, washing away roads, and even houses and farms. The water rose so fast that people had to leave in a hurry and did not even have time to pack their belongings.[15]

Soon afterwards, those left behind have to deal with swarms of desert locusts, as high temperatures and extreme rainfall seem to be the ideal conditions for large swarms to form.[16] In 2019, we saw the largest locust infestation in Somalia in 25 years. Swarms the size of the city of Paris migrated across the country, stripping everything bare in what was a disaster for the country and, of course, for the population. A swarm of one square kilometre contains 40 to 80 million locusts and can eat as much in one day as 35,000 people put together, according to calculations by the global food and agriculture organisation FAO.[17] That means even more destroyed crops and even more people looking for food and a safe haven, and thus even more desperate people living in tents.

In 2022, severe drought in Somalia killed 43,000 people. Famine is also looming for 2023. Almost half the population is in urgent need of humanitarian aid, according to the UN. About 8.3 million people are affected. Five rainy seasons have already failed to materialise, causing 1.4 million Somalis to flee to other areas. According to UN chief António Guterres, 80% of those people are women and children.

"The drought has had a huge impact on this country where most of the population depend on agriculture and especially livestock. Millions of goats, sheep and cows have died because they could no longer find grass or water", the UN chief said. "It is unconscionable that Somalis, who have done almost nothing to cause the climate crisis, are suffering the terrible consequences. Climate change is causing chaos".[18]

Another factor is the impact of the conflict in Ukraine. The Red Cross reports that high food prices due to the war in Ukraine are making it even more difficult for families to buy food. At the same time, violence is increasing in Somalia, making areas hardest hit by drought difficult for humanitarian aid workers to access.[19]

Winning souls

Climate-related shocks, such as drought and extreme rainfall, are robbing people in Somalia, as in Afghanistan, of the ability to support themselves and driving them to seek a better livelihood. Many end up in hopeless conditions. This renders many young people in Somalia likely to engage in illegal activities, such as piracy, or to recruitment by extremist groups, such as Al-Shabaab. Since the year 2000, Al-Shabaab militias, for example, have been controlling large parts of southern Somalia, including vast agricultural areas, in order to consolidate their stronghold in the region. They are building canals in certain areas to reduce Somali farmers' dependence on rainfall, thus attempting to build goodwill and recruit young men.

During the severe drought in 2011, the year in which our Task Force Barracuda was operating, we also saw Al-Shabaab preventing access to humanitarian shelters, preventing people from getting the help they needed.[20] The armed militias were able to benefit from the resulting food insecurity by exploiting the hunger and desperation. And again in 2017, Al-Shabaab was able to take advantage of flooding and drought to assert its dominance. The terrorist group provides services and aid to regions of Somalia outside government control. They set up drought committees to coordinate relief operations in different parts of the country and position themselves as post-drought service and relief providers. Not infrequently, they offer people money to persuade them to join or blackmail people into paying "tax" despite the fact they have no money.[21] In some cases, people are forced to hand their children over to militia members for military training so that those children can go on to fight.[22] So it is not surprising that some people will do anything to get away. To Ethiopia, for instance, or further, to Yemen, to continue their journey to Europe from there.

Bad cocktail

This bad cocktail of insecurity and poverty, desperation and extremism is therefore at the root of the maritime piracy for which our military was deployed at the time. If a young Somali cannot grow crops due to severe drought and his livestock is dying because of drought or indeed flooding due to intense rainfall, and European, Iranian and Asian fishermen are meanwhile scooping fish out of the sea with impunity, leaving him unable to provide food for himself or his family, then he is ripe for recruitment as a pirate. Someone who is poor and has no prospects might as well attempt to hijack a ship which could potentially generate around 10,000 US dollars very quickly.[23] If there is no longer any local authority to stop this, and fundamentalist groups are proclaiming that this is the best course of action, there are always people willing to sail some 200 kilometres across the ocean in a tiny boat with a full tank of fuel. What have they got to lose?

So the risk-reward ratio is just too attractive for a young Somali at that point. Especially when it turns out that shipowners pay huge sums of money easily and quickly after a ship has been hijacked (many transactions remain out of the press). The resulting "piracy bubble" economy just serves to fuel the greed and opportunism even more. With one successful hijacking, you can support your family for a generation. It is not surprising, therefore, that in those years around the start of the major counter-piracy missions, we were actually seeing more pirates, who were more heavily armed with machine guns, rocket launchers and ladders. They were thus able to attack much larger, fully laden merchant ships sailing through the Gulf of Aden and the Suez Canal towards the Mediterranean and back. So what basically started as local fishermen using force to defend the fishing grounds off the coast of Somalia against invaders in the mid-1990s has evolved over the years into well-organised and extremely lucrative criminal pirate networks. That revenue model becomes even more professional as financiers move in and pay people to carry out hijackings.

Meanwhile, units from various navies continue to have their hands full combating that piracy. That is our mandate. We can only "monitor" fishing in the region itself; intervening in illegal fishing is simply not part of our mandate. Those are the agreements made in Brussels and represent political choices, which means that the military cannot stop a fishing vessel that is secretly fishing off Somalia; they have to allow that ship to sail through the Suez Canal to Europe to unload the catch. I realise that not everyone is comfortable with that. And that is quite understandable: it is like putting sticking plasters on festering wounds without disinfecting them first. Our broad international engagement off the coast of Somalia does eventually have an effect. That is, no more ships are hijacked there. However, the root causes remain unaddressed and well-organised criminal groups are now increasingly adept at smuggling anything and everything, such as drugs, weapons and people. For international organised crime, this provides opportunities to link the supply chain of drug producers in Asian countries, for example, to drug dealers in Europe.[24]

We should be thankful that the broad international counter-piracy effort and the measures taken by shipowners have ultimately proved so effective, but at the same time we have little or no insight into what criminal gangs are doing now. We have no presence in Somalia's hinterland, where crime is rampant for a variety of reasons and the consequences are of great concern to Europe. What we saw in the Gulf of Aden, and later in the western Indian Ocean, is in fact the tip of the iceberg; the web of challenges in Somalia is highly complex, to put it mildly, not least because that web extends to many other parts of the world. Somalia has shown us that climate change can make weak states slip even further. Further weakening can push an already weakened state affected by climate change over a tipping point to become a failed state where warlords are in control. The bad cocktail then becomes a toxic cocktail.

Notes

1. Prior to the EU mission launched in 2008, Operation Atalanta, HNLMS Evertsen and HNLMS De Ruyter were deployed at the request of the UN to protect food shipments from the UN Food Programme (WFP). But the threat of piracy grew in 2008, increasing the need for escorts for both the WFP and merchant shipping. This need is being met by Operation Atalanta, which started on 8 December 2008.

2. The naval patrol comprises ships and aircraft from Belgium, Germany, France, Greece, Italy, the Netherlands, Spain, the UK, Sweden and non-EU member Norway. The mission has three main tasks: protecting UN food programme food shipments, protecting vulnerable shipping and disrupting and reducing piracy.

3. Leonard, E. & Ramsay, G. (ed.) (2014), "Globalising Somalia: multilateral, transnational and international repercussions of conflict" (pp. 3-14). London: Continuum Press.

4. Singh, C. & Singh Bedi, A. (2013, 7 November), "Regional Dimensions of Somali Piracy and Militant Islamism: Anthropological and Econometric Evidence", *Peace Economics, Peace Science and Public Policy* 19(3), pp. 369-380

5. United Nations intervention took place from 1992 to 1995, consisting of UNOSOM I, UNITAF, UNOSOM II and Operation Restore Hope.

6. Murphy, M. (2011), "Somalia, The New Barbary? Piracy and Islam in the Horn of Africa." Oxford University Press.

7. Houben, M. (2010), "The fish is paid dearly. Images of modern pirates". In: Schokkenbroek, J. & ter Brugge, J. (ed.), "Hijackers & Pirates. Villains or Heroes" (pp. 109-122)

8. Murphy, M. (2010), "Small boats, weak states, dirty money. Piracy and Maritime Terrorism in the Modern World." New York: Columbia University Press.

9. World Bank, "The Pirates of Somalia. Ending the Threat, Rebuilding a Nation" p. 115-117

10. Official Journal of the European Union (2008, 12 November), Act adopted under Title V of the EU Treaty Council joint action 2008/851/CFSP of 10 November 2008 on a European Union military operation to contribute to the deterrence, prevention and repression of acts of piracy and armed robbery off the Somali coast. The Council of the European Union. http://eur-lex.europa.eu/LexUriServ/LexUriServ.do?uri=OJ:L:2008:301:0033:0037:EN:PDF

11. Food and Agriculture Organization of the United Nations (2017), Rapid Results Drought Response Plan Somalia 2016/17

12. Federal Government of Somalia (FGS), World Bank (WB), United Nations (UN) & European Union (EU) (2018), Somalia Drought Impact & Needs Assessment. Synthesis Report (1), https://documents1.worldbank.org/curated/en/901031516986381462/pdf/122991-v1-GSURR-Somalia-DINA-Report-Volume-I-180116-Digital.pdf

13. Eveleens, I. (2017, 27 March), "Saeed Ibrahim from Somaliland has lost everything due to drought", *Trouw*, https://www.trouw.nl/nieuws/saeed-ibrahim-uit-somaliland-is-door-de-droogte-alles-kwijt~bdfb22ab/

14. UNHCR (2019, 23 September), "Drought and insecurity drive Somalis to Ethiopia", online *via*: https://www.unhcr.org/nl/2019/09/droogte-en-onveiligheid-drijven-somaliers-naar-ethiopie/

15. UNDP (2020, 8 May), "Conflict and heavy floods force tens of thousands of people to flee their homes in Somalia, amidst COVID-19 threat", online *via*:

https://www.unhcr.org/news/briefing/2020/5/5eb50d2d4/conflict-heavy-floods-force-tens-thousands-people-flee-homes-somalia-amidst.html

16. BBC (2020, 2 February), "Somalia declares emergency over locust swarms", online *via*: https://www.bbc.com/news/world-africa-51348517

17. Food and Agriculture Organization of the United Nations (s.d.), FAO Desert Locust Information Service. Accessed 3 December 2021, from https://www.fao.org/resilience/resources/resources-detail/en/c/278608/

18. Quoted in NOS (2023, 12 April). "UN chief: Somalia suffers climate crisis it is not to blame for." NOS, https://nos.nl/artikel/2471134-vn-chef-somalie-lijdt-onder-klimaatcrisis-waar-het-geen-schuld-aan-heeft]

19. Red Cross (2022, 22 December). "Somalia at risk of famine: what can we do?" https://www.rodekruis.nl/nieuwsbericht/somalie-dreigt-in-een-hongersnood-te-belanden-wat-kunnen-we-doen/

20. Hammond, L. & Vaughan-Lee, H. (2012, 18 April), "Humanitarian space in Somalia: a scarce commodity". HPG Working Paper, https://odi.org/en/publications/humanitarian-space-in-somalia-a-scarce-commodity/

21. United Nations Security Council (2020, 4 March), Children and armed conflict in Somalia. Report of the Secretary-General, https://reliefweb.int/sites/reliefweb.int/files/resources/N2005820.pdf; Fulo Regilme, S. & Spoldi, E. (2020, Children in Armed Conflict: A Human Rights Crisis in Somalia. *Global Jurist* 21(2), pp. 365-402

22. United Nations Security Council (2020, 4 March), Children and armed conflict in Somalia. Report of the Secretary-General, https://reliefweb.int/sites/reliefweb.int/files/resources/N2005820.pdf

23. Eichstaedt, P., "Pirate state: Inside Somalia's Terrorism at Sea", p. 36; UNODC and Oceans Beyond Piracy (2015), "Somali Prison Survey Report: piracy motivations and deterrents", (23-05-2016)

24. Voorhoeve, J. et al (2016). "Security and stability in Northern Africa". Advisory Council on International Affairs, The Hague.

Chapter Three
Free rein for jihadists

"There are risks and costs to action. But they are far less than the long-range risks of comfortable inaction."
John F. Kennedy

While many Dutch people are enjoying a sunny summer in 2015, I am on a troop visit to Iraq as the Chief of Defence. I have just arrived from the Netherlands. *Via* sweltering Baghdad, where it is 40 degrees Celsius at the time, I fly on a C-130 Hercules to the Kurdish city of Erbil in the late afternoon. There, in northern Iraq, Dutch soldiers are training Kurdish Peshmerga fighters to prepare for the fight against the terrorist group Islamic State (IS) in Iraq and al Sham, also known as ISIS or Da'esh. When you see the city of Erbil, you actually imagine yourself in a modern western city with tall glass buildings, wide roads and lots of people on the streets. Driving through like that, you can hardly imagine that it there is a war going on, with the front line only a few dozen kilometres away.

It is also near the front line where the various training sites are located. I am driven safely in an armoured vehicle to the central training site the next morning. There I meet the Kurdish trainees and award diplomas to the graduates. How proud they are. The men cheer and triumphantly wave the newly awarded diplomas in the air. Some bearded students even give enthusiastic kisses to our soldiers. For a down-to-earth Dutchman, that looks a little odd, but when you consider what these men have been through, you understand. These are people who have in some cases been fighting different enemies for 30 or 40 years, and have seen loved ones brutally murdered and women and girls abused and trafficked by ISIS. Some have relatives who are currently in refugee camps, having fled from their villages and homes in fear of ISIS. Those guys know what they are training for: for greater protection of their families from ISIS and for enhanced security of their surroundings. In that case, I would be motivated myself, especially if I knew that the lessons and training would make me better prepared for battle.

What we hardly realised at the time, and something that does not seem at all relevant when it comes to religious extremism, is that climate change has also exacerbated the security situation in Iraq.[1] Drought, water shortages and floods are not uncommon here and lead to great social misery in an agricultural region such as Iraq, in addition to the long-standing political instability and lack of prospects for large groups of young people in particular.

It takes a while for this wider view to sink in, if only because there are so many more urgent problems. For our Dutch military personnel, despite everything, training Kurdish Peshmerga fighters is highly rewarding work. Our soldiers also hear the horror stories, about decapitations, female slaves and murdered children. Because of the horrific attacks in Paris and Brussels, for example, everyone knows that ISIS is capable of creating victims outside Iraq and Syria as well. The goal for all Western military personnel in Iraq therefore seems very clear: "We train Pesh, to fight Da'esh", as the adage goes within the international coalition. In practice, the training amounts to what we Westerners would consider basic but which could be life-saving in Iraq.

Lessons for Peshmerga fighters

Lesson 1: learn to shoot properly. Don't just fire away at random, but choose your position properly, learn the right shooting positions, look and think before you shoot. Adjusting your weapon correctly, adopting the right shooting stance to be able to hit your target at 200 metres and coordinating fire sectors are basic aspects that make you much more effective with less ammunition. Even after a shooting incident, know what to do. So don't immediately run towards a comrade if he has just been shot by ISIS, otherwise you will be shot yourself.

That sounds logical, but people are less trained there and it is a natural human reaction to run straight to your mate if he is wounded. Our advice is not to do that. Or as a Dutch soldier dryly remarked at the time: "That's not useful from a tactical point of view." Better to just coordinate your actions and make sure everyone is in position to cover you, so you really can save that comrade.

Lesson 2: provide the right kind of leadership. This means that, as an officer, you do join the battle, but you do not always lead it if it is not necessary. That might seem very brave – and it is – but by doing so you will get ahead of the troops, lose the overview and will be the first to be killed. And then how effective will your unit be without a commander?

Lesson 3: Recognise the incredible diversity of roadside bombs in Iraq laid by ISIS. Learn to dismantle them to avoid more casualties. That lesson does not need much explanation. However, it quickly becomes apparent that the input of the Peshmerga during that lesson is extremely valuable. For instance, they have experience of roadside bombs not described in our Dutch syllabus. Our trainers then include these in the course material, thus helping to keep all participants alert to and prepared for any potential threats.

Lesson 4: Apply simple medical procedures to save lives at the front. For example, you really don't have to die from a shoulder wound, but in Iraq people often bleed to death unnecessarily. My people teach the Peshmerga how to prevent that and also what alternative medical procedures are available. How do you apply a tourniquet or pressure bandage? How do you treat a wound? If you don't have bandages or antiseptic cream handy, for example, you can also put a slice of tomato on the wound to disinfect it. Anything is better than the more familiar Peshmerga method: sprinkle gunpowder into a wound and hold a flame near it to cauterise the wound, which, as we know, is life-threatening and unnecessarily painful.

After four weeks of training, the time has come. All classes and training are over and the fighters receive their diplomas. That means they are leaving the relatively safe training environment to go back to the war zone where the battle against ISIS is being fought. A battle in which there is much at stake, namely the survival of their families. That motivates these men to give their all. For the Dutch personnel, the farewell is also a special moment. After all, you have been training people to go and fight against ISIS, a barbaric enemy. How will they get on? Can the Peshmerga keep themselves and others alive? Happily, some of them manage to do so, but at that point ISIS is spreading across the region like an oil slick. That is also the reason why we deploy another 150 troops and six F-16s in Jordan around that time in order to push back ISIS in Iraq and eastern Syria.

The birth of ISIS

Just as in Afghanistan and Somalia, I realise that climate change has further aggravated the situation in Iraq, a country that is no stranger to severe drought, water shortages and devastating floods. And here, too, many young people are disillusioned and radicalised. Yet it is also important to note that agriculture in Iraq has been in decline for decades, due in part to bad policies and poor governance under Saddam Hussein, and that oil extraction in Iraq – which requires a great deal of water – is prioritised over securing water supplies for Iraqi farmers. To produce one barrel of oil, you need at least twice that amount of water. Additional water is then needed for cleaning and maintenance. Oil accounts for 65% of GDP and 90% of Iraq's government revenue (pre-Covid-19 pandemic figures).[2] People in the vast marshlands in southern Iraq suffer greatly from water abstraction, including from the oil fields. The underlying ideological divisions between Shiites and Sunnis are becoming more visible due to the US-led military intervention to end the rule of dictator Saddam Hussein. That intervention has unfortunately not led to any stability, but has in fact had quite the opposite effect.

In a nutshell, when Saddam Hussein and his Sunni supporters lost power through military intervention, Iraqi Shiite (clerical) leaders saw an opportunity to seize power. The Sunni minority – previously in power and in a privileged position – felt oppressed and turned against old rivals, or the new Shia regime in Iraq, attacking Shia holy sites as well as Shia residential areas and innocent civilians. The Shiite majority got involved in the fight, which meant that insurgents in several Iraqi regions began using guerrilla tactics, such as car bombs, snipers and suicide bombings, to harm both the military forces and each other.

Despite frantic attempts by the US, and later the UN, to stabilise Iraq, sectarian violence only increased and a year later an al-Qaida splinter group also entered the fray. The result was a situation resembling civil war, with ISIS eventually managing to seize large parts of Iraq because of its Sunni base. The result was that many more people fled. In 2008, for instance, according to Red Cross estimates, 2.3 million Iraqis fled within the country itself and 2 million left Iraq altogether.[3] So after the 2003 invasion of Iraq, although the country was rid of a brutal dictator, it lacked any kind of political stability. Iraqi democracy was weak, contributing to a power vacuum that various rebel and terrorist groups tried to fill, resulting in widespread violence and huge numbers of refugees. As a result, we saw a breeding ground for jihadists, which intensifies when there is a sudden severe drought or devastating flood. "Join us, and you will never have to worry about supporting your family again", was the sales pitch in 2006 and 2007 from members of a group that soon afterwards became known as ISIS. This was at a time when thousands of people in western Iraq no longer had any income due to the water shortage.

Many farmers, including many young people, found themselves in similar hopeless situations at that time and in the years that followed. They could no longer grow crops and their livestock was dying, destroying any prospect of a decent livelihood. This is the critical moment at which young men in particular are easily recruited by jihadists. The moment at which baskets of food or cash are also used as lures. Little wonder that desperate farmers and farm workers who are struggling to survive are often receptive. The ISIS following grows as a result.

As we have seen, the emergence of ISIS has various causes. Experts point, for instance, to the colonial legacy, the maintenance of dictatorial regimes in Egypt, Saudi Arabia, Iraq and Syria – because of oil and arms interests – or the financial support for Sunni militias from families in Saudi Arabia. ISIS also manages to win over many officers and other military personnel from the large and well-equipped army of former dictator Saddam Hussein. Now, however, there are indications that villages hardest hit by drought and/or floods are the most fertile recruiting grounds for jihadists.[4]

Drought and rainfall are in any event cyclical phenomena in the region. Interestingly, around the city of Tikrit, Hussein's birthplace in northern Iraq, ISIS has many more followers in farming communities facing water shortages than among farmers not suffering from a lack of water. In a desert-like area west of the Tigris river, farmers with fields closest to the encroaching desert sands join ISIS in far greater numbers than those near the green valley. It is clear that the growth in ISIS' following in Iraq is partly due to the effects of climate change and water scarcity.[5]

Iraq is now in the throes of a water crisis due to a shortage of drinking water, poor water quality, outdated and damaged infrastructure and inefficient water use. In recent years, basic water supply services in the south also failed repeatedly during the summer months, contributing to widespread protests against the government, most notably in 2018.[6]

Drought in Syria

In neighbouring Syria too, in addition to all sorts of political and socio-economic developments, drought was the proverbial straw that caused disruption and instability in the region. Indeed, Syria, despite the debate among scholars, is for many still the best-known example of a water shortage, partly caused by drought, and the resulting loss of income from agriculture, which set the scene for the horrific conflict that developed subsequently. It was in 2006 that a four-year period of unprecedented drought began in Syria. At that time, the country was already parched due to years of poor policies. For instance, existing irrigation projects were inefficient and Bashar al-Assad's regime encouraged the cultivation of export crops that required huge amounts of water, such as cotton and wheat.[7] Because many farmers in Syria were particularly dependent on groundwater and many of them pumped water unchecked from their own wells, groundwater resources were also dwindling sharply. That meant that the water reserve available for use during dry periods disappeared and the soil degraded further. And that dry period soon followed: between 2006 and 2011, the worst drought ever recorded in the entire region.[8] This created a huge water shortage and crops failed in much of Syria. The result was a doubling of grain prices, a greatly reduced livestock population and a sharp rise in childhood diseases that can be linked to poor food or even a lack of food altogether.[9]

Assad's agricultural policy poured oil on the fire. He was liberalising the economy and abolished food and fuel subsidies, a measure that affected the weakest even more. It was thus understandable that some people would look for a better life for themselves and their children. Some 1.5 million people, including many pastoralists and farming families, migrated to major Syrian cities such as Aleppo, Damascus, Homs and Hama to look for work, in most cases unsuccessfully. They ended up in shanty towns, where their future certainly did not look bright. Before this influx of Syrians to the major cities got under way, the same cities were already having to cope with large population increases due to an influx of an estimated 1.2 to 1.5 million Iraqi refugees.[10]

Add to this nearly 1.5 million people from rural Syria, and the social consequences became incalculable. Rents increased by 400% in a short space of time and food prices were following a similar pattern.[11] What did not help was that the Syrian government was doing little or nothing to combat this crisis; in fact, the opposite was true. Peaceful demonstrations were being quashed. Young men aged 17 or older who were going about their studies and demonstrating in the streets were thrown into torture prisons. People were fleeing. It is still not clear how or why incidents involving young people escalated so quickly. Some believe one explanation is that southern Bedouin tribes with weapons got involved, in other words, tribes whose nomadic nature meant they had relations extending far into Saudi Arabia and did not have a large enough share in the power of the Assad regime.

Another toxic cocktail

It was remarkable that nobody in the international community actually predicted that things would go wrong in Syria of all places. After all, under the repressive regime of dictator Assad, the country was still pretty stable. But Syria was being pushed over the edge. Partly because of prolonged drought, partly because of ethnic tensions that mushroomed and groups that received support from neighbouring countries, and partly due to the wrong policy choices in areas such as agriculture combined with Assad's repressive regime. This led to a situation in which numerous factors aggravated each other, turning the bad cocktail into a toxic one here too.

While scholars differ on the extent to which drought and climate change contributed to the eruption of the conflict in Syria, it is clear that they served to boost the effect on the various other factors influencing the conflict or its origins. "Syria's rapidly growing suburbs, characterised by illegal settlements, overcrowding, inadequate infrastructure, unemployment and crime, were ignored by Assad's government and formed the core of the growing unrest", researchers at Columbia University wrote in 2015.[12] These are also the reasons why, according to the same experts, other regions and countries, such as Turkey, Lebanon, Palestine, Israel and Jordan, face similar security risks. Throughout the Middle East, similar situations of authoritarian regimes, social deprivation, limited opportunities and oppression as well as drought, water shortages and agricultural decline are at play. As a result, there too, a young generation is growing up without prospects, embittered and angry.

Where people – especially young people – see no prospects, they become susceptible to ideologies that offer them a way out and hope for a better future. Terrorist groups are keen to exploit this; we should not underestimate that. In our eyes, they sow only death and destruction, but on the ground they offer the prospect of security and an income to support families. They also offer an escape from the failing regime and the prospect of a new future. And this is how they manage to recruit so many.

Notes

1. Jaafar, B. (2021). The water shortage crisis in Iraq: perspective paper no. 2140. Begin-Sadat Center for Strategic Studies, Ramat Gan. https://besacenter.org/the-water-shortage-crisis-in-iraq/

2. Nakhle, C. (2021), "How Iraq can move beyond the oil sector", Italian Institute for International Political Studies, https://www.ispionline.it/en/pubblicazione/how-iraq-can-move-beyond-oil-sector-32014

3. Margesson, R., Bruno, A., Sharp, J. (2009), "Iraqi refugees and internally displaced persons: a deepening humanitarian crisis?" Congressional Research Service, Washington DC

4. Schwartztein, P. (2017, 14 November). "Climate Change and Water Woes Drove ISIS Recruiting in Iraq. Battered by shifting resources, desperate farmers were driven into terror recruiters' clutches. Can it happen again?", *National Geographic*, Climate Change and Water Woes Drove ISIS Recruiting in Iraq (nationalgeographic.com)

5. Zhang, J. (2020, 6 February). Framing the climate crisis as a terrorism issue could galvanise action. Columbia Climate School Student Blog: Consilience Considers, https://news.climate.columbia.edu/2020/02/06/climate-crisis-terrorism-framing/

6. Lossow, T., et al. (2022, 12 September). Water governance in Iraq: enabling a gamechanger. Clingendael, https://waterpeacesecurity.org/files/245. See also Birkman, L. Kool, D. & Struyken, E. (2022, 17 September). Water challenges and conflict dynamics in Southern Iraq. Water, Peace and Security. https://waterpeacesecurity.org/files/208

7-8. Gleick, P.H. (2014), "Water, Drought, Climate Change, and Conflict in Syria", *Weather, Climate, and Society*, 6(3), pp. 331-340, http://www.jstor.org/stable/24907379

9. Kelley, C.P., Mohtadi, S., Cane, M.A., Seager, R. & Kushnir, Y. (2015), "Climate change in the Fertile Crescent and implications of the recent Syrian drought", *Proceedings of the National Academy of Sciences* 112(11), pp. 3241-3246, https://doi.org/10.1073/pnas.1421533112

10. Leenders, R. (2008), "Iraqi Refugees in Syria: Causing a Spillover of the Iraqi Conflict?", *Third World Quarterly* 29(8), pp. 1563-1584, http://www.jstor.org/stable/20455130

11. Kelley, C., Mohtadi, S., Cane, M., Seager, R. & Kushnir, Y. (2015). "Climate change and the recent Syrian drought", *Proceedings of the National Academy of Sciences* 112 (11), pp. 3241-3246

12. Kelley, C.P., Mohtadi, S., Cane, M.A., Seager, R. & Kushnir, Y. (2015, 17 March), "Climate change in the Fertile Crescent and implications of the recent Syrian drought", *Proc Natl Acad Sci USA* 112(11), p. 3241-3246, https://pubmed.ncbi.nlm.nih.gov/25733898/

Chapter Four
Water as an instrument of power

"Whiskey is for drinking, water is for fighting over."
Quote by farmers in western USA

At quarter past seven in the morning on a summer Friday in August 2014, I walk through the Ministry of Defence in The Hague. I hand back to my secretary the stack of formal documents I had to sign, as well as the unclassified documents I was given the night before. Together, we go through today's agenda. Each topic comes with a pile of documents. Most of them I have already read, the last I go through. At ten to eight, my secretary pokes her head around the door and says it's time to go to the morning briefing by the Directorate of Operations. However busy it is, I make time for that every day, because that's what Defence work is all about. We are constantly part of various missions, and then there are the thousands smaller operations every year to support the civil authorities in the Netherlands. These range from helping to search suspicious sites with specialised equipment to securing our airspace or clearing explosives. This daily morning briefing is crucial for me to be kept up to date. We always want to know the ins and outs of everything, as I could be called upon at any moment to make a decision about starting or stopping an operation. At such a point, there is no time to study a pile of paperwork. A senior military officer simply has to be up to speed.

Together with Lieutenant-General Hans Wehren (my deputy), I walk to the protected directorate with its heightened security. After passing through the security lock, I put my phone in a safe, as everyone does here, and proceed to the Director of Operations' office. A few years ago, I sat there myself.

I greet the few colleagues I find there every morning and ask the director to start his briefing. He immediately starts talking about an action by ISIS fighters who left the Iraqi village of Wana at high speed the day before in pickup trucks and captured US Humvees. The aim was to seize Iraq's largest dam, the Mosul Dam. Two months earlier, Sunni ISIS had already captured the city of Mosul, home to nearly two million people. It appears to be the next step in a ruthless campaign to establish a new caliphate in the Middle East and it would seem to be a cunning strategic move. ISIS has unerringly figured out where the weak spots are and how dependent everyone is on the already scarce water supply. They know that this huge dam controls the flow of water to the city of Mosul, and thus the water supply to millions of Iraqis living along the Tigris. So whoever controls that huge dam has the power. Indeed, that is the aim of the ISIS fighters, because as soon as they arrive at the Mosul Dam, they attack a group of Kurdish soldiers stationed there and then move on, fighting as they go. When the fighting around the dam is over and most Iraqis working at the dam, some 1,500 people, have fled, much of the immediate area has been destroyed. Soon an ISIS propaganda video appears online showing a fighter with a flag, saying: "The flag of unification is flying over the dam."

Conflict dams

It is an unusual development in an area close to where a Dutch mission is to start a few months later: our training mission in Erbil, where Dutch soldiers are training Kurdish Peshmerga for their fight against ISIS. I notice that my colleagues are concerned, which is understandable. For a year now, ISIS has been making huge advances in Iraq, and everyone knows that ISIS has used water as a weapon in Iraq before, when they captured the Fallujah Dam in western Iraq. ISIS used this dam as a means to deprive people downstream of water, but also to stop advancing Iraqi forces by opening the sluices and making areas inaccessible. The same water was then diverted through an irrigation canal towards a nearby valley, leaving the city of Abu Ghraib under four metres of water, as well as other large areas up to 100 kilometres away.

Between Fallujah and Abu Ghraib, ten thousand homes were destroyed by the water, as well as almost the entire crop covering 200 square kilometres of fertile farmland. Many animals drowned too.[1]

So now ISIS fighters control another dam, the colossal Mosul Dam, on which so many people depend. What will they do with it? One scenario is to destroy it. Based on information gathered, we know that certainly in the upper reaches (depending on the amount of water present at the time and whether people in the area have had sufficient warning), a tsunami-like wave could develop, surging through the area, carrying debris, household goods, unexploded bombs, cars, hazardous chemicals, rubbish and dead bodies. Few would be able to escape the violent surge, which would also destroy entire wheat crops, endangering food supplies. The water could even reach the capital Baghdad, including the airport and the "Green Zone", where government buildings and most embassies are located. And if Baghdad's international airport floods, foreign aid has little chance of arriving in time. Getting food or water to those in need would then be virtually impossible, let alone setting up hospitals or restoring electricity. At that moment in that briefing room in The Hague, I realised that the worst-case scenario, the destruction of the Mosul Dam, thus threatened to be an outright catastrophe.

Another scenario is that ISIS decides to leave the dam intact, but to cut off the water to the Shia population in southern Iraq. That would trigger a massive famine. And a final scenario is that ISIS wants to keep the Mosul Dam under control to provide people with water and electricity, but on their own terms. This would allow them to retain power in the region and also raise taxes on the water to fund their terrorist operations. So the options for ISIS are to either flood Iraq, cut off the Shiite areas south of the capital from the water, or, in the most "favourable" case, use the dam as an instrument of power to force the local population to cooperate.

Saved in the nick of time?

The concern within the Directorate of Operations is therefore more than justified. So it is a huge relief that Kurdish forces in Iraq, with the help of international air support, finally manage to retake Mosul Dam over a week later. It is a fierce battle, however, and everyone knows afterwards that the danger is not over yet, as the Mosul Dam is considered one of the most dangerous dams in the world due to the ever-deteriorating state of its foundations in particular. Ever since the dam opened in 1984, Iraqi engineers have pumped more than 100,000 tonnes of concrete (an average of 10 tonnes a day) into the cavities under the dam to prevent the water from one day breaking through. At a time when ISIS is still in control of the Mosul Dam, engineers and scientists are therefore deeply concerned about its condition. Indeed, no concrete has been added under the dam to prevent weakening of the foundation for almost two weeks. Moreover, not only is the dam in the hands of ISIS; the engineers have also fled and are no longer monitoring the dam. With the help of satellite photos and a variety of data, experts are therefore constantly trying to assess the state of the dam. According to the US Army Corps of Engineers, it appears that numerous cavities appeared under the dam during that time; some 23,000 cubic metres in total. John Schnittker, an economist who has been working on water issues in Iraq for more than a decade, says at the time that the consensus among experts is that the dam "could burst at any time". Any suggestion of this possibility to the average Iraqi, however, is just met with a shrug as people there do have other, more pressing problems on their minds. Besides, the question is whether it will happen in their lifetime. Or, as an Iraqi once told a reporter from *The New Yorker*: "We survived Saddam, we survived ISIS, and we will survive the Mosul Dam."[2]

Nevertheless, at the time, the US government was spending huge sums of money on strengthening the Mosul Dam. Even today, various engineers are permanently engaged in what amounts to an endless battle against nature. Using obsolete pumps the size of truck engines, they drive huge amounts of liquid concrete into the earth. They only stop when the holes appear to be full. This does not mean that the hole is actually full, because the engineers cannot tell whether somewhere at the bottom, cement may be washing away. There is simply no other solution. They have to do it this way, unless a decision is made to demolish the dam completely and use, for example, Turkish dams north of the border, for a fee of course. That option is far from ideal, given the political instability in the region and the strategic dependence it creates. An alternative would be to invest billions of dollars to build a concrete curtain against the dam wall, a kind of adhesive seal. But even that option is not feasible, because it involves so much money and would be a slow process. So the risk remains that much of Iraq could flood in the (near) future if the Mosul Dam fails. Then the consequences of the first scenario, namely the repercussions of an ISIS attack on the dam, would become a horrific reality.

Dam as a bargaining chip

For me at least, the temporary takeover of the Mosul Dam by ISIS is a clear example of how people can use water as an instrument of power. The greater the control of a dam, the more control you have over an area, the safety and well-being of hundreds of thousands of people. This is precisely why we see dams being used in many more places as bargaining chips by governments, but also as terrorist weapons by adversaries. The Taliban in Afghanistan, for instance, have also captured and destroyed dams on a regular basis. To prevent this, the Kajaki Dam in the south at the intersection of Uruzgan, Helmand and Kandahar, for example, was a key strategic object for the ISAF coalition to protect. This dam on the great Helmand River is vital for the local population for irrigation for agriculture and for the generation of electricity. We also see tensions rising in neighbouring India and Pakistan (arch enemies since 1947) due to water scarcity and the construction of dams on the Indus River. This long and mighty river flowing through Asia is fed by meltwater from the Himalayas in spring and summer and is the lifeline for 270 million people in the region. But the snow and glaciers of the Himalayas are dwindling, reducing the water supply for irrigation and drinking water, which is probably another reason why Kashmir is such an important region to fight over and why hundreds of thousands of soldiers of Pakistani and Indian origin are now stationed there. It is not only a fertile region and a major source of raw materials, but it is also an extremely important source of water which comes from the glaciers and on which India and Pakistan depend.

Water from the Indus is also needed for the energy security of the three emerging Asian countries; hydroelectric power requires water, in this case fresh water. Countries like China, Pakistan and India are therefore under increasing pressure to secure their national water resources and are taking action by building dams and reservoirs. As a result, Asia now has more dams than the rest of the world. China has built dams to capture water in the upper reaches of the Indus, as the river's source is in China. India, in turn, is particularly vulnerable to the Chinese construction frenzy, because more than half of the river water leaving Chinese territory flows into India. Over time, therefore, it has built dams in rivers that also flow through Pakistan, as well as in the Indus. This in turn causes concern in Pakistan, as its own water supply may be reduced as a result; so Pakistan too is now building mega dams on the Indus, with all the socio-economic and environmental implications that entails.[3]

The first water war?

As well as using water as a means of defence, as in the case of the Dutch Water Line, there are numerous examples of how water can be used as a means of (offensive) power. In 2023, a dam collapsed near the Russian-controlled town of Nova Kachovka. This dam was in the southern Ukrainian region of Kherson. It was apparently blown up, but there was no evidence of this. Neither was it known who was responsible, but it soon became clear that this was a major environmental disaster. The dam served as a crucial source of water for millions of people in the region and was a major source for agricultural irrigation in southern Cherson and for Crimea. The disappearance of this water source would potentially have major repercussions for agriculture and food production.

Many places were also temporarily flooded due to the collapse of the dam and thousands of people had to be evacuated. Immediately after the collapse, the fast-flowing water caused the spread of mines and other explosives, as well as dirt and pollutants, such as fuel from gas stations. It shows what the impact can be when people use dams as weapons.

Unfortunately, this is nothing new. Consider, for instance, the construction of the Great Renaissance Dam on the Blue Nile in Ethiopia. Construction began in 2011, the year Egyptian President Mubarak was deposed during the "Arab Spring", just as I became Director of Operations in The Hague. The construction could be seen as a logical strategic move by Ethiopia, as Egypt is downstream of the Nile and dependent on Nile water. That would increase power over, as well as tensions with, Egypt. At the time, Ethiopia claimed it would only use the huge dam as a hydropower plant to generate more energy.

The fight over the dam between Ethiopia and Egypt predates 2011. Egypt cites an old 1959 treaty on water rights to the Nile with neighbouring Sudan, the country sandwiched between Egypt and Ethiopia that also depends on the Nile. To be clear, this is an old treaty to which Ethiopia was not a signatory, and which states that Egypt has exclusive rights to water in the Nile basin. While Egypt invokes ancient laws with this treaty in hand, Ethiopia lets it be known time and time again that it wants to go ahead with construction of the dam. This results in escalating tensions between the two countries and threats from both sides. Ethiopia argues that the dam is an existential necessity for Ethiopia, while Egypt argues that building the dam is an existential threat to Egypt, but goes on to state that it is prepared to "protect" the "vital interests" of the country's 100 million inhabitants.[4]

It is not inconceivable that both countries will one day defend their interests by military means. Many different countries, observers and international organisations would therefore be involved in a conflict: the US, the EU,

South Africa, the African Union and the World Bank. The question is whether Egypt would give up its monopoly of the Nile with the necessary diplomacy; in other words, whether the issue of the dam could bring about greater regional cooperation and integration. Should Egypt and Ethiopia fail to agree on the distribution of Nile water, however, we could easily be facing the first modern "water war".

In any case, further discussions on water use are expected to be in the offing; the climate is becoming drier and a growing number of people have no access to drinking water. Ethiopia is building a series of dams on the southern Omo River, leaving Kenya fearful that Lake Turkana will run dry. And Uganda is building dams on the White Nile. Dams are also being built elsewhere in the world. Worldwide, there are plans for 3,700 new dams, according to the Netherlands Environmental Assessment Agency (PBL),[5] which are being built in areas of high prosperity, such as Latin America, Southeast Asia and sub-Saharan Africa. Back in 2018, the PBL wrote that the combination of the rising demand for water and the growing water shortages was increasing the risk of water wars.[6]

Lack of water treaties

Previous analysis shows that dam construction increases the risk of social, political or economic conflict, either because many regions have not agreed on a water treaty, or because the issue is not yet the subject of any consultation or negotiation.[7] This poses a particular risk in countries where the demand for water is rising sharply due to water scarcity, such as in the Middle East, Central Asia, the Ganges Basin and the Orange and Limpopo river basins in southern Africa.[8] The question therefore arises as to whether it is conceivable that more dams could be added in the future. That seems very likely, at least if we look at the number of transboundary river basins. There are almost 300 of them worldwide, such as the Nile in West Africa and the Rhine and the Danube in Europe. Other well-known river basins are the Mekong in Asia (where Cambodia, Myanmar, Thailand and Vietnam are victims of dam construction by China and Laos) and the Indus River. The latter largely runs first through the Indian part of the disputed Kashmir region before reaching Pakistan. India has already built dams on the Indus.[9]

One of the few major rivers in the Middle East that still flows "freely" and on which millions of people depend is the Great Zab with a length of some 400 kilometres. This powerful river rises high in southeastern Turkey and flows into the Kurdish region in northern Iraq. There, south of Mosul, the Great Zab empties into the Tigris, which in turn is crucial to the lives of millions of people and animals in southern Iraq, as it hardly ever rains there. Yet dozens of dams have already been planned on the Great Zab by both Iraq and Turkey, as the river is ideal for hydropower plants.[10] Should all the plans currently on the table, which have already been awarded to Chinese and other construction companies, actually go ahead, the Great Zab is certain to become a series of reservoirs providing 1.1 million households in Turkey with 1,100 megawatts of electricity and up to 4,000 megawatts in the Iraqi part.[11]

Dam victims

So the question is what does the future hold when we look at all the dams that have already been built and the construction plans for new ones? It is difficult to predict, but I fear that many river basins will become sources of great concern, as the growing population will also require an increasing amount of water. Meanwhile, however, there is less and less water available due to climate change and poor water management. In addition, we now know that reservoirs and dams have significant long-term consequences and actually even trigger climate change. Several US studies show that some large reservoirs in locations where the vegetation in the basin has not yet disappeared emit even more greenhouse gases than coal-fired power plants due to the decomposition of organic material. In tropical climates, this involves large amounts of methane and, in more temperate climates, carbon dioxide.[12]

Also, when a dam or reservoir is built, trees are cut down and entire villages disappear, as is now the case in Pakistan. People are then forced to move, not knowing where to go or how to earn a living. Millions of people who depend on farming or fishing see water drying up downstream and fish disappearing due to ecosystem degradation. This is because fish can no longer swim upstream to spawn, and nutrient-rich silt can no longer be carried by the river and deposited on farmland. Elsewhere, aquatic life also disappears in the same way and traditional agricultural systems perish, sometimes even thousands of kilometres away. And since river water can no longer flow into the sea because of the many dams, seawater penetrates deeper into the land. This can lead to salinisation of the soil and agricultural land thus becomes unusable. This too can be a powerful impetus for communities to migrate in search of a better life.

Dams also have a major impact on river life and sediment runoff. Without the river as a "conveyor belt" of sediment, river life disappears. The biggest drawback is that sediment no longer enters river deltas and sea estuaries, causing coastlines to disappear into the sea. The Mississippi River has now become a canal and Louisiana's coast is shrinking to the tune of one football field per hour.[13] Combined with groundwater abstraction in urbanised areas and for agriculture, the soil is sinking, making river deltas even more vulnerable to extreme weather and the rise in sea levels.

Turn the tap back on

Dam construction therefore comes at the expense of the environment and in many cases, on the backs of local people. This is why countries like the US, Canada and Australia have passed what they call "wild river laws", under which dams are no longer allowed. This legislation aims to preserve the function of rivers now, and for generations to come. Indeed, an increasing number of dams in those countries are being demolished. The US, for example, once a leader in dam construction, has removed 1,300 dams, not only because the dams were considerably outdated, but also because the importance of nature and the free migration of the salmon population outweighed the need for electricity generation.[14]

For those who want to know exactly what happens when a dam is demolished, Bart Geenen – dam expert at the World Wildlife Fund (WWF) – has the answer. In an interview, he says it is like a tap you turn back on, and so is often "the beginning of something beautiful".[15] It is clear to me in any event that many dams also have an important and useful purpose, as they provide electricity and irrigation, for example, and thus also business, trade and economic prosperity. Furthermore, dams and weirs are often needed for river navigation, which in turn contributes to trade and prosperity. And without prosperity, there is no climate control. So besides the danger and adverse effects, dams also have undeniable benefits.

The arguments for and against therefore need to be carefully considered. And that balancing act should be performed with all stakeholders for reasons of stability and security. This becomes all the more important when you realise that dams are increasingly becoming another instrument of power. In a world that is warming and where water is increasingly scarce, they are a potential trump card for both those with good and those with evil intentions, as the example of ISIS in Iraq shows. In combination with increasing water scarcity, therefore, dams all over the world have the potential to become conflict dams.

Either way, it is clear that people need to use water more sparingly and that agreements on the distribution of water are crucial to avoid conflict.

Notes

1. Tobias von Lossow, Stiftung Wissenschaft und Politik, German Institute for International and Security Affairs, "Water as a weapon: IS on the Euphrates and Tigris", p. 2; Strategic Foresight Group (2014), Water and violence: crisis of survival in the Middle East. SFG, p. 20

2. Filkins, D. (2016, 25 December), "A bigger problem than ISIS?", *New Yorker*, https://www.newyorker.com/magazine/2017/01/02/a-bigger-problem-than-isis

3. Jorgic, D. (2017, June 13), "Pakistan eyes 2018 start for China-funded mega dam opposed by India", *Reuters*, https://www.reuters.com/article/us-china-silkroad-pakistan-dam-idUSKBN1941P9

4. Roussi, A. (2020, 23 July), "Row over Giant Nile Dam Could Escalate, Experts Warn", *Nature* 538, pp. 501-502, https://media.nature.com/original/magazine-assets/d41586-020-02124-8/d41586-020-02124-8.pdf

5-6. Netherlands Environmental Assessment Agency report (s.d.) (2018), The Geography of Future Water Challenges. https://www.pbl.nl/nieuws/2018/toenemende-waterrisicos-staan-duurzame-ontwikkeling-in-de-weg

7. Milne, S. (2021, 17 August), "How water shortages are brewing wars", *BBC News*, https://www.bbc.com/future/article/20210816-how-water-shortages-are-brewing-wars

8. UNEP-DHI & UNEP (2016), Transboundary River Basins: Status and Trends, Summary for Policy Makers. United Nations Environment Programme (UNEP), Nairobi, http://www.geftwap.org/publications/river-basins-spm

9. Gupta, J. (2021, March26), "Indus water talks resolve little, but raise hope for dialogue", *The Third Pole*, https://www.thethirdpole.net/en/regional-cooperation/indus-water-talks-resolve-little-but-raise-hope-for-dialogue/

10. Çabuk, S.N., Bakış, R., Göncü, S., Gümüşlüoğlu, E. & Çabuk, A. (2013), "Investigation of Hydroelectric Energy Potential of the Zab River basin using geographic information systems and remote sensing methods", *Journal of Renewable and Sustainable Energy*, 5(6), 063131, https://doi.org/10.1063/1.4850526

11. Kemman, A. (2020, 9 August). "Who will conquer the Great Zab?", *Allegiance, via*: https://verhalen.trouw.nl/grotezab/

12. Song, C., Gardner, K.H., Klein, S.J.W., Souza, S.P. & Mo, W. (2018), Cradle-to-grave greenhouse gas emissions from dams in the United States of America. *Renewable and Sustainable Energy Reviews*, 90, 945-956, https://doi.org/10.1016/j.rser.2018.04.014

13. Kolbert, E. (2019, 25 March), "Louisiana's disappearing coast", *New Yorker*, https://www.newyorker.com/magazine/2019/04/01/louisianas-disappearing-coast

14. The American Rivers Project maintains an online database of these: https://www.americanrivers.org/conservation-resource/62-dams-removed-2015-benefitting-rivers-communities-nationwide/

15. Down to Earth editors (2017, 12 September), *Down to Earth*, online at: https://downtoearthmagazine.nl/stuwdammen-verwijderde-dam-is-begin-iets-moois/

Chapter Five
Sahel, the canary in the coal mine

"The earth is crumbling, the topsoil floats into the air like dust. It is grimly quiet; in the evening the crickets no longer chirp and there is no pungent smell of raindrops prompting frogs to sing in drunken chorus. The sound of bleating goats and braying donkeys is absent from the corrals of the herdsmen: 3.5 million cattle have died in southern Ethiopia in recent months, 2.5 million in Kenya."[1]

Koert Lindijer, Africa correspondent of Dutch newspaper NRC *Handelsblad*, on 1 January 2023

"When do we leave?" The journalist dabs his forehead as he looks questioningly at my spokesperson. We are in a small white UN plane that is supposed to take us from the Malian capital Bamako to the city of Gao. It is late May 2014, Minister Jeanine Hennis' first visit to the mission in Mali. The engines have been roaring for a while and the door is wide open, letting the dry Saharan air blow into the plane like a hot foehn. "We are still waiting for the minister," my spokesperson mutters. I look up from my papers and peer through the plane window; the air above the tarmac of the runway shimmers. To my relief, I see her approaching with her aide in her wake. As soon as the aircraft doors are closed and the minister is ready for departure, the cool air from the air conditioner flows into the cabin. I see the relief on the faces of those travelling with her.

We take off and the metropolis of Bamako grows smaller and smaller. When you see this capital in south-west Mali below you like this, you realise that you are flying over one of Africa's poorest countries. Along the banks of the Niger, there are only two real tower blocks. Apart from a monumental bank and a huge hotel once built by the Russians, Bamako consists mainly of a multitude of low-rise buildings, many of which are earthen houses on countless dusty streets. But also many walled green gardens and, in quite a few places, goats and free-range chickens. It is actually a huge, sprawling village; a "village" in a country that is 70% desert or semi-desert, where new people from the countryside arrive daily to seek their fortune.

Our journey to Gao in the north is clearly taking longer than the travelling party has anticipated. Someone at the back of the plane asks several times how long it will be. I quite understand, as Mali is 33 times the size of the Netherlands, and flying from the capital Bamako to the northern city of Gao takes just as long as flying from Amsterdam to Nice in the south of France. When we step off the plane after a few hours, the heat hits us in the face. Although it is extremely hot in Bamako, the heat in the desert city of Gao is really stifling. It is midday and, at 50 degrees Celsius, the hottest time of day. The two accompanying journalists from news agency ANP and RTL News look around. They know they are at an airport, but that is not the right word to describe this location. This is a bare concrete strip in the desert, with a small, dilapidated airport building next to it.

The Dutch soldiers who have been waiting for us take the two of them to a Bushmaster, a large armoured wheeled vehicle in desert camouflage, which we use to drive to the Dutch camp Castor, which is a little further out in the desert. I'm going there myself on a working visit to my 380 military personnel who are there right now. The minister and journalists have come along to see for themselves how the UN mission in Mali is going and what Camp Castor, which is in fact annexed to the large UN camp, is like now. Although this mission is usually talked about in purely military terms, there is also a clear link here to drought, crop failures, famine, water shortages and migration: all factors that are exacerbated by climate change, as we will see.

Dark pee is bad news

Just before we board the vehicle, we are each handed a flak vest and helmet – "in case missiles are fired at the camp." The journalists look at them silently. They get into a different Bushmaster. The dirt road to the camp is bumpy and dusty. When we get out 15 minutes later, everyone is trying to get from one spot of shade to another. In the full sun, it is unbearable. With a large bottle of water in hand, we walk along gravel paths past tents and containers. The Sahara sand has coloured them red. This is where the Dutch military sleep.

While we are walking, someone tells the two journalists what to do if they hear the alarm, which indicates a missile attack. A protracted signal means put on your helmet and take cover. An intermittent signal means that the coast is clear again. They seem to know, nodding. These are the standard signals at all camps, including those in Afghanistan and Iraq. Moments later, a military colleague in charge of hygiene and healthcare at the camp tells the journalists to keep drinking throughout the day. There are bottles of water everywhere. "If you feel thirsty, it may already be too late", he says. "That's why you should keep checking your urine. Dark pee is bad news." It reminds me of my time in Afghanistan, where the men would say to each other: "If you pee Fanta Orange, you haven't been drinking enough."

A little while later, Fons Lambie, one of the journalists, stops and looks at his shoes. The heat is making his soles peel off. A couple of soldiers laugh; that's not the first time something like that has happened here. Suddenly, the wind gets up. It is a tourbillon, a small but violent local cyclone that almost sandblasts us. In no time, the red sand is in our hair, eyes and nose. That's how quickly the weather can turn here. "As can the security situation", notes Bert Koenders dryly. He is head of the UN mission in Mali in 2013 and 2014. In that capacity, he has visited the large UN camp in Gao many times. He is travelling with us today.

He is right. Mali was recently top of the class in terms of democracies in Africa. The country is ostensibly one of the most stable in the Sahel region.

The crux of course lies in that "ostensibly", because the country is a mix of peoples with tensions and conflicts between them. The north is Arab and that is where the nomadic Tuareg (Berbers) reside. Other parts of the vast country are home to the Bambara, Peul, Soninké and Malinké, among others. The Tuareg are often seen as the slavers for the Maghreb, the northwestern part of Africa. That old hurt still lives on. In the 1980s, a drought caused massive cattle mortality, as a result of which the Tuareg became "beggars". They never really recovered from this. Meanwhile, other population groups benefited from the extraction of oil, gas and minerals, which exacerbated the divisions. So there is always something brewing under what appears to be a calm surface. And every now and then it boils over. Former Libyan leader Moamar Gadaffi regularly fanned the flames during his reign by first supporting one group and then another. *Divide et impera*, as the Romans said.

Tipping point

The situation escalates when Gadaffi is deposed in 2011, however. Libya, northeast of Mali, lapses into chaos after the dictator's demise. Arms and mercenaries flow easily into northern Mali through neighbouring countries. So the warring Tuareg there are well placed to arm themselves and see their opportunity to fight alongside jihadists for the creation of the independent state of "Azawad". At the time, the Malian government is powerless; its control does not extend much further than the outskirts of the capital, Bamako.

As a result, the militants can easily recruit poor and underprivileged youth. They say to them: "You see, the government does nothing for you." The fighters also offer the youths money to fight for them, sometimes as much as $300 a month. Most of that money is earned from drug smuggling and arms trafficking. Thanks to youth recruitment and the help of several thousand Islamist-extremist fighters from, for example, al-Qaida and ISIS, the Tuareg soon gain control of half of Mali. They seize underprivileged and poverty-stricken northern Mali, an area larger than France, before bringing large, more southerly cities, such as Timbuktu, Gao, Mopti and Segou, under their influence and control. Using pick-up trucks and heavily armed, they then advance further towards Bamako, where the Malian government is based. Mali's army looks on helplessly. They are poorly armed, undermanned and hopelessly disorganised.

Help is in sight, however: thousands of French soldiers land in Mali to fight the Tuareg, and thus thwart their attempts to establish their own state. Operation Serval has begun.

"We will continue to attack: now, tonight and again tomorrow", French Defence Minister Jean-Yves Le Drian said on television. Many residents of Mali are in party mood after the intervention. "We can listen to music again, dance, drink alcohol and do whatever we feel like", one resident says.

Calm is restored in 2013 thanks to the French effort, but not for long. Tensions persist between the Malian government and the Tuareg in northern Mali. The Tuareg are still there, although they have been driven out to the northeast. The violence spreads to other places, the so-called "waterbed effect". Alongside the French intervention, the UN peacekeeping mission MINUSMA is now getting under way,[2] which aims to protect civilians in Mali and restore order. The mission should also help the Malian state restore its sovereignty in the north of the country so that other countries and UN aid organisations can begin development programmes.

Dutch military personnel in Mali

In 2013, the Dutch armed forces are brought into the mission, and in 2014 we are on the ground. This is the first time since Srebrenica that we have contributed to a UN mission on a larger scale. The political decision-making process is therefore quite involved and I invest a lot of time in technical briefings to parliament to explain what lessons we have learned from Srebenica and what that means for our contribution to MINUSMA. For example, I ensure that our officers in the mission at all levels can exert sufficient influence on the decision-making within MINUSMA and that the unit has sufficient combat power to be able to stand its ground independently if situations escalate. We also opt for a Dutch contribution that can strengthen the mission as a whole by focusing on the intelligence chain. So we are not responsible for area security, but for providing intelligence to UN units. Based on our experiences in Afghanistan and other missions, we know that in this way we can gain a clearer picture of the root causes of the conflict and thus help the UN make a switch from monitoring and response to addressing those root causes in a more targeted way.

For the UN, this is a new concept. Never before have they worked with an intelligence chain like this. And never before have they been able to make use of the associated scarce technological capabilities, such as intelligence units with drones, special forces covering large areas in small independent teams, and Apache combat helicopters. We also send mortar gunners, scouts, explosive ordnance disposal units, fire support teams, communication systems specialists, doctors and nurses to Mali. But above all, intelligence specialists. They have to map out the areas in northern Mali, gather information from the local population and analyse it. This will enable the UN to identify potential security risks at an earlier stage and to deploy troops early to prevent deterioration of the situation.

For example, if there are rumours of an imminent attack, Dutch military personnel travel to the village in question and set up their vehicles out of sight. They then move into the village on quads and with an interpreter, to avoid overwhelming the residents any more than necessary. Once they arrive, they talk to tribal elders, officials or school teachers and ask what is going on. This approach works, as it prevents escalation. So it is fair to say that we are the eyes and ears of the mission and thus enable the UN to anticipate developments.

And is this sufficient? I see that many soldiers have doubts about the work they are doing there. Much important information may be transmitted, but they don't know what happens to it in the end. Some wonder whether it does actually contribute to the effectiveness of the mission in such a large area. The UN clearly still has to get used to operating in a more information-driven way, but it is already experiencing the enormous added value of that anticipatory capability.

Our intelligence experts pick up confirmation from the population that it is not only the desert that is advancing to the south, but also insecurity. Back in 2015, they predicted that rising tensions would trigger a wave of attacks in central Mali, a prediction that would sadly prove accurate in later years. Little was done with the intelligence at the time, however, as neither the Malian government nor MINUSMA was ready to handle it.

The competition for fertile land

It is clear from our intelligence that drought and water shortages are contributing to the relocation of large groups of people in Mali. Crop failures due to drought in the Sahel are not just a recent phenomenon; the area has been subject to climate cycles with more and less rainfall for centuries. During certain periods, therefore, it is highly susceptible to drought and famine, while it can also be exposed to severe flooding. It is now clear that there are no longer any constants in this respect; research shows that climate change not only intensifies but also prolongs these episodes.[3] Periods of drought in the Sahel are thought to be caused by shifts in jet streams and what is known as the intertropical convergence zone, which in turn may be triggered by changes in solar radiation intensity, ocean water temperatures or air pollution and greenhouse gases.[4] To combat these drought phenomena, an organisation to combat drought in the Sahel, the Comité permanent Inter-État de Lutte contre la sécheresse dans le Sahel [Permanent Interstate Committee for drought control in the Sahel] (CILSS), was set up as early as 1973. It aims to tackle drought and invest in food security. A challenge, especially when you realise that the population of the Sahel, which includes Mali, is growing.[5] All those people are cutting down the few trees still left for firewood and keeping livestock that need to graze.

So there are going to be problems, as tree roots normally serve to retain the soil and run-off water, and thus also the fertile farmland which is now being either washed or blown away. In addition, many farmers are sowing fields in areas that are actually unsuitable for agriculture, resulting in soil erosion. And that in turn leads to greater drought. Less vegetation usually means less precipitation, and when rain does fall, it largely runs off superficially and barely replenishes the groundwater reserves. Water sources therefore dry up and it becomes increasingly difficult to grow food. A prolonged drought thus undermines the resilience of entire ecosystems.

Nomads found themselves facing exactly this scenario in northern Mali in 2010, three years before the French intervention. After the long droughts of the 1970s and 1980s, they were once again exposed to prolonged drought. In many places, livestock was dying and hunger was on the increase. Many people were leaving Mali in search of better pastures. But when pastoralists arrived at their winter grazing grounds (their dry season coincides with our winter) after a trek of hundreds of kilometres in many cases, they found that they no longer existed. Indeed, those stream valleys where their traditional dry season pastures lay were not only drying up due to climate change, but more and more of them were also being cultivated: fields for and by local farmers. So the pastoralists moved on, not only fleeing the erratic rainfall and changes at the start of the rainy season, but rather in search of fertile grazing land. They thus ended up in growing numbers in southern Mali, or moved on to places like Niger, Burkina Faso or northern Nigeria.

Herdsmen are now coming into contact with communities with which there has been no agreement to share natural resources. Farmers in southern Mali, who consider the land there as their property, do not exactly welcome the northerners and block their passage. Clashes and violent confrontations between different ethnic groups are always just around the corner. This situation is being exacerbated by the rapid population growth, with greater numbers of people depending on water every year, and by the felling of countless trees for houses, furniture and ovens, all of which combines to create a downward spiral.

Al-Qaida as an employer

Severe drought caused another famine in Mali in 2012. Grain was almost impossible to buy, and when it was, it cost twice as much as the year before. Children were sick with hunger.

More and more people were forced to eat the seeds they actually needed to sow and grow for the next harvest. By eating them, they could get by for one or two days, but after that they ran out completely. Consequently, more and more people were dying, if not from hunger, from exhaustion or as a result of diarrhoea. The number of people fleeing to the cities, hoping to find work there, was increasing. And in addition to all that, there was the mismanagement and self-enrichment of the government elite.

So in the years that followed, Mali's young people, seeing their parents' lives ruined by the dry years of the preceding decades, reached for arms much more readily. They were willing to accept dollars from warring groups in exchange for tasks. Not so much because these young people felt like jihadists, but mainly because they were driven by poverty and unemployment. We see all this in our intelligence. But our mission is not to ensure these young people get jobs, to provide sustainable agro-ecological farming techniques to cultivate their fields, to plant trees or to help set up sustainable water management. Our mission in Mali is to find out for the UN what is really going on, who is in charge in a particular destabilised region and how the warring factions can be contained.

For some, intelligence work in such a vast country with all its complex issues seems futile, especially when you consider that the UN mission itself is having quite an adverse ecological impact on the local environment.[6] A large-scale UN camp extracts a considerable amount of groundwater, which means that wells for the local population are more likely to run dry. Some military personnel realise this and rightly question it. The knowledge that the military are extracting water that is already scarce is likely to have an adverse effect on the already fragile peace process. In 2016, for example, a local community in Kidal protested against our mission. Their complaint, justified in itself, was that an increase in the number of troops in the camp would deplete the local water supply.[7]

In response, the UN drills deeper wells to improve the availability of water for the local population, but the negative image is not so easily shed. In the Sahara, the water supply often consists of fossil water that is not replenished by groundwater streams from elsewhere. This poses a risk that even the deeper wells will eventually dry up.

Opponents of the UN mission strategically use the protests and local grievances to step up resistance and their attacks against MINUSMA. They convince locals that with their income (mostly earned through crime or smuggling), they can offer a better alternative for their welfare and livelihood than an organisation which claims to bring peace but in the meantime uses the water that is already scarce. It shows that reducing the ecological footprint is not only important from the perspective of climate goals, but that it also facilitates acceptance and enhances the effectiveness of missions. Furthermore, it shows once again that military and civil reconstruction efforts must go hand in hand. There is no doubt that a military contribution is needed to stabilise the country after the initial intervention by the French, but military solutions alone are certainly insufficient in Mali.

Refugees: the calm before the storm

Almost eight years later, not only has the situation not improved, but it has actually deteriorated even further. Seasonal flooding and drought are contributing to internal displacement.[8] In 2020, more than 80,000 people were affected by exceptionally severe flooding, many of them killed or injured. More than 6,000 homes were destroyed, as were more than 7,000 tonnes of food.[9] Extremists further exploited the situation and recruited swiftly among young people; there were brutal killings of innocent people almost every day.[10] Farmers and herdsmen fought each other over land and to keep their cattle alive. Cows that were still alive ate plastic waste for lack of food. Entire communities from rural areas moved to the big cities, which buckled under the strain and desperate situations abounded.

I witnessed this myself in the smog-shrouded capital of Bamako, on the foul-smelling and murky Niger River. The suburbs and areas around the city, the barren fields, were strewn with rubbish, plastic waste in particular. On the way to and from the airport just outside the city, where a UN base and our intelligence unit were stationed, huge numbers of smouldering piles of rubbish that had been set alight could be seen in every direction. There are no prospects here. The average income in Bamako is €1.50 a day, and the city is growing by 100,000 people every year. Most of them are farmers fleeing from violence and drought and all are looking for a means to survive.

Many young people are trying to cross over to Europe out of desperation. Terrorism expert Liesbeth van der Heide, with whom I was lecturing on climate and security in 2020 and who has done extensive fieldwork in Mali, said: "If I had been born in Mali, I would also try to cross the Mediterranean in a boat." And she is not alone in that point of view. "If Europe thinks it has a problem with migration today, wait another 20 years", US general Stephen Cheney said back in 2017, according to a report by the Environmental Justice Foundation (EJF), an NGO fighting for human rights and environmental protection. According to this retired general, the Sahel in particular will see mass displacement. "We are not talking about one or two million people, but 10 or 20 million. And they will try to cross the Mediterranean."[11] In Europe, we already have huge problems with tens of thousands of migrants and discussions are rife about whether we stop them or let them in. Either way, migration pressure is going to increase significantly. In my experience, it is better not to turn a blind eye and leave the problems for the next government. It is better to face the problem and consider in a European context what we can do to prevent these flows.

According to Sweden's independent Stockholm International Peace Research Institute (SIPRI), there also seems to be a link between child recruitment and scarce rainfall in central Mali. SIPRI's researchers spoke with military personnel from the UN mission and found that during times of scarce rainfall, some families in Mali were more likely to send their children to armed groups as a way of generating income. When there is less rainfall, there is noticeably more recruitment. The SIPRI researchers also noted that in places where corruption and nepotism by government officials is rife, armed groups took over the role of the government. Katiba Macina, for example, an armed jihadist group led by the charismatic Imam Amadou Koufa and which operates in Mali from the Inner Niger Delta to the Mauritanian border, has built wells and set up agricultural projects, appearing to have the people's best interests at heart. But in reality, the al-Qaida-linked terrorist organisation is all about power and influence.

The researchers also concluded from military accounts that the recruitment of herdsmen in Mali by armed groups was directly linked to water scarcity. "No work, no schools and no water in an already difficult situation means that young people are easily recruited by terrorist groups and have to survive by supporting these groups in smuggling operations *via* routes through the Sahara", said an anonymous MINUSMA soldier. "There is nothing we can do about that." The lack of natural resources combined with unemployment, according to this source, is the reason why young people are "taking up arms and trying to get whatever they can". He believes it is the "only option they have". Another factor here is that these desperate youngsters end up lower in the social hierarchy of their environment, creating a kind of identity vacuum. They are then more inclined to join armed groups, because it gives them higher status and prestige.[12]

Epicentre of instability

Meanwhile, in the remote areas of the Sahel, stretching from Senegal to Sudan, state institutions are so weak or corrupt that governments cannot offer any alternative. Extremists are therefore able to mobilise support in failing states and regions. For instance, armed groups have penetrated areas previously untouched by extremist violence. Along the Indian Ocean coastline, al-Qaida-linked militants control large parts of the countryside, and further south, in Mozambique, a rebellion with only a few dozen fighters escalated into a full-scale war a few years ago.

The central part of the Sahel – Mali, Burkina Faso and Niger, as well as southern Libya, northern Nigeria and Chad – has also become an epicentre of instability and constitutes a veritable transit point for refugees, migrants, organised crime and terrorism. Both ISIS and al-Qaida are gaining ground there. Should the entire Sahel region become a haven for extremists, smugglers and terrorists, it will become a hotbed of discontent that will soon make its presence felt at home; a breeding ground and a base of operations for jihadists.

In short, the threat is growing in an almost unimaginably vast area separated from Europe only by the Mediterranean Sea. What happens if it gets drier? Long and severe droughts have become commonplace in East and Southern Africa as well as in the Sahel. When people greet each other, the question is often: "Is it raining where you come from?" And what happens if more trees are cut down? Today, researchers estimate that two-thirds of Africa's farmland is affected by drought and deforestation.[13] "My big fear", says Solomon Hsiang, climate researcher and economist at the University of California (Berkeley), "is that Africa's transition to a new order in response to climate change will lead to a constant flow of migrants."[14] Any prospect of a better future is thus getting further and further away, to put it mildly, because this just feeds the recruitment pool fished by groups such as al-Qaida, ISIS and Boko Haram in countries such as Nigeria, Cameroon, Niger, Chad and the Central African Republic.

An additional problem is the fact that more than 64% of the Sahel region's 150 million inhabitants are under the age of 25 (in Mali, the figure is as high as 70%).[15] With such high percentages of young people in a barely developed region plagued by drought, the threat of destabilisation and conflict is enormous, precisely because a lack of prospects drives them to extremes. Or as Liesbeth van der Heide says: "In a family of shepherds in Mali, the eldest son always takes over his father's work. But what will his eight brothers do? Those boys can move to the cities, but there too, inequality is rife and you often have to pay to get a job. So young people have limited choices: either remain destitute, try to get to Europe, or go to work for well-paying local groups that promise the earth."

The last choice would appear to be the preferred option, given the extremist violence increasing in the Sahel. In this respect, it is not only Mali but the entire Sahel region that is the canary in the coal mine; it is a serious warning of the shape of things to come if we stand back and do nothing.

Notes

1. Lindijer, K. (2023, 1 January). "After four years I have lost almost all my cattle, my end is coming". NRC, https://www.nrc.nl/nieuws/2023/01/01/na-vier-jaar-heb-ik-vrijwel-al-mijn-vee-verloren-mijn-einde-komt-in-zicht-a4153029?t=1689837134

2. United Nations Multidimensional Integrated Stabilisation Mission in Mali (French: *Mission multidimensionnelle intégrée des Nations Unies pour la stabilisation au Mali*).

3. Wang, S. & Gillies, R. (2011), "Observed Change in Sahel Rainfall, Circulations, African Easterly Waves, and Atlantic Hurricanes Since 1979", *International Journal of Geophysics*, http://www.hindawi.com/journals/ijge/2011/259529/abs/

4. World Bank (n.d.), "Population growth (annual %)", accessed 3 December 2021, from https://data.worldbank.org/indicator/SP.POP.GROW?locations=ML

5. World Bank, "Population growth (annual %): Mali", (n.d.) (3% per annum in Mali)

6. MINUSMA did become one of the first UN missions to mention the ecological footprint in its mandate. In 2012, the UN Environment Programme released a report entitled "Greening the Blue Helmets", in which the UN recognised that peace missions could have an impact on the natural environment. The report also highlighted that the environment and natural resources affected peace missions (Nairobi: UNEP, 2012).

7. Hegazi, F., Krampe, F. & Seymour-Smith, E. (2021), Climate Related Security Risks and Peacebuilding in Mali. SIPRI Policy Report. Stockholm International Peace Research Institute, https://www.sipri.org/sites/default/files/2021-04/sipripp60.pdf

8. Extract from Parliamentary letter from the Ministry of Foreign Affairs, July 2021: "As a result of the military coup, France temporarily suspended bilateral military cooperation with Mali to keep pressure on a transition to a constitutional and democratic order. Following consultations with Malian transition authorities, France decided on 2 July to resume this cooperation. On 10 June, President Macron also

announced a reorganisation of French military deployment in the Sahel, including the end of the French regional counterterrorism operation Barkhane in its current form. The French decision is in accordance with the long-standing French view that it is desirable to further internationalise the deployment in the region and place more responsibility with the Sahel countries themselves to ensure their own security and counter security threats, including terrorism. The government shares the view that it is desirable for Sahel countries to take more responsibility for their own security."

9. Hegazi, F., Krampe, F. & Seymour-Smith, E. (2021), Climate Related Security Risks and Peacebuilding in Mali. SIPRI Policy Report. Stockholm International Peace Research Institute, https://www.sipri.org/sites/default/files/2021-04/sipripp60.pdf

10. Van der Heide, L. (2019, 20 April), "Dumping One Government Won't Fix Mali", *Foreign Policy*, online *via*: https://foreignpolicy.com/2019/04/20/dumping-one-government-wont-fix-mali-security-west-africa-sahel-ogossagou-fulani-dogon-tuareg-azawad-terrorism/

11. EJF (2017). Beyond borders: "Our changing climate – its role in conflict and displacement", https://ejfoundation.org/resources/downloads/BeyondBorders-2.pdf

12. Hegazi, F., Krampe, F. & Seymour-Smith, E. (2021), "Climate Related Security Risks and Peacebuilding in Mali", *SIPRI Policy Report*. Stockholm International Peace Research Institute, https://www.sipri.org/sites/default/files/2021-04/sipripp60.pdf

13. Vives, L. (2015, 13 January), "More than half of Africa's arable land 'too damaged' for food production", press release Relief Web, https://reliefweb.int/report/world/more-half-africa-s-arable-land-too-damaged-food-production

14. Lustgarten, G. (2020, 23 July), "The great climate migration", *New York Times*, https://www.nytimes.com/interactive/2020/07/23/magazine/climate-migration.html

15. Up-to-date demographic figures *via* IndexMundi: https://www.indexmundi.com/mali/demographics_profile.html

Chapter Six
Hurricane after hurricane after hurricane

"Humanity is waging war on nature. This is suicidal. Nature always strikes back – and it is already doing so with growing force and fury."

António Guterres, UN Secretary-General

"It looks like a scene from a bizarre Hollywood movie", says a colleague at the scene to whom I'm speaking *via* a satellite phone. "From *Armageddon* or something." It is 6 September 2017. Hurricane Irma, a storm of the most powerful category, has just left a trail of devastation on Sint Maarten in the Caribbean. It is an extremely traumatic experience for the people who live and work there. The howling of the wind, the driving, horizontal rain, flying roof tiles and debris and the utter chaos left behind. Boats thrown onto the shore, cars blown away like toys and thrown in a heap, planes rolled upside down, huge masts snapped like matchsticks, and a harbour under a metre of water. No phone coverage, no internet, and so many homes destroyed or completely disappeared. Just gone.

As Sint Maarten is a country within the Kingdom of the Netherlands, the Dutch armed forces are immediately deployed to provide emergency relief. Fortunately, we always have units in the area, and immediately deployed small forward groups to the island, which means that we can link and scale up rapidly. That soon proves necessary and it enables us to respond quickly and assess the situation. Because of the gravity and scale, we swiftly send further reinforcements from the Netherlands to the disaster zone.

As soon as you arrive on site in a disaster zone like this as part of a military team, you immediately "flip the switch", as a colleague so aptly put it. Get up at six o'clock, have something to eat, and then you're flat out until it gets dark at six in the evening. And then prepare for the next day. Day in, day out. That may sound obvious, but nowhere does it tell you what the military should do in that chaos after such a violent natural disaster. Where do you start? What are you going to do? It is important to get a good picture of the situation as soon as possible, but it is also vital to provide help where it is time-critical. Rescue people where you can, then ask questions. How do you create order and safety when there is nothing but chaos and a multitude of desperate people? How do you ensure that people can survive the first few days and then move on? What kind of help is needed immediately and how can you deliver it? Where can we land a helicopter or where can we land a rubber boat? Fortunately, in situations of chaos and uncertainty, the military know what to do and how to establish order. They are well organised, can continue to operate under dire circumstances and, above all, have incredible improvisation skills and perseverance.

Dutch military personnel

Our marines patrol to stop the looting, to give prisoners access to fresh air, to distribute food, water and medicine and to create shaded areas for men, women and children waiting for hours in the blazing sun. Soldiers flown in from the air assault brigade guard the airport, clear debris from the runway, keep roads clear for police and ambulances and help to evacuate patients and tourists. From the guard ship, the combat camera team is deployed by helicopter to capture footage of the disaster area, giving us a quick picture of the devastation and areas where immediate help is needed. These are images that the US news channel CNN and our own NOS also like to use.

Medical personnel care for the elderly and injured, helicopter crews and doctors bring medical aid, food and water to poorly accessible areas, and search for missing persons. The supply ship HNLMS *Karel Doorman* brings in equipment: emergency shelters, bulldozers, excavators, radio masts, water tankers and medical equipment. Military personnel also distribute food and medical supplies around the islands. They constantly fill jerry cans on the huge ship at every tap they can find, distributing thousands of litres of drinking water produced from seawater to the islanders, and thus also helping dialysis patients being treated in local hospitals.

As well as working on the ship, the mechanics and technicians go ashore to perform vital work such as restoring power to buildings where emergency assistance is being provided. Logistics personnel, such as Lieutenant Lisa, keep track of who and what comes in and make sure items get to the right place as quickly as possible. Lisa, who initially thought she would be away for a fortnight, ends up staying for two months because help is so badly needed. "You don't complain, you just get on with it", she says determinedly. And in the meantime, the engineers haul away nearly a thousand truckloads of debris, repair the hospital, get the airport operational again, repair school roofs, fix toys in between, and help where they can with temporary repairs to homes. Like building a new ramp at the house of a young, disadvantaged woman with multiple sclerosis (MS). She is in a wheelchair and can now get in and out of her house again. Her brother is moved to tears when he sees it.

Heavier storms

It never fails to impress when you see how quickly and decisively military personnel can step in in situations like this, how they keep their cool and how rewarding that work can be. But it also makes me realise how vulnerable populations and societies are when natural disasters strike with such devastating force and how much military support is needed immediately. At the peak of the operation, more than 600 Dutch military personnel were working on St Maarten from early morning to late evening, while another 400 men and women were supporting them from nearby ships and from the Leeward Islands. And that is just one example of deployment after a hurricane. There are many more examples of global military deployment after storms and hurricanes in recent years.

I remember Hurricane Katrina, which swept across the US in 2005 with devastating consequences. For weeks, parts of New Orleans were flooded. Hundreds of people died. There was $125 billion worth of damage. Looting and violence followed hot on the heels of the storm. Only with the deployment of as many as 65,000 military personnel could order be restored.[1] Hurricane Sandy left more than half a million Americans in the New York region without power in 2012, and hundreds of people had to be rescued from the floods.[2]

More and more US military personnel are feeling the effects of climatic conditions at home as a result of heavy floods and hurricanes over the past 20 years.[3] For example, in 2018 and 2019, hurricanes Florence and Michael caused severe flooding in the interior of the US, causing US$3.6 billion worth of damage to Marine Corps Base Camp Lejeune in North Carolina[4] and more than US$5 billion worth of damage to Tyndall Air Force Base in Florida. About 10% of the military aircraft based at Tyndall needed repairs after the storm and 95% of the buildings at the military base were severely damaged or completely destroyed.[5] This led to a statement by NBC News that the damage at Tyndall was worse in material terms than that caused by missile strikes in the Middle East.[6]

Extreme weather conditions are the reason the Pentagon has been factoring in substantial extra costs at home for years. On top of this are the costs incurred by the Defense Department on missions in other countries. A 2019 Pentagon report states that 79 US military bases worldwide are affected by regular flooding and rising sea levels. The world's largest naval base, in Norfolk, Virginia, may even become unusable in the near future due to flooding caused by rising sea levels and increasingly frequent storms.[7] There is also a risk of damage to military facilities in Alaska due to rising temperatures as the permafrost on which facilities are located begins to thaw.[8] Furthermore, wildfires are creating a dangerous situation for military personnel on or near military bases in California, and in places where military personnel are deployed outdoors, extreme heatwaves pose health risks, such as heatstroke or sunstroke.[9]

In short, many US military personnel are not just seeing on the news what a huge impact natural disasters are having worldwide, nor are they just being deployed to countries where people need help because of climatic conditions. They are also experiencing firsthand the impacts of climate change at military bases at home.

In fact, 2020 appears to be a record year in terms of storms. As many as 30 storms worldwide were named that year, 13 of which developed into hurricanes, storms with wind speeds of at least 119 kilometres per hour. Six of these developed into major hurricanes. There were so many that the traditional hurricane names ran out and the weather service switched to the Greek alphabet. Many of these storms, it also turned out, remained active for longer, and mostly on land. This is due to the warming of the world's oceans.[10] Scientists explained it as follows: "If you think of a hurricane as an engine, the warm seawater is the fuel. And when the seawater is exceptionally warm, as is regularly the case in the Caribbean and the Gulf of Mexico, that warm water can 'charge' hurricanes into extremely severe storms. When a hurricane makes landfall, it is suddenly cut off from that fuel and begins to disintegrate and then weakens. But because seawater is the fuel, the greater amount of water vapour carried in the boosted atmosphere can act as an extra battery."[11]

So there is a clear link between warmer seawater and climate change. The warmer the seawater, the more fuel the hurricane absorbs, and the hotter the air, the more rain a hurricane will contain. This is also evident when we look at the statistics showing that both the frequency and intensity of such natural disasters are increasing, with new records being set every year.

The year 2021 saw more of the same. After the violent earthquake in Haiti in mid-August, tropical storm Grace hit the same area two days later. The Netherlands sent naval vessel HNLMS *Holland* to the affected area to provide emergency aid. The same month, category 4 hurricane Ida hit the coast of the southern US. New Orleans braced for a hurricane more severe than Katrina in 2005. The dams that had been constructed fortunately withstood the onslaught, but Hurricane Ida nevertheless left a trail of devastation and took New York and New Jersey by surprise. The result: 95 deaths and $65 billion worth of damage.[12]

More and more emergency aid needed

The repercussions of such major disasters are immense, and a country like Mozambique is all too aware of this. Mozambique, with a population of some 30 million, is one of Africa's most vulnerable countries. The country was already facing massive debt when tropical cyclone Idai passed through in 2019 and cyclone Kenneth followed shortly afterwards. According to the Red Cross, this destroyed at least 90% of the capital Beira, damaged more than 180,000 homes and flooded large tracts of land, leaving behind a cholera outbreak and hundreds of thousands homeless.[13]

The estimated cost of the damage was some $870 million, for which Mozambique had to borrow even more.[14] This is an unwelcome prospect for all those other countries that are vulnerable because of their coastal cities. Europe is no exception. There, too, the seawater temperature is rising because of climate change. Recent calculations by the KNMI show that Europe could be hit by a powerful hurricane such as Sandy every other year by the end of this century. Given the implications of these results for our society, the KNMI, together with other climate institutes around the world, is investigating what this means not only for our own safety,[15] but also for that of people worldwide.

This rising trend is highly likely to lead to many more evacuations worldwide. After all, most cities are now located on coastlines and rivers and they are rapidly increasing in size as they act as a magnet for people looking for a better life. It also means more extensive property damage from storms and flooding to homes and infrastructure in coastal cities. And that in turn leads to a greater need for international emergency assistance. The Red Cross estimates that the cost of international emergency aid – if no timely action is taken – will have risen to some €18 billion a year in ten years' time.[16] And this only takes account of the cost of "immediate emergency relief", not the necessary post-disaster reconstruction, which is many times higher.

An additional problem is that relief workers in those countries are affected by the disaster themselves. Their focus is therefore more likely to be on their own family and neighbourhood, to provide assistance there first. The same applies to government officials. They are expected to act decisively and take quick decisions after a disaster, but they too have to deal with missing family members and damage to their homes at such times. We saw this in the aftermath of Hurricane Irma.

Another factor is that while women often take the lead in doing what needs to be done immediately after a natural disaster, they themselves are often the most vulnerable. Natural disasters worldwide thus claim more female victims than male, according to a 2014 World Health Organisation (WHO) report.[17] Many women have never learned to swim or do not otherwise know how to get to a place of safety. In countries hit by severe floods, women are also more vulnerable to hunger, abuse of power and rape in the aftermath of a natural disaster.[18]

The fact is that in a natural disaster, a lot of women die. Mothers who could have provided food and water for their children. Women who could have helped to distribute food fairly in the aftermath of a disaster. Women who would have been aware of the needs of those around them and could thus have helped to come up with solutions.

In any event, we can assume that with more and more powerful hurricanes and natural disasters, the demand for emergency support will rise proportionally, and we can expect an ever-greater call to be made on the armed forces for this kind of mission. Emergency relief is shifting from a sideline to an important sub-task for the military, and this places demands on the civil-military and international coordination of such support, as well as on the composition, equipment and training of units.

Notes

1. Welzer, H. (2009), *The climate wars. Why people will be killed in the 21st century* (pp. 33-34). Ambo

2. CBC News. (2012, Oct 30). Superstorm Sandy: More than 7 million without power. *CBC News*. https://www.cbsnews.com/news/superstorm-sandy-more-than-7-million-without-power/

3. "Between 1980 and 2021, 29 Drought, 35 Flooding, 136 Severe Storm, 19 Winter Storm, 18 Wildfire, 52 Tropical Cyclone, and 9 Freeze billion-dollar disaster events affected the United States (CPI-adjusted)", summary of all natural disasters in the US over the past 20 years, Billion-Dollar Weather and Climate Disasters: Events | National Centers for Environmental Information (NCEI) (noaa.gov)

4. https://www.marinecorpstimes.com/news/your-marine-corps/2020/07/20/heres-where-the-corps-north-carolina-bases-stand-22-months-after-hurricane-florence/

5-6. https://www.nbcnews.com/think/opinion/u-s-military-terrified-climate-change-it-s-done-more-ncna1240484

7-9. US Department of Defense (2019), Report on effects of a changing climate to the Department of Defense. US Department of Defense, Washington DC

10. "Slower decay of landfalling hurricanes in a warming world", 11 November 2020, Nature 587, p. 230-234, Lin li and Pinaki Chakraborty, https://www.nature.com/articles/s41586-020-2867-7

11. Gibbens, S. (2020, 16 November), "The effects of climate change: hurricanes stay powerful longer, including on land", *National Geographic*, https://www.nationalgeographic.nl/wetenschap/2020/11/de-gevolgen-van-klimaatverandering-orkanen-blijven-langer-krachtig-ook-aan-land

12. Kramer, K. & Ware, J. (2021). Counting the costs 2021: a year of climate breakdown. Christian Aid, London.

13. International Federation of Red Cross & Red Crescent Societies, Mozambique Red Cross Society, UN Office for the Coordination of Humanitarian Affairs (2019, 29 March), Assessment Report Tropical Cyclone IDAI, Mozambique, Beira City, https://reliefweb.int/sites/reliefweb.int/files/resources/Beira_Rapid_Assessment_Report_29March2019.pdf

14. UNDP (2019), Mozambique Cyclone Idai: post disaster needs assessment, https://www.undp.org/publications/mozambique-cyclone-idai-post-disaster-needs-assessment-pdnadna

15. https://www.knmi.nl/kennis-en-datacentrum/achtergrond/zware-herfststormen-in-europa-door-orkanen-in-een-warmer-klimaat

16. Red Cross (2019), The cost of doing nothing: the humanitarian price of climate change and how it can be avoided, https://reliefweb.int/sites/reliefweb.int/files/resources/2019-IFRC-CODN-EN%20%281%29.pdf

17-18. WHO (2014). Gender, climate change and health, https://www.who.int/publications/i/item/gender-climate-change-and-health

Chapter Seven
Stratego in the Arctic Circle

"It could easily be the largest oil reserve on Earth.
Big enough to kill for...?"

Quotes from the Swedish television eco-thriller *Thin Ice*

In my final year as Chief of Defence (CDS), in 2017, a senior official from the Dutch Ministry of Infrastructure and the Environment gives a guest lecture to senior officers in Breda. At the time, they are taking the Advanced Defence Studies (HDV) course, an internal course at academic level. The officer talks about climate change and the consequences if the earth's temperature rises by 2 degrees. One of the servicemen in the class, James, is struck by the impact this could have, he tells me later when he is working in The Hague. He is also surprised, as he realises that this topic is not actually an issue for the defence organisation. How strange, he thinks. "We know exactly what the threat is, we can even predict it and yet we do nothing about it. And we're supposed to be concerned with security." At that moment, he knows: "This will be the subject of my final thesis."

It is shortly before I speak out at the Peace Palace on the relationship between climate and security. James then has little idea of where his quest will lead him. First, he researches the US military and NATO. He finds out that NATO has no policy on the subject at the time. However, in the US, under President Barack Obama, the issue is high on the agenda. James also discovers that the US military leadership has been tasked with actively planning and taking action on this. But what about the Dutch military? Nowhere in any policy documents can James find the issue of climate change in relation to security. So he makes an appointment with the then director of strategy at the Ministry of Defence, who tells him that at higher levels, climate change is considered "not that relevant" for an organisation like our armed forces. It is indicative of the situation at the time, when the organisation was overloaded with the constant trade-offs between the growing demands on the military and the increasing spending cuts that were eroding the organisation.

In official policy documents, James does read about the geopolitical game arising from the melting of polar ice in the Arctic region, which, I assure him, is certainly important. As CDS, I have been in regular contact for years with my NATO and EU colleagues from Norway, Sweden, Finland and Denmark. For them, security does not mean the same as it does to the eastern and southern EU and NATO member states. Whereas in eastern Europe people are mainly worried about Russia's military power and influence and in southern Europe concerns relate to instability on its borders, countries in the far north have long been concerned about the military-strategic consequences of the rapidly melting ice caps in the northern polar region.

Snowball effect

For years, the North Pole, the top of the earth – also called the Arctic region – has been of little or no military-strategic importance, the one exception being during the Cold War, when NATO and the Warsaw Pact shared a border and the region was a safe haven for nuclear submarines that played a crucial role in the doctrine of mutual deterrence. But now the area is warming rapidly, according to researchers. "In the past 40 years, three quarters of the sea ice has disappeared. If this trend continues, the Arctic region will be ice-free in 14-15 years. It could take another 20 or 25 years, but most Dutch people alive now will still experience that", according to weatherman and climate scientist Peter Kuipers Munneke in 2020.[1]

A year later, in April 2021, came the news that sea ice in the Arctic region is melting twice as fast as previously thought. This was reported by scientists from University College London in a new study, the results of which appeared in the trade journal *The Cryosphere.*[2] A satellite from the European Space Agency (ESA) had been used to calculate the thickness of the ice.

In 2021, the UN climate panel, the IPCC published its sixth Assessment Report, showing that the melting of the ice sheets in Greenland and the Antarctic may start to accelerate. If warming is high, the sea level rise due to accelerated melting could average about 2 metres by 2150.[3] These figures are uncertain because melting processes are complex and not yet properly understood. The report has therefore also been criticised. The IPCC's scenario is said by some to be exaggerated, too far-fetched. However, the UN report by climate experts is reminiscent of military planning. The military also analyse all environmental factors and then, on the basis of that comprehensive picture, develop scenarios that form the basis for our operational planning. Our intelligence people then develop a most likely and a most dangerous scenario. Our planners use the most likely scenario to develop a strategy. It is then tested against the most dangerous scenario to develop a Plan B in case the approach is not successful. This way, you focus on the most likely scenario, but you are also prepared for the worst.

International climate experts in effect do the same. They too develop likely scenarios with a certain range, but each time the most dangerous scenario actually turns out to be the most likely one. What this IPCC report shows is that, for whatever reason, we have been far too optimistic in our expectations. We have lulled ourselves into a false sense of security. We have to keep adjusting the forecasts because the ice is melting at a higher rate and temperatures are rising faster than expected. Our international community is playing catch-up and losing precious time.

According to the UN report, the melting of the permafrost, the subsoil that is normally frozen all year round, is also out of control. This releases large quantities of CO_2.[4] It has to do with the fact that when the ice melts, it gets warmer on Earth. Just as it is warmer if you wear a black T-shirt in summer instead of a white one, dark water absorbs more heat than white ice.

Consequently, melting ice in turn makes the Arctic region warm even faster, thus turning global warming into a vicious circle.

We have now reached the point at which the last decade was probably the warmest period in the past 125,000 years. Due to a combination of emissions and deforestation, the amount of carbon dioxide in the atmosphere is at levels not seen for about two million years, according to climate experts.[5]

What if the ice melts?

Much of Russia's territory is in the northern polar region. It is a country where people are already directly affected by the heat and melting of the permafrost, which covers two-thirds of the total land (sub)surface there. This is all to do with the relatively steep temperature rise in the Arctic region. In the summer of 2021, temperatures reached as high as 38 degrees Celsius. As far as we know, it has never been that hot north of the Arctic Circle.[6] For instance, the frozen ground in Siberia, in the far north of Russia, is melting faster and faster, making it unstable and causing roads, buildings, gas pipelines and oil storage tanks to subside.[7] And the environmental disaster in Norilsk on 29 May 2020, in which a major fuel leak turned nearby rivers blood red, caused significant damage to the local ecosystem. There are now about 35,000 incidents involving major oil and gas pipelines in Western Siberia every year, 21% of which are related to loss of stability and structural integrity.[8]

As elsewhere in the world, we are seeing longer periods of heat and drought and shorter periods of increasingly intense rainfall. As a result, northern Russia is also facing floods that are increasing in magnitude and frequency. In addition, forest fires caused by drought are not only laying waste to large parts of the region, but are also affecting air quality and further increasing CO_2 emissions. This is why scientists are warning of an ecological disaster that will be felt worldwide. In 2020, nearly 10 million hectares of Siberian Forest, an area the size of Portugal, went up in flames, according to the Russian branch of Greenpeace.[9] A year later, when forest fires took hold again, 10 regions in Russia declared a state of emergency.[10] The figures circulating vary, but nearly

2 million hectares are reported to have gone up in smoke in July 2021, about half the area of the Netherlands.[11]

Arms race

My northern military colleagues are particularly concerned, however, about the potential geopolitical repercussions of the rapidly melting ice. Estimates from the United States Geological Survey show that 13% of the world's oil reserves are located within the Arctic Circle, and as much as 30% of the world's gas reserves.[12] Besides living natural resources such as fish, minerals such as coal, zinc, lead, silver, diamonds, manganese, chromium, titanium, nickel and copper are also present in the Arctic region. There are also ample supplies of rare earth metals used to produce items such as mobile phones and electric cars, as well as modern weapons.[13] The melting ice is clearing the way for the exploitation of these resources and making the Arctic Ocean navigable for merchant shipping. The US, Canada, Russia, Denmark and Norway all border the North Pole and lay claim to part of the area. But besides these five states, there are other countries with interests in the changing situation in the region, including China. As a result, the Arctic region has effectively become a battleground for power and competition.

The race began on a quiet morning in August 2007. Russian submarines sank to 4,000 metres in the Arctic Ocean and planted a titanium flag on the ocean floor below the North Pole. The images of the Russian national flag at the bottom of the sea quickly spread around the world. The West immediately condemned the action in the strongest possible terms. Soon afterwards, scientists issued a statement based on satellite images announcing that the amount of sea ice had shrunk to a record low, whereupon the world suddenly realised how fast the ice in the area was melting. Indeed, never before in human history had so much ice disappeared from the North Pole.

In the months and years that followed, we saw Russia building military bases and expanding its Northern Fleet with submarines and frigates equipped with long-range and cruise missiles.[14] They were also conducting missile tests from new nuclear-powered submarines capable of carrying nuclear warheads. China was not sitting idly by and issued a policy document in 2018 stating that it was a "near-Arctic state", which wanted to build a "polar Silk Road" with other countries for trade and research purposes.[15] This move was probably prompted by the mineral resources to be found in the area, but also by the prospect of access to new sea routes that shorten travel time between Asian ports and European markets by up to two weeks. It is also a route lying outside Russian jurisdiction which circumvents the piracy in the Gulf of Aden and the "toll route" through the Suez Canal.

Greenland "not for sale"

The US is also interested in the Arctic region.[16] They train there in case Americans come into conflict with a Russian ship carrying a nuclear cargo. The US is also concerned that China may gain access to rare earth metals, which could be a trump card in a potential trade conflict with the US. In 2018, perhaps for this reason, US President Donald Trump suddenly sent out an extraordinary tweet. He tweeted that he wanted to buy Greenland, an area that not only has precious resources, but is also part of the northern polar region, with a key strategic location on the northern flank of the US continent, between Canada on the one side and Europe and Russia on the other. However, Greenland is also an autonomous part of Denmark. Danish Prime Minister Mette Frederiksen quickly responded publicly that the purchase was an "absurd idea", whereupon President Trump abruptly postponed his planned visit to Denmark. He is not actually the first US president to suggest buying Greenland. In 1946, President Harry Truman also offered money for Greenland: $100 million to be exact. Another fact that may not be widely known is that in 1867, the US bought Alaska from Russia for a little over $7 million.

Meanwhile, countries such as Denmark, Norway and Canada are paying close attention to what happens around the North Pole, as they are entitled to part of the area through legitimate claims. The region is thus monitored by countless satellites, submarines and aircraft working overtime in and above the Arctic Circle, as well as patrols with sled dogs (by Denmark and Canada)[17] and increasingly frequent military exercises (by the US and Canada).[18] At the same time, China seems intent on installing advanced satellite communications equipment, which Western security services fear could be used for military purposes, such as tracking and control of spy satellites and ballistic missiles.[19] It is a major source of concern for the Americans, and for the rest of the world.

Geopolitical hotspot

Fortunately, countries are for now continuing their discussions on the Arctic region, particularly through the Arctic Council, a consultative body which represents all countries bordering the Arctic region and to which the EU is also admitted as an observer. Since 1996, there has been an Arctic consultation between indigenous populations and Canada, the US, Russia, Finland, Norway, Sweden, Iceland and Denmark (which includes Greenland and the Faroe Islands). What was initially intended to protect the environment and the people of the Arctic region has taken on an increasingly political function over the years. Those who have a say in the Council obviously also have a say in the new transit route for the global economy, as well as joining the discussions about oil and gas resources, and about the ores and earth metals that still lie hidden under the Greenland ice.

Although these countries are still talking to each other, they remain active in military terms in the meantime. China is not represented in the Council. The purpose of the latter is not to mediate in disagreements, nor is it in a position to direct or mediate in matters of national security, conflict and confrontation. It is mainly a platform for members to talk to each other about issues such as nature and the environment, but not about military security, in accordance with its founding statement.[20]

Given the huge geopolitical and economic implications of the melting ice, however, the question remains as to how long countries will remain in dialogue with each other. We have seen diplomatic consultations shutting down in

2023 and geopolitical tensions rising sharply following Russia's invasion of Ukraine. The accession of Sweden and Finland to NATO is also leaving its mark on Arctic cooperation, and in June 2023, the US opened a diplomatic mission in the Norwegian city of Tromsø. It will be the most northerly mission for the US and also the first above the Arctic Circle.

For Russia, a melting Arctic region presents a wealth of opportunities. Not only does it create entirely new trade routes in the region between China and Europe, but the thawed Barents Sea also offers Russia open access to the oceans all year round. Not surprisingly, Russia has launched an extensive military modernisation programme for the region. Many new bases have been built along the 6,000-km-long northern coastline and the Northern nuclear Fleet has been upgraded to a full-fledged fifth military district. Russia has also announced a new maritime doctrine with greater emphasis on the Arctic region.[21] All this shows how it is becoming increasingly relevant in geopolitical terms.

Thin ice

Who knows what the future holds? Swedish television makers have at least discovered that the battle for the melting North Pole makes for exciting and grim tales about a geopolitical confrontation. They broadcast a thriller series entitled *Thin Ice* in 2020. The first episode is ominous from the start: a research ship is attacked off the coast of Greenland, just as the Arctic Council is trying to reach agreement on a treaty banning oil extraction in the Arctic region.

This may be good news for its creators, who are no doubt delighted with the popularity of the series, but on the other side are the ecologists, climate experts and environmental organisations who are deeply concerned about what is to come. With all the activity, there is an increasing risk that oil on board a ship will leak into the remote area. The task of cleaning up such a spill would be virtually impossible, and that means crude oil could end up in the ice, causing it to melt even faster. Environmental organisations therefore take the view that countries should stay away from the North Pole and – as some Western countries are doing – call for more protected marine areas to be established, a move which is being vetoed by China and Russia in the UN Security Council.

The melting of the polar ice is inevitable and poses an acute danger to everyone. The effects in Siberia are already evident, but coastal cities worldwide are also going to feel the huge repercussions of melting ice, with some eventually being submerged altogether. It is clear that climate change is causing the Arctic region to undergo geostrategic changes, and that this has implications for the security policies of NATO, the EU and all the countries involved.

Notes

1. Ekker, H. (2020, 6 November). Not since measurements began has there been so little Arctic ice in autumn. NOS, https://nos.nl/artikel/2355433-niet-eerder-zo-weinig-ijs-op-de-noordpool-in-het-najaar-sinds-begin-metingen

2. Mallett, R.D.C., Stroeve, J.C., Tsamados, M., Landy, J.C., Willatt, R., Nandan, V., Liston, G.E. (2021). "Faster decline and higher variability in the sea ice thickness of the marginal Arctic seas when accounting for dynamic snow cover", *The Cryosphere* 15, p. 2429-2450

3. Schutterhelm, R. (2021, 26 November), "Faster Antarctic melt poses major threat to Netherlands". Nu.nl, see https://www.nu.nl/klimaat/6149888/snellere-afsmelting-antarctica-vormt-grote-bedreiging-voor-nederland.html

4. ANP Productions (2021, Aug 9). Sea level rise due to global warming irreversible, says IPCC. Noordhollandsch Dagblad

5. The IPCC does not conduct research itself, but every few years summarises how experts from many countries view the state of climate change. They also publish a summary for policymakers, to be approved by country representatives.

6-7. Kamphorst, J. (202, 22 July), "Siberia is melting: schools are sinking", *Trouw*, see https://www.trouw.nl/cs-bcbd18a8

8. Shapovalova, D. (2020, 11 June), "Oil spill in Siberia: are we preparing for permafrost thaw?", *The Arctic Institute*, see https://www.thearcticinstitute.org/oil-spill-siberia-prepared-permafrost-thaw/

9. Davydova, Y. (2021, 18 August), "Record breaking fires in Siberia", *Greenpeace*, see https://www.greenpeace.org/international/story/49171/russia-record-breaking-fires-siberia/

10-11. Torfs, M. (2021, 30 July), "Forest fires in Siberia get further out of control, firefighters can't control fire for long", VRT, see https://www.vrt.be/vrtnws/nl/2021/07/30/ook-siberie-staat-opnieuw-in-brand/

12. Stauffer, P. (ed.) (2008), "Circum-Arctic resource appraisal: estimates of undiscovered oil and gas north of the Arctic Circle." United States Geological Survey, Washington DC, see also https://www.eia.gov/todayinenergy/detail.php?id=4650

13. Gronholt-Pedersen J. & Onstad, E. (2021, 2 March), "Mining magnets: Arctic island finds green power can be a curse", Reuters, see https://www.reuters.com/article/us-rareearths-greenland-usa-china-insigh-idUSKBN2AU0FM

14. Walsh, N. (2021, 5 April), "Satellite images show huge Russian military buildup in the Arctic", CNN, see https://edition.cnn.com/2021/04/05/europe/russia-arctic-nato-military-intl-cmd/index.html

15. State Council Information Office of the Peoples' Republic of China (2018), China's Arctic Policy, see http://english.www.gov.cn/archive/white_paper/2018/01/26/content_281476026660336.htm

16. Greenhaw, T. et al. (2021). "US military options to enhance Arctic defence", Brookings, Washington DC

17. CBS News (2016, 28 September). "Canadians Turn to Native dog sleds for Arctic sovereignty patrols", see https://www.adn.com/arctic/article/canadians-turn-native-dog-sleds-arctic-sovereignty-patrols/2011/12/02/

18. Luhn, A. (2020, 16 October), "Freezing cold war: militaries move in as Arctic ice retreats", The Guardian, see https://www.theguardian.com/environment/2020/oct/16/arctic-ice-retreats-climate-us-russian-canadian-chinese-military

19. Humpert, M. (2019, 4 September), "China looking to expand satellite coverage in Arctic, experts warn of military purpose", *High North News*, see https://www.highnorthnews.com/en/china-looking-expand-satellite-coverage-arctic-experts-warn-military-purpose

20. The Founding Declaration of the Arctic Council (the 1996 Ottawa Declaration) is available online at https://arctic-council.org/about/

21. Humpert, M. (2022, 22 September). "From Ukraine to the Arctic: Russia's capabilities in the region and the war's impact on the north". *High North News*, https://www.highnorthnews.com/en/ukraine-arctic-russias-capabilities-region-and-wars-impact-north

Chapter Eight
Water bomb in Asia

"It is baffling that we are continuing knowingly to sow the seeds of our own destruction, despite the evidence that we are turning our only home into an uninhabitable hell for millions of people."

Mami Mizutori, UN researcher

"My vision is that by 2018 we will have an influential global community of experts with practical experience and policymakers. A community that meets regularly in The Hague, and also elsewhere..." Bert Koenders, Minister of Foreign Affairs in 2016, reads the words from his paper – in English – and looks briefly at the audience in the auditorium of the Peace Palace in The Hague. Behind him hangs a large screen meant for PowerPoint slides. On either side of the speaking area is a huge wall of glass, offering a splendid view of the palace garden. The afternoon is dedicated to the Planetary Security Initiative, a conference on climate change and security organised by Foreign Affairs. "The presence of the Dutch Chief of Defence illustrates that we are convinced of the importance of an integrated approach", says the smartly dressed speaker. He looks at me for a moment. Then he goes on to talk about the impact of climate change on our security. He argues that swift global political action is needed to adapt to changing climatic conditions.

Now it is my turn to speak. I know I am not the first general to warn of the consequences of climate change. When President Barack Obama was awarded the Nobel Peace Prize in 2009, he warned that climate change would fuel more conflicts for "decades to come". He took that analysis not from a few environmental organisations, but from a group of US generals and admirals.

Among them was retired admiral David Titley. Years later, in November 2016, Titley addressed presidential candidate Donald Trump directly in a column in *The Washington Examiner*. "Just as any good businessman or CEO does not knowingly ignore a risk to his or her business, a president cannot ignore the risks of climate change. They are real, they are happening now and they affect all the men and women serving in our armed forces today. As well as our millions of veterans at home."

In the Netherlands, I did become the first general to speak out publicly on the effects of climate on our security. This was not anticipated or planned, because only a fortnight ago my secretary received an invitation by e-mail from staff at the Ministry of Foreign Affairs and the Clingendael think tank asking if I would be interested in participating. They had presumably seen just before the news item in *De Telegraaf* about my remarks on climate and security at a security conference in Halifax, Canada, in November 2016. There, too, I warned about the effects of climate change in relation to our wider security, and that this should be at the top of everyone's agenda. People probably now think that makes me a great addition to this international conference.[1] Scientists, delegates from NGOs, policymakers and military officials are gathered here to make the world a little safer.

However, I am all too aware of how sensitive the issue is, especially when it is addressed by the most senior military officer in the Netherlands. I have therefore prepared my speech meticulously and I illustrate my story with appropriate and powerful images in the background. Every time I see the audience waving their phones in the air to take pictures, I know that something new has appeared on the screen behind me. I talk about water in particular, quoting the Anglo-American poet W.H Auden: "Thousands have lived without love, none without water." When this slide appears, it seems as if half the audience want to take a picture. I am sure an image like that will do well on Twitter: a Chief of Defence in uniform and behind him a quote in large lettering on a screen about "love" and the importance of water.

The other general

Suddenly I see a journalist and a cameraman at the back of the room, from the national tv, busy positioning the camera so that I am in the picture. In the meantime, I try to concentrate on the text, because little is as uncomfortable as stumbling over an English text while a few hundred people in a room are looking at you, and a television camera is rolling in the background. Later in the break, several people tell me how they were moved by the speech. That is obviously good to hear, although I also realise that I am speaking mainly to the converted here: the people who are already convinced that there is a link between climate change and security.

Who actually makes a much greater impression on me that day is retired general Anm Muniruzzaman, a small and friendly looking man, who had served in the Bangladesh military for thirty-eight years. He is president of the Bangladesh Institute of Peace and Security Studies and also chairman of the Global Military Advisory Council on Climate Change. We have something else in common: we are among the few senior military officers who are attending the conference and talking openly about the impact of climate on our security. It is clear that the general is extremely concerned about the future of his country. He starts speaking as soon as he appears. "The biggest threat facing Bangladesh is the loss of land mass, which is probably due to rising sea levels", he tells the audience. Muniruzzaman is referring to 2007 research by the Intergovernmental Panel on Climate Change (IPCC), which shows that a one-metre rise in sea level means a loss of 17-20% of Bangladesh's land mass. "If that happens, 20 to 30 million people are expected to become refugees", he continued. "The political system in my country is already under pressure. What if all those people run out of homes, food, water or have little to no access to health and hygiene facilities and so they have to flee?"

The general starts talking faster as the audience listens intently. "Bangladesh could just collapse in that case. That is the worst-case scenario. People are already fleeing my country. In our case, really the only possible escape route is towards India, except for a short stretch of border with Myanmar. We share a long land border of 4400 kilometres with India. But we can't go there. Surrounding Bangladesh on the border with India is a fence of concrete and barbed wire. Three metres high. Every few kilometres, a watchtower rises above it. There, Indian border guards stand watch, and they shoot at people approaching the border." The general pauses for a moment. "And the sea level keeps rising", he adds.

Like the Netherlands, Bangladesh is a delta country, but much larger, much more vulnerable and much poorer. Here, most of the population live in areas at risk of flooding from rivers and seawater. They cannot afford major delta works. Each flood from the sea causes more salination and takes another bite out of the fertile landscape. Floods not only cause great humanitarian distress but also migration flows. The vast, densely populated agricultural areas are so threatened by floods that large parts of the population have to move to safer areas in Bangladesh and beyond. But those areas are already inhabited by other population groups, so that could in turn lead to heightened tension.

I can see that my colleague from Bangladesh is struggling, which is completely understandable. When you see your country being so affected by climate change and the pressure on a weak system becoming almost unsustainable, you want to do something for the people in your country. If you then find that you are invited to just about everywhere in the world to speak about the effects of climate change, but very little is actually done to keep the people of your country safe, the frustration is understandable. You are just a lone voice in the wilderness.

I later learn from another conference participant that six years earlier, in 2009 – the year I was serving in Afghanistan – General Muniruzzaman had published a paper along with a Pakistani general and former defence minister, and an Indian general on what climate change meant for the security of the Indian subcontinent, and what should be done.[2] This is significant, as the authors represent three countries that under normal circumstances do not exactly get along with each other. On the contrary, in fact, as Pakistan and India have been arch enemies since their inception in 1947, building huge dams, amongst other things, partly because they do not trust each other in matters relating to water management. It is telling in the extreme when three former top military officers from those countries then set aside those hostilities and decide to join forces in calling for a collective approach to prevent the looming consequences of a changing climate for their countries.

Effects of climate change in Asia

As I drive back to the ministry a little later, I find that I cannot get the Bangladeshi general's story out of my head, even when I receive an email from my spokesperson about a news report that my statements are now trending. Maybe it is because I feel guilty. In my contribution, I talked about the effects on the Netherlands and how we experienced the 1953 flood disaster here, and also what the effects of the changing conditions are on the Middle East. I did not mention the rest of the world, not even Southern Asia, where the problems are so pressing and the repercussions so immense.

So did I underestimate the problem? Or is it because in the Netherlands we have become accustomed to the images of floods in that part of the world? Year in, year out, we see distraught people on television who have lost everything. And then we move on to the next news item. Such is the phenomenon of the emotionally diminishing impact the further away the misery is. And now I had just been talking to another officer, to a general like myself, who lives in one of those very countries where all those distraught people live. A country where millions are at risk. People who, like us, also live in a large river delta, but are in constant danger of finding themselves in the same chaos and misery that befell us in the Netherlands in 1953. And their crisis would in all likelihood be many times greater in scale and a truly horrific scenario.

There is not much time to dwell on this. Before I know it, I find myself back in the hustle and bustle of the day. The day-to-day business in the mission areas where there is always something happening invariably takes priority. So does the almost daily deployment back home to support the civil authorities, such as fire service, police and local authorities. And of course there is the endless stream of correspondence, documents and the countless meetings and discussions that are pretty much back to back in my diary, filling the entire day.

The IMCCS Expert Group

The pace of life is different in retirement a few years later and I take the time to really delve into the impact of climate change. It all starts with a telephone conversation with American Sherri Goodman from the Center for Climate Security in Washington. For many years, Sherri was the US Department of Defense's deputy undersecretary for environment and sustainability. In 2007, she founded the Center for Naval Analysis (CNA) Military Advisory Board, made up of several top US former military officers, to advise the federal government on national security in relation to the growing impact of climate change. We quickly agree that there is also much work to be done in Europe in terms of spreading the word to get the relationship between climate and security onto the international agenda, both within and outside the security institutions. Because one thing we know for sure: no one is safe. No one can hide behind dykes, national borders or oceans. Climate change affects us all and it is going to affect our environment and our lives. But the question is: how can we get this message across clearly? It is practically non-existent on the agenda in the security world.

What is more, many security experts have been writing analyses for years in which the word "climate" does not even appear. Neither is climate change ever a topic at security conferences attended by politicians, knowledge institutions, policymakers, the military and defence industry representatives. In the five-and-a-half years I have been a member of the NATO Military Committee, a gathering of all the NATO Chiefs of Defence, climate change has never been seriously discussed. In 2010, NATO did decide that crisis management was a core task, but climate change was swallowed up in a list of factors that could potentially affect operations. It appears between health risks and water scarcity.[3] I think this also explains the commotion that arose briefly when, in 2017, during the Planetary Security Initiative mentioned earlier, I did establish a clear link. It is still the old, familiar threats and security risks that dominate the international security agenda as well as our own, such as the threat from Russia, the harmful role of North Korea, the threat of terrorism from Iraq and Afghanistan, the dispute between India and Pakistan over Kashmir, the relationship between Israel and the Palestinians, the role of Saudi Arabia and the situation in and around the Persian Gulf.

Sherri Goodman tells me in that first phone conversation that she founded the CNA Advisory Board at a time (2007) when there was no money available for such initiatives. The topic of climate change in relation to security was certainly not popular in the US at that time. She believes it is therefore better to make use of existing conferences and the power of a network approach. I soon find out that I am not the only senior military officer who is concerned about this. All over the world, militaries are experiencing the impact of climate change. This is reason enough to join forces within the security sector.

Growing awareness

That opportunity arose at the next Planetary Security Initiative in The Hague in 2019. There, I met Sherri Goodman in person for the first time and her idea that we discussed earlier became a reality. Four knowledge institutes, one from the US, one from France and two from the Netherlands, got together to create a global military network dedicated to the issue of climate and security. And so the International Military Council on Climate and Security (IMCCS) is born, with Sherri Goodman as Secretary-General, and for which I am approached for the role of chairman. As a "green" general, I was of course delighted to accept. It soon proved a successful formula and grew into a network of top military and security experts from some 40 countries across every continent. The four knowledge institutes formed the supporting consortium; the Center for Climate and Security in Washington, the Institut de Relations Internationales et Stratégiques (IRIS) in Paris, The Hague Centre for Strategic Studies (HCSS) and the Institute of International Relations "Clingendael" in the Netherlands. As the theme gained momentum, interest grew and more and more knowledge institutes linked up with the IMCCS. There are now 16 institutes from different continents and a research network has been created within the IMCCS.

Our first goal was to raise awareness among the major international institutions (UN, EU, NATO), among countries, among defence and security organisations. Awareness of the fact that climate change is also a security issue, and that the security sector is therefore a vital partner that needs to accept and develop its responsibilities. But where do you start? At that point, I felt a bit like Don Quixote tilting at windmills. We decided to set our sights on the world's leading security conference, the Munich Security Conference. We did not have much time or money for expensive new research or campaigns, but what we did have was the knowledge and experience from our network, and the scientific analysis capacity of the four institutes. And so in 2019, we developed our first World Climate and Security Report, which we presented in Munich in February 2020. The report held up a mirror to the security community by showing how all regions of the world were already experiencing the security consequences of climate change.

It hit home. Together with people like John Kerry, former US Secretary of State and special climate envoy in the Biden administration since January 2021, and former UN Secretary-General Ban Ki-moon, I talked about these changes in various panel discussions. In between, I presented the findings to the Luxembourg parliament at the invitation of the country's deputy prime minister, after which Luxembourg decided to support our IMCCS network.

This was the first time in the history of this leading "hardcore" security conference that climate change was on the agenda, and it was having the desired effect. Munich was proving to be a stepping stone to the global stage. I receive one request after another to explain our findings at a wide range of conferences at home and abroad. The message of climate change and security, proclaimed by a military officer, makes people think; from NATO ambassadors to young people who help to develop new NATO strategy, and from research institutes to the organisers of various European security conferences.

There is now a high level of awareness: climate change and security are related. This is fortunately also true for the more traditional climate organisations. Initially, there appeared to be some suspicion among some climate movements, possibly because of a concern that "their" issue would be hijacked by the big security organisations and that climate would become much more of a security issue. But this is obviously not the case, and the suspicion gradually started to diminish. Everyone realises that the security sector should not only be part of the solution, but must also be part of the overarching and coherent approach required to achieve it.

Melting glaciers

One of the first in-depth studies conducted by IMCCS involved a specific report on the worrying effects of climate change in South-east Asia. Not only because the story of the Bangladeshi general had made such an impression on me two years earlier, but also to further build our knowledge about that region and expand our network there. In addition, it is now very clear that millions if not billions of people in Asia are directly affected by climate change. This is not just in Bangladesh and the low-lying areas of the Philippines, which scientists believe will eventually be largely wiped out by rising sea levels,[4] but it also concerns the livelihoods of 240 million people who depend directly on the ecosystem in the Hindu Kush Himalayan region, whose mountain ridges stretch from Afghanistan to Myanmar.

Nearly two billion people live in the basins of the rivers that originate in these mountains, and melting glaciers pose a direct threat to the stability of their habitats.[5] The river basins are lifelines for the countries in that region because they supply water for drinking and irrigation. High in the mountains, glaciers hold precipitation in the form of ice in winter, and in spring and summer the ice melts, providing fresh water to people downstream. Global warming is causing glaciers to melt faster, which means that much more water flows downhill in a short period of time in summer, which, combined with torrential rains, can cause major flooding and landslides. In the longer term, however, the water supply in the glaciers diminishes, which actually increases the risk of drought downstream. This includes the Indus, whose source is in China (Tibet) and which flows through both Pakistan and India before emptying into the Arabian Sea. In August 2010, when the Indus was already filled to the brim with meltwater from the snow peaks, a heavy monsoon struck. As a result, some places saw as much rainfall within a few hours as they would normally see in a whole year. There was severe flooding downstream, resulting in two thousand deaths and damage to the tune of 10 billion euros.[6]

Climate change is thus increasing the likelihood of flooding in Asia, as more ice melts and glacial lakes become more likely to overflow, as discussed in Chapter 1 in relation to Afghanistan. The increased rate of glacial melt can also lead to landslides and avalanches, especially if mountain slopes of rock and glacial ice become unstable due to increasingly violent freeze-thaw cycles. In February 2021, for example, a tidal wave of water, rocks, debris and silt came down in the mountains in India's Uttarakhand state, where a section of glacier from the Indian Himalayas is breaking off. It is an area in northern India where many dams are also being built. Besides killing dozens of people, the deluge destroyed many bridges, roads and homes, and cut 13 villages off from the outside world.[7] Hundreds of rescue workers were deployed, equipped with search dogs, thermal sensors and drones to rescue as many people as possible.

So what else does the future hold for people in that part of the world, knowing that by the end of this century at least a third of the glacial ice in the Himalayan region will have disappeared?[8] Even if the goals of the Paris Climate Agreement are met? And if global warming is even greater than the one-and-a-half degrees stated in the Paris Agreement, as much as two-thirds of mountain range glacier ice could be lost, according to the research team.[9] That would be an unimaginable catastrophe for the 2 billion people there who depend entirely on those glaciers for their water and food supplies.

Heat in India

In addition to all this is the almost unbearable heat in Asia, which scientists predict is only going to get worse. Aletta André, a correspondent in India for the Dutch newspaper *Trouw*, describes what the heat felt like in the Indian capital New Delhi in 2019: "The summer temperatures of above 45 degrees Celsius, day in and day out, add an extra layer of sluggishness. The blanket of heat is heavy and suffocating. You feel it in your eyes and limbs, it permeates your entire body. As if we all have to move through water in slow motion." She goes on to say: "The water stored in black tanks on the roof is scalding hot when it comes out of the tap. So we just fill a bucket and let it cool in the air conditioning for an hour. India's heatwaves are becoming more frequent, longer and hotter. For those who live or work on the streets, the heat can be fatal. Those who can do so stay indoors and close the curtains. Like vampires, we avoid sunlight. Family activities and fun evenings with friends move to the bedroom where the air conditioning is running."[10]

Fortunately for the Dutch correspondent, she can afford air conditioning and can always book a one-way ticket to the Netherlands in the event of an emergency. That is not the case for the vast majority of India's inhabitants. Many work outside in the fields or have to search for scarce drinking water in the searing heat. I remember clearly that in the same year, 2019, India's water shortage coincided with a massive heatwave. Cities like Bangalore, Chennai, Mumbai and New Delhi were in the news for one reason: they were running out of water. We saw images on television of hundreds of thousands of residents who had no choice but to wait for hours in the blazing sun for their turn to fill their bottles, tanks or jugs with water. This was a real crisis, partly caused by inadequate rainwater harvesting and rapid urbanisation, which meant that supply roads to ancient lakes, ponds and wells had been closed or filled with buildings.[11] The message behind the images on television was crystal clear: India had a serious water problem with dire consequences for its people, and those consequences were only going to get worse.

That is because it is getting even hotter. Scientists expect that half a billion people will have to endure heatwaves of 56 degrees Celsius by 2100, and in some cases even higher than 60 degrees Celsius.[12] These heatwaves will not just last for a few days, but for weeks. That will undoubtedly have devastating repercussions for countries in Southern Asia, such as India, Pakistan, Sri Lanka, Myanmar and Bangladesh, where humidity does not decrease with rising temperatures and where some 60% of the working population work outdoors in agriculture. In those temperatures, even if you sit in the shade, you will not survive. Heat combined with high humidity means that drops of perspiration do not evaporate easily, so the body cannot get rid of its heat and overheats as a result. This is what happens in the event of heat exhaustion. Many people in those regions will no longer be able to work outside during the day. Not only that, but many will die from the effects of climate change.

What will happen when much of the water that has been used up to now for drinking water, sanitation, agriculture, hydropower and tourism has disappeared? What will all those tens of millions of disadvantaged people in Asia do then? Consider Pakistan, where more than half the people in the country's largest cities already have no access to clean water. In the huge city of Karachi, the 20 million inhabitants are facing more and more water shortages. Hardest hit are the millions of people in deprived neighbourhoods and the lower middle class.[13] There, we see a veritable "water mafia" emerging; organisations that steal containers and jerrycans of clean water to sell at a high price to areas with severe water shortages.[14] In India too, this "water mafia" has been a phenomenon for years. "They pump from wells in the dead of night. Criminals control the liquid economy in one of the world's most densely populated areas", *Foreign Policy* wrote about Delhi in 2015.[15] And in the same year, the BBC showed rows of men and women clinging to a circulating water truck which left after 15 minutes, leaving some empty-handed.[16] Another reminder that thousands can live without love, but no-one can live without water.

In large countries such as India and Pakistan, home to a quarter of the world's population, with hundreds of millions below the poverty line, people are going to experience more and more floods and increasingly extreme heatwaves. Those people are going to find that soon no more water will flow in their irrigation systems, no more fruit trees will grow and fields will no longer flourish, or homes will be crushed by a devastating surge of water, mud and boulders that destroys everything in its path and hits settlements downstream. The choice for all those people is then very simple but at the same time highly complex. You flee or you die.

And that in turn creates tensions in the region. It is conceivable, for instance, that provinces above and below those rivers could come into conflict with each other, and that these tensions could culminate in separatist movements that want to secure their own water supply and will not hesitate to use violence to do so. What will governments do when the stability of a region or country is at stake? Everyone wants their own people to live in security and stability. After all, power itself benefits from that. But what are people capable of when they are desperate? Will it lead to water conflicts? To interstate wars that affect the rest of the world too? What eventually happens in Pakistan and India will affect the rest of the world in equal measure.

Agricultural crisis in China?

Let us not forget about that other vast country in Asia: China. It is also being hit hard by climate change. In June 2020, hundreds of thousands of people were evacuated in the south; dozens of people died as a result of floods and mudslides caused by downpours. According to China's Ministry of Emergency Management, the economic damage was estimated at 500 million euros.[17] A month later, China was again having to contend with heavy rainfall, said to be the heaviest in 30 years.[18] Over 2 million people had to evacuate to higher ground and more than 140 people died. The economic damage that month amounted to $8.5 billion.[19] China's meteorological service reported unpredictable, extreme weather.

In 2020, for instance, the Yangtze River burst its banks, pushing dangerously against a dam. In July 2021, the month of disasters, there was massive flooding due to extremely heavy rains in Henan province with an estimated $17.6 billion of damage. The severe weather was caused by areas of high pressure over the South Pacific and typhoon In-Fa, and resulted in at least 1.2 million people being affected. Towns and villages were flooded and some 30 dams of overflowing reservoirs were about to breach. In Dengfeng, a flooded aluminium factory exploded, and in the city of Luoyang, a large dam was blown up by the military to prevent the population from being caught unaware by another dam breach.

More than 100,000 people were evacuated from hotels, schools, residential areas and hospitals struggling with flooding and power shortages. A hospital in Zhengzhou had to manually ventilate hundreds of critically ill patients when the power failed. Train stations and airports were home to many thousands of stranded travellers. Most of the deaths in China occurred in the provincial capital Zhengzhou, where the metro network was partially flooded. Water had broken through a wall and was pouring into the metro tubes; it was up to passengers' necks or even over their heads. The media later reported that, exhausted, they tried to comfort each other, before sending farewell messages to their loved ones. Five hundred victims were eventually rescued from the underground, but at least 12 died. Is this a harbinger of things to come? China still faces big problems, Chinese scientists warned in the *South China Morning Post*. Not just from rainfall and overflowing rivers, but also from drought and rising sea levels.

Water scarcity is also a growing problem in China. This is because of drought, the uncertain state of agriculture, the uncertain state of water resources, and the rapid pace of glacial melt in the Himalayas. Too much water comes down at an accelerated rate, resulting in much lower water levels for the rest of the year. If sea levels rise at the same time, China runs the risk of salt water penetrating faster and deeper into the coastal area, salinising the farmland there. This will adversely affect wheat and rice production. If the water supply from the "eternal" snow of the Himalayas melts faster, which will increase water shortages in certain periods, experts say we can be sure of an agricultural crisis in China.[20] As a result, China's own exports will decrease and it will be forced to source food from developing countries. Should China, with its huge population, do so, it is likely that global food prices would rise, causing global shortages and food riots.

We have seen this happen before. Over a decade ago, in 2010, China was buying huge quantities of wheat on the world market because of the drought at home. Interestingly – or rather, worryingly – during the same period, Syria, Russia, Ukraine and Argentina were also experiencing drought.[21] At the same time, a Canadian wheat-growing region experienced severe rainfall[22]. All these factors combined have put the world wheat market under severe pressure. As a result, many countries tried to stockpile wheat in good time to at least feed their own population, and bread prices soared. We now know that bread price increases like this trigger uprisings, such as the Arab Spring.[23] Extreme weather events such as droughts thus create turmoil within global food chains, with all the repercussions that entail, and all this adds to the regional tensions that can arise from flooding and water shortages. Flooding in southern China and a water shortage in the north, for instance, can lead to tensions between different regional alliances within the Communist Party. It was for good reason that China's water management minister said in 2015: "Fight for every drop of water or die."[24]

I believe that all these examples show the disruptive effects of climate change, which threatens the lives of hundreds of millions of people. I look at this mainly from the point of view of my security experience and worry about its regional security effects. It will not only lead to major humanitarian crises, but in all likelihood also to large-scale migration flows of people seeking refuge elsewhere. But then again, where can they go? It is a complex, and above all alarming, development in a fragile and densely populated region.

Notes

1. Rigter, N. (2016, 20 November), "Army chief: fighting climate change", *De Telegraaf*, see https://www.telegraaf.nl/nieuws/1291109/legerchef-vechten-tegen-klimaatverandering

2. Tariq Waseem Ghazi, A.M.M. Uniruzzaman, A.K. Singh, "Climate Change & Security in South Asia, Cooperating for peace", GMACCC, Paper number 2, May 2016

3. Lippert, T. (2016). NATO, climate change, and international security: a risk governance approach. RAND Corporation, Santa Monica.

4. Tye, S., Waslander, J., Chaudhury, M. (2020), "Building Coastal Resilience in Bangladesh, the Philippines, and Colombia: Country experiences with mainstreaming climate adaptation." World Resources Institute, Washington DC

5. Sharma E. et al. (2019), "Introduction to the Hindu Kush Himalayan Assessment". In: Wester, P., Mishra, A., Mukherji, A., Shrestha, A. (ed.), "The Hindu Kush Himalayan Assessment", Springer

6. Vaidya R. et al. (2019), "Disaster Risk Reduction and Building Resilience in the Hindu Kush Himalaya". In: Wester, P., Mishra, A., Mukherji, A., Shrestha, A. (ed), "The Hindu Kush Himalaya Assessment", Springer, p. 393.

7. Van Raaij, B. (2021, 11 February), "Is deluge the result of climate change?", *de Volkskrant*

8-9. Carrington, D. (2019, 4 February), "A third of the Himalayan ice cap doomed, finds report", *The Guardian*, see https://www.theguardian.com/environment/2019/feb/04/a-third-of-himalayan-ice-cap-doomed-finds-shocking-report

10. Andre, A. (2019, 22 June), "How do you survive the heat in New Delhi?", *Allegiance*, see https://www.trouw.nl/nieuws/hoe-overleef-je-de-hitte-in-new-delhi-be975728/

11. Janakarajan, S., Llorente, M. & Zérah, M-H. (2005), "Urban water conflicts in Indian cities: man-made scarcity as a critical factor". Paper presented at the International Workshop on Urban Water Conflicts, 27 and 28 October 2005.

12. Saeed, F., Schleussner, C.F. & Ashfaq, M. (2021), "Deadly heat stress to become commonplace across South Asia already at 1.5°C of global warming", *Geophysical Research Letters*, 48(7), p. 1-11. See also: Radford, T. (2021, 29 March), "Half a billion people may face heat of 56°C by 2100", *UNDRR Prevention Web*, see https://www.preventionweb.net/news/half-billion-people-may-face-heat-56degc-2100

13-14. Hashim, A. (s.d.), "Parched for a price: Karachi's water crisis", *Al Jazeera*. Accessed November 26, 2021, from https://interactive.aljazeera.com/aje/2017/parched-for-price/index.html

15. Sethi, A. & Das, S. (2015), "Midnight Marauders", *Foreign Policy* no. 213, pp. 54-65

16. Majumder, S. (2015, 28 July), "Water mafia: why Delhi is buying water on the black market", *BBC News*, see https://www.bbc.com/news/world-asia-india-33671836

17. Foreign Editor (2020, 11 June), "Dozens killed by floods in China", *Algemeen Dagblad*, see https://www.ad.nl/buitenland/tientallen-doden-door-overstromingen-in-china-ac78a303/

18-19. *de Volkskrant*, (2020, 17 July), "Record rain ravages China".

20-23. Lieven, A. (2020). "Climate change and the nation state: the realist case", Allen Lane, 25-26

24. Charlie Parton, "China's Looming Water Crisis", *China Dialogue*, April 2017, p. 6; Ben Abbs, "The Growing Water Crisis in China", *Global Risks Insights*, 10 August 2017; "China: A Watershed Moment for Water Governance", World Bank, 7 November 2018

Chapter Nine
Devastating floods

"In China's Zhengzhou, underground train passengers became trapped by heavy rainfall and drowned. In Madagascar, people eat mud to fill their stomachs during a famine caused by unusually prolonged drought. In Siberia, forest fires that appear to have been smouldering all winter flare up again. In the US state of Oregon, forest fires generate so much energy and heat that they affect the weather. And the Amazon region cannot be relied upon: due to fires, the rainforests currently emit more CO_2 than they absorb. But even in Western Europe, homes, roads and bridges are now being swept away by what were once charming rivers…"

Journalist Titia Ketelaar, NRC Handelsblad, 23 July 2021

It is July 2021, a summer plagued by natural disasters. Heatwaves, droughts, forest fires, extreme rainfall, landslides, floods. While natural disasters elsewhere in the world often seem far removed from our own lives, things are now happening very close to home. In the news, I see how extreme rainfall and flooding in Germany and Belgium are causing many casualties and unprecedented damage. It later emerges that the total damage in the affected area is $43 billion.[1] According to scientists, this is undeniably a consequence of climate change. The warmer the air, the more moisture it can hold, which causes more rain. And that leads to swollen rivers that burst their banks more often. Rivers which are already filling up as ice from glaciers melts faster, and which now have less space because of growing urbanisation on the banks. This is because two-thirds of all the people on earth now live along the rivers and coastlines that are our lifelines.

We saw the consequences in Germany, where 165 people were killed by devastating storms in 2021. Entire villages were cut off from the outside world. Countless houses collapsed and were swept away by the hugely swollen and wildly flowing rivers. Many people sought protection in trees and on the roofs of buildings. Military personnel were deployed and helicopters with rescue workers flew back and forth to rescue people. Bodies of people overwhelmed by the sudden rising waters were found in flooded basements, and firefighters also perished during rescue operations. "We have never experienced such a disaster. It is really exhausting", Rhineland-Palatinate state premier Malu Dreyer told journalists.[2] Armin Laschet, at the time the minister president of North Rhine-Westphalia, spoke of "the disaster of the century".[3] Based on an estimate of the flood damage, he is demanding a federal recovery package of 20 to 30 billion euros.[4]

Our other neighbour, Belgium, also suffered widespread havoc. Homes and bridges collapsed and many residents were evacuated. People there also lost their lives. It later emerged that Germany and Belgium were experiencing what are known as flash floods, where the water flows in lower-lying areas very quickly. A raging torrent of water takes people completely by surprise. Within minutes, the water level can rise by several metres. If you are lucky, you might just make it up your stairs in time.[5]

Later, as Belgium and Germany licked their wounds, the scientific journal *Geophysical Research Letters* issued a shocking report. In a worst-case scenario, the same kind of storms that caused the flooding will be 14 times more common by 2100 than they are today. They would be slow-moving, severe storms that would completely overwhelm a region's river system.[6]

Country behind the dykes

In the Netherlands, no lives were lost due to the extreme storms, but even here the damage was extensive, especially in Limburg. There, the storm flooded homes and in some places the high water pressure caused sewage to overflow into people's homes *via* the toilet. The Dutch armed forces deployed some 800 personnel to provide emergency assistance. They filled sandbags, took them to where they were needed to hold back the water or put up flood fences. They also evacuated people from homes and hospitals, rescued animals, lifted old people in wheelchairs out of their care homes and set to work with chainsaws to clear trees washed away in the flood water.

In the Netherlands, we should count ourselves lucky. If we had not spent more than 10 billion euros over the past 25 years to relocate and raise river dykes, and to expand and deepen flood plains – so that we can store more water in them and thus have a controlled discharge for a river like the Meuse – we would have suffered more chaos and misery.[7]

"It looks like war"

The fact that we have been spending money to make space for rivers in the past 25 years is all to do with the flooding of the 1990s. In 1993, our alarm bells went off. At the time, I was attending the Advanced Military Studies course (HMV) in Rijswijk, the training for higher positions in Defence. The Meuse River burst its banks due to persistent rainfall and flooded entire villages. Even cities like Venlo and Roermond became inaccessible due to high water levels.

Anyone turning on the television could see Dutch military personnel taking boats and trucks into neighbourhoods to tell people to leave their homes. The river dykes threatened to breach at any moment. "It looks like war", a friend said to me as he watched the images. Limburg did indeed look like a disaster zone, which is exactly what it was. Some 8% of the province, an area of 18,000 hectares, was under water. In five days, 12,000 people were evacuated. Defence set up a command post in Venlo, and army helicopters were flying over the disaster area to rescue people who had been cut off.

There was no longer any traffic in the area. No cars or bikes to be seen; there were not even any walkers. Many cows and sheep had drowned. It was clear that this was a national disaster. Soon afterwards, on 31 January 1995, disaster struck again. Extreme rainfall in northern France and the Belgian Ardennes caused the water in Limburg to rise again to terrifying levels. In the

Gelderland river area, 250,000 people and one million animals were evacuated as a precaution. Military personnel from across the country rushed to the affected area with sandbags and equipment to hold back the water and to help with evacuation.

Defence set up a helicopter operations centre at Volkel Air Base to rescue people and asked other countries for help. In Germany, for example, 40 German and British military helicopters, which could also be used for night operations, were ready for us. At Laarbruch Air Base, just across the Dutch border, British Chinooks were on standby for larger-scale evacuations. That risk was significant now that the dykes could breach. At the request of the Dutch Directorate General for Public works and Water management (*Rijkswaterstaat)*, Dutch F-16s therefore made infrared recordings so that analysts could determine if and where the dykes were saturated: this was known as Operation Wet Feet. Rescue helicopters were flying at night with a "night sun", a huge spotlight under the aircraft, so that the crew could see what was happening on the ground and locate anyone in distress in the water.

The Netherlands, world champion in adaptation

Fortunately, things ended well in the 1990s. The dykes held, and after two weeks most residents were able to return to their homes. There were no fatalities, but the damage was enormous. It was clear to everyone that this must never happen again, and the then prime minister, Wim Kok, immediately announced a new Delta Plan, "Room for the River". Shortly afterwards, the government started reinforcing the dykes along the Meuse, Rhine and Waal rivers, and outflow areas were created, giving rivers and floodplains more space to cope with larger amounts of water.

To this day, in the Netherlands we are constantly improving our dykes, flood defences and other measures to be prepared for high water. We have to be, because 9 million people (more than half the population) live in flood-prone areas. A quarter of the Netherlands is below sea level (Amsterdam Ordnance Datum, NAP) and 55% of our country is prone to flooding, 30% of which is river flooding. The Netherlands therefore has over 17,000 kilometres of dykes: the distance from Amsterdam to New Zealand. According to experts, this makes us the best protected delta country in the world. We constantly monitor the water level, the weather, the height of the waves, and calculate the required strength and height of dykes.

We in the Netherlands know that water is our oldest enemy and ally, and that water also unites us in times of need. Young and old, rich and poor, all population groups and all political movements stand together in the fight against the rising water. We have even institutionalised our fight against water in elected water boards, whose task is to "manage" the water in Delta Region Netherlands and keep us safe from floods. And we are quite prepared to release billions of euros to strengthen our defences against floods.

Storm drain

Nevertheless, we were once again faced with a similar scene in the southern province of Limburg in the summer of 2021. Much damage, but fortunately no casualties. Once again, we found out how vulnerable the Netherlands in the river delta actually is. The question is: how long will we remain safe in the Netherlands? That remains a cause for concern. Because the climate is changing and the earth is warming rapidly, we are facing more volatile weather in our region; much more precipitation and in shorter periods of time, but also more meltwater from the Alps due to glacial melt. The Netherlands is a kind of storm drain for rainwater from our neighbouring countries and meltwater from the Alps. Everything comes together here. If it rains really heavily in nearby countries, we are vulnerable to flooding. But melting ice in the polar regions also increases our vulnerability to flooding. We will soon have the "highest sea levels in eight thousand years", for instance, because the vast ice sheets in the polar regions have been thrown out of kilter, says Sybren Drijfhout, sea level rise project leader at the KNMI and professor of physical oceanography at the University of Southampton.[8]

According to Drijfhout, we should be aware – and this is confirmed by the UN's latest climate report – that we have now thrown the major ice sheets out of kilter and that it will take hundreds or thousands of years for them to rebalance in a warmer world. Those parts of the ice sheets that are in direct contact with ocean water could disappear particularly quickly. If that scenario repeats itself and the coastline is not better protected, large parts of the Netherlands will be consigned to history.

We should therefore start to consider a "controlled retreat from the Netherlands in the long run", according to Dutch experts such as polar meteorologist Michiel van der Broeke. He is a researcher at the Institute for Marine and Atmospheric Research (IMAU) at Utrecht University.

Stay or leave

To make us aware of this danger, the Dutch government has created the overstroomik.nl website, where anyone in the Netherlands can see whether their hometown will be flooded if the water rises. In my case, there is already a 10% chance that I will experience a flood of up to 3 metres in my lifetime. That could be as early as tomorrow, according to the website. That would mean no water, no electricity, no gas, no toilet and no internet. Moreover, I would be on my own for several days. I would have two options, the website says: stay or leave. That is quite a sobering thought and one that would undoubtedly be alarming for many people.

Sea level rise and increased risk of flooding also pose a growing threat to some of our critical infrastructure. For instance, a country's military infrastructure can be severely damaged by floods. Think of naval ports, airfields and coastal installations, such as radar stations. The US naval base in Norfolk (the largest in the world), which floods several times a year, is a striking example. In the US, heavier rainstorms also cause flooding at military airfields, rendering them non-operational for extended periods. And what are the risks for radar stations in coastal areas and for nuclear power plants, which are usually located on rivers and coasts?

And what are the implications for our agriculture? In the Netherlands, for instance, the need to keep our agricultural land dry is causing the groundwater level to remain low while the sea level is rising, which means that the soil is becoming increasingly salty. The higher the sea level, therefore, the saltier the groundwater in our coastal provinces, and the harder the pumping stations in the polders have to work, which in turn causes more salt water to seep up at the bottom of the dykes. The Dutch agricultural export business, which requires significant amounts of freshwater, is a billion-dollar industry. For now.

I also wonder about all the other costs involved in a major flood. A third of Europe's population lives in coastal areas. The European Commission has calculated that the annual cost of flooding will explode if stringent measures are not taken. Currently, sea floods in Europe cost €1.4 billion a year. By 2100, that figure could rise to €240 billion a year.[9] Of these costs, 95% could be prevented with simple and sensible measures such as dyke heightening. These are not cheap investments, but they are extremely cost-effective, as Europe's coastal areas are not only densely populated but also filled with businesses, ports, industry and real estate. The annual damage from flooding will not only cause much unnecessary suffering for residents, but also considerable damage to the economy. Measures are not only needed to protect people's homes and jobs; they are also a wise and profitable investment.

In November 2019, for instance, images of the flooded Basilica San Marco in Venice shocked the world. The 1,600-year-old lagoon city on the Adriatic Sea was facing its worst flooding in 50 years. A rise in sea levels combined with subsidence due to the settling of the lagoon floor was the cause, resulting in billions of euros of damage. It is important, therefore, for Italy to invest as soon as possible in dykes and seawalls to hold back the sea.

Research shows that European countries are all preparing differently for a rise in sea levels.[10] That makes it all the more important for them to learn from each other, especially now that the problem is becoming so urgent.

Who is still safe?

Elsewhere in the world, other people are also at risk due to the increased likelihood of severe weather and flooding. In China, as described earlier, and also in Russia, cities like St Petersburg are vulnerable to rising sea levels in the medium term.[11] In the US, low-lying coastal cities such as New York, Los Angeles, New Orleans, Miami and Seattle are at risk. In the US, it is even expected that by the year 2045, less than 25 years from now, 300,000 American homes will be uninhabitable due to the danger of floods and hurricanes.[12] On top of that, there are numerous cities without coastal protection, and without the resources for multi-billion dollar flood defences, such as coastal cities in the Sahel and Asian megacities in India and Vietnam, where many people are already vulnerable.

So the risk of dangerous flooding is growing everywhere; the lives of hundreds of millions of people are at stake. "If we do nothing, we will drown", says Henk "the water guy" Ovink. After hurricane Sandy, he was a member of the reconstruction task force set up by President Obama, and responsible for ensuring that reconstruction efforts take into account the increased risks of future flooding.[13]

A former water envoy to the Dutch government, Ovink travelled around the world to help other countries in their fight against rising water levels, such as vulnerable coastal cities that are set to grow significantly in size in the coming decades as more and more people want to live and work there.[14] According to a study by the US research firm Climate Central, 300 million people already live in coastal areas and river deltas which, without coastal protection, will suffer severe flooding on average once a year from around the year 2050.[15]

Notes

1. Kramer, K. & Ware, J. (2021). "Counting the costs 2021: A year of climate breakdown", Christian Aid, London.

2. Nu.nl (2021, 16 July), "More than 100 dead and many missing due to severe weather in Germany and Belgium", see https://www.nu.nl/wateroverlast-limburg/6145917/meer-dan-100-doden-en-veel-vermisten-door-noodweer-in-duitsland-en-belgie.html

3. Mudde, T. (2021, 18 July), "How 'the disaster of the century' could have hit Germany so hard", *de Volkskrant*, see https://www.volkskrant.nl/nieuws-achtergrond/hoe-de-ramp-van-de-eeuw-in-duitsland-zo-hard-kon-toeslaan~b70a3051/

4. Hofman, F. (2021, 9 August), "German flood damage amounts to possible €30 billion", *NRC Handelsblad*, see https://www.nrc.nl/nieuws/2021/08/09/duitse-schade-door-overstromingen-bedraagt-mogelijk-tot-30-miljard-euro-a4054237

5. Thus Matthijs Kok, professor of water safety at TU Delft, quoted in Van der Schoot, E. & Timmer, E. (2021, 17 July), "Netherlands has a lucky escape", *De Telegraaf*, see https://www.telegraaf.nl/nieuws/1900772269/nederland-ontsnapt-aan-nog-erger

6. Kahraman, A., Kendon, E.J., Chan, S.C. & Fowler, H.J. (2021), "Quasi-stationary intense rainstorms spread across Europe under climate change", *Geophysical Research Letters* 48(13), https://doi.org/10.1029/2020gl092361

7. Thus Pim van der Knaap, Boskalis board member, quoted in Van der Schoot, E. & Timmer, E. (2021, 17 July), "Netherlands has a lucky escape", *De Telegraaf*, see https://www.telegraaf.nl/nieuws/1900772269/nederland-ontsnapt-aan-nog-erger

8. Quoted in Hoving, W. (202, 27 January), "No, things are not OK with the sea level rise", *Friesch Dagblad*, see https://frieschdagblad.nl/regio/Nee-het-valt-ni%C3%A9t-mee-met-de-zeespiegelstijging-26804795.html

9. Vousdoukas, M., Mentaschi, L., Mongelli, I., Ciscar J-C, Hinkel J., Ward, P., Gosling, S., Feyen L., (2020). "Adapting to rising coastal flood risk in the EU under climate change", Publications Office of the European Union, Luxembourg, https://publications.jrc.ec.europa.eu/repository/handle/JRC118512 https://www.google.com/url?sa=t&rct=j&q=&esrc=s&source=web&cd=&ved=2ahUKEwj4maLYs5zyAhV4h_0HHbxQBZYQFnoECAsQAw&url=https%3A%2F%2Fpublications.jrc.ec.europa.eu%2Frepository%2Fbitstream%2FJRC118512%2Fpesetaiv_task_6_coastal_final_report.pdf&usg=AOvVaw1DowpfSBa3R3b2QTal6mCL

10. McEvoy, S., Haasnoot, M., Biesbroek, R. (2021), "How are European countries planning for sea level rise?", *Ocean & Coastal Management* 203, 105512. https://doi.org/10.1016/j.ocecoaman.2020.105512

11. Kozin, D. (2019, Feb21), "St Petersburg's dam is holding back the floods, for now", *The Moscow Times*, see https://www.themoscowtimes.com/2019/02/21/st-petersburgs-dam-is-holding-back-floods-for-now-a64066

12. Union of Concerned Scientists (2018), Underwater: Rising Seas, chronic Floods, and the Implications for US Coastal Real Estate. *Union of Concerned Scientists*.

13. Broer, T. (2017, August 22). This is "Henk the water guy", the Dutchman who is teaching the world not to drown. *Vrij Nederland*, https://www.vn.nl/henk-ovink-watergezant-uit-nederland/

14. UN (2018), World Urbanisation Prospects. UN Department of Economic and Social Affairs, New York, see https://population.un.org/wup/

15. Climate Central (2019), Flooded future: global vulnerability to sea level rise worse than previously understood. Climate Central, Princeton NJ

Chapter Ten
Ruthless wildfires

"We farmers, we sit here every year when the rains fail and we say: next year. Well, next year ain't gonna save us, nor the one after that. This world's a treasure, Donald, but it's been telling us to leave for a while now."
Matthew McConaughey, as Cooper in the film *Interstellar*

From the moment it was set up in 2019, more and more former military personnel, scientists and researchers from home and abroad were joining the IMCCS. It was good to see that interest in the issue is so widely shared among security experts around the world. All are experiencing the repercussions in their own countries and regions, and all want to become part of the solution. But first and foremost, we need to increase our own knowledge and understanding of the relationship between climate and security. We therefore worked hard that first year to organise the network, partly by participating in a variety of security conferences, where we approached security officials and researchers from different countries and continents to exchange experiences and insights so that we could take stock of the impact of climate change worldwide. Former colleagues from the US and Central America, for instance, pointed out the increasing danger of large forest and wildfires due to drought caused by global warming.

It appears that it is not only climate and climate change that are having a major impact on forest fires, but also direct human actions. Between 2004 and 2017, a total of 43 million hectares of nature spread across Asia, Africa and Central America were destroyed due to deforestation. That is an area 10 times the size of the Netherlands. Tropical forests disappeared mainly to make way for agricultural land, writes the World Wildlife Fund (WWF) in 2021. European countries are thus also indirectly responsible for deforestation on other continents, the WWF reports. One of the main causes of deforestation is the demand for agricultural products such as palm oil, soya for animal feed and cocoa. Deforestation makes it warmer and drier and rainfall patterns change, making it easier for new fires to start. In its report, the WWF therefore calls for international legislation to tackle deforestation. The wildlife organisation is also calling on consumers to eat more plant-based food and urging companies to become more sustainable.[1]

In the course of the IMCCS assessment, experts from our network also pointed out the danger of forest fires in southern Europe, an understandable move as there is cause for concern in Europe too. In 2019, more than 400,000 hectares of European natural areas were destroyed by fire. That year, for instance, there were 235 wildfires in Austria, 668 in Bulgaria, 1,963 in Czechoslovakia, 1,458 in Finland, 5,435 in France, 1,523 in Germany, 4,351 in Italy, 1,107 in Latvia, 548 in the Netherlands, 9,635 in Poland, 10,832 in Portugal and 10,883 in Spain. These include forest fires, vegetation fires, and the burning of grasslands and agricultural land.[2]

Fire in Portugal

Dutch people holidaying abroad are increasingly confronted with wildfires. In 2018, shortly after my retirement, I experienced this firsthand when I wanted to go to the Algarve in Portugal with my wife to recharge the batteries. At the time we wanted to go, however, a huge fire was raging there. An army of 700 firefighters was needed to contain the blaze, which by then had already destroyed more than 1,000 hectares of forest and farmland. Record-breaking temperatures were making it difficult to extinguish the fires, and new ones were flaring up and putting the whole area at risk.

Portugal's civil protection agency sent urgent warnings to locals and tourists to prepare for evacuation. Those watching the images on the news saw the huge blaze and people fleeing from it: "This is the latest place in Europe to feel the effects of the scorching summer of 2018", said one reporter. Interviews with local firefighters revealed just how exhausting and dangerous the operation to contain the blaze was. Two fire engines had already caught fire, and residents and tourists were forced to leave. Another fire was raging further north on the border with Spain.

Fanning the flames in Australia

In 2019, therefore, when I read the observations, studies and reports by the experts from the IMCCS network on the risk of wildfires, I was no longer so surprised by their intensity. However, it was an eye-opener for me when I read how unprepared governments were and how little account they were taking of this natural hazard. In 2019, in a country like Australia, climate change was not yet high on the political agenda. Indeed, Australia was one of the foremost objectors at the UN climate summit in Madrid that year.

Critics claim that Australia's government is too protective of its own coal industry. This is not really surprising, given that Australia is the world's largest exporter of coal, accounting for about a third of global exports. It is also the reason why Australian prime minister Scott Morrison repeatedly took a piece of coal to the Australian parliament two years earlier to make the point that the country's power supply was ensured by mining coal. The prime minister also refused to believe that ambitious climate policies can prevent drought, drinking water scarcity and forest fires.[3]

This is causing great annoyance and frustration among security officials in his country, such as former Australian defence boss, Admiral Chris Barrie. Barrie wrote in a foreword to a 2019 report by Australian climate experts that "apart from nuclear war, global warming caused by human activity is the greatest threat to humanity on Earth".[4] Humanity could cease to exist by 2050 due to destabilising factors in society and the environment, he wrote. He believes that there is little the Australian government can do about nuclear war, but all the more about the effects of climate change.[5] "It is a leadership issue", Barrie rightly argues.

Fatal short-sightedness

When a year later, in 2020, wildfires had been raging for months in Australia, covering areas ten times larger than those in the Amazon rainforest and killing thirty-four people, things were about to change. Australian firefighters were seen on television refusing to shake the hand of the Australian prime minister and they accused the government of fatal short-sightedness.[6] Former fire chief Greg Mullins said in a radio interview that he had twice warned the prime minister of unprecedented fire risk and asked him to agree to increase funding for the fire service, as well as take action to combat climate change. The government's response, however, was that it was "not convenient" at the time.[7]

Meanwhile, television news broadcasts were full of footage of fleeing people losing their homes, as well as gruesome images of injured and fleeing animals. We were all shocked by the images of those huge fires and towering flames, but especially by the picture of a charred baby kangaroo that appeared to be stuck in barbed wire. Those are images that are difficult to forget. In response, tens of thousands of people took to the streets in Melbourne, Sydney, Brisbane, Perth and other cities. Dermot O'Gorman, top executive of the World Wildlife Fund in Australia, called the bushfires "one of the worst natural disasters in modern history" and could not recall any other place in the world where so many animals had fled or been killed. Three billion animals were killed by the fires, scientists reported to indicate the staggering loss.[8] The scientists say they have been "conservative" in their estimate because of a lack of reliable data. The impact on other animals, such as fish and turtles, for instance, was not included in the study because there was not enough relevant information.

At the time, the deployment of the military in Australia was one of the largest peacetime operations. Navy ships and military aircraft brought water, food and fuel to the affected areas, and military personnel helped thousands of residents and tourists on the east coast. This help was badly needed, as tens of thousands of people were without power. Some places had run out of drinking water and there were long queues at supermarkets and petrol stations because of hoarding.

Firefighters from numerous countries were flown in to provide assistance, a necessary move given that the fire destroyed an area five times that of the Netherlands. "It is like driving from Groningen to Maastricht and beyond, and only seeing blackened forest", writes *Volkskrant* correspondent Jeroen Visser.[9] In the end, only heavy rains were able to extinguish the fires in Australia. In mid-February, that redeeming rain finally arrived, putting an end to this unrelenting and destructive force of nature after eight months.

Scientists wrote afterwards that the fires were a foretaste of climate disasters ahead.[10] "The 2020 bushfires were unprecedented, but may well become the norm in years to come", according to Richard Thornton, head of the Bushfire and Natural Hazards Cooperative Research Centre in Australia, which coordinates natural disaster research. He believes that people living in areas where bushfires are common, which is actually most of Australia, need to become resilient to such disasters.[11] It also appears that the fires caused a surge in local CO_2 emissions, which are now reaching record levels.[12]

Hobbit in a wine bar

Even after the bushfires, the Australian prime minister did not seem to be particularly moved, at least not enough to take any targeted action. What is more, he said that net zero would not be achieved in the wine bars of the inner cities. Not everyone appreciated that. A former Australian air force general, Air Vice-Marshal John Blackburn, who was committed to combating climate change, told a journalist: "I served in the armed forces for four decades; you can't dismiss us as left-wing hobbits living in a wine bar."[13] He also said of himself and his colleagues: "We are serious individuals with extensive experience who look at the risk and want to do something about it."

Blackburn is the initiator of the Australian Security Leaders Climate Group (ASLCG) established in April 2021, affiliated to the IMCCS. The security experts and former senior military officers associated with this network argue that Australia will begin to experience a range of security threats as a result of climate change. The group of concerned experts feel compelled to call urgent attention to this, as they say their own government is failing to address the growing impact of climate change or to protect its own population. For instance, besides the danger of wildfires, which have caused such devastation in their own country, they also mention other major risks in places such as Southeast Asia. Sea level rise, cyclones, scarcer drinking water, floods, climate refugees: all are phenomena that could affect Australia in some way, either directly or indirectly.

The scorching summer of 2021

These are all issues covered in our IMCCS reports and we are therefore monitoring developments with great concern. The ferocious fires in Australia may have been extinguished for now after eight months thanks to the rain, but elsewhere new fires just keep breaking out. In Siberia, for instance, gigantic forest fires were visible from space in 2021, and uncontrollable blazes were also developing in Norway. Forest fires were also ravaging northern Algeria. More than 60 people died there, including 28 soldiers who were helping to fight the fires and evacuate local people. The area where most of the fires were raging, Tizi Ouzou, some 60 kilometres east of the capital Algiers, is remote and water is scarce, which hampered the firefighting efforts.[14]

Closer to home, in France, forest fires were threatening the densely populated Massif de la Clape, and in eastern Austria, hundreds of firefighters were tackling a huge forest fire. In Greece, Turkey and Italy, temperatures were exceptionally high at 40 to 45 degrees, causing forest fires in many places. In Turkey, thousands of residents had to leave their homes and entire villages burned down. In a fortnight, more than 160,000 hectares of forest had been reduced to ashes, more than is normally seen in an entire year.[15] In Greece, the army was helping firefighters and local authorities to fight the dozens of forest fires. NIGHTMARE WITHOUT END and FIRES

EVERYWHERE, screamed the headlines in Greek newspapers. There was further concern in Greece about the effects of the high temperatures. Because so many Greeks use air-conditioning, the authorities feared that too much power was being consumed. Prime Minister Mitsotakis said that Greeks should not set their air conditioning below 26 degrees Celsius, otherwise too much electricity would be required and the grid would be overloaded.[16]

In southern Italy, thousands of hectares of forest, pastures and olive groves burnt down in 2021. Harvests of cherries, peaches and nectarines were at risk of being halved; fires threatened nature reserves in Calabria and Sicily. At the same time, elsewhere in Italy, extreme rainfall led to flooded cellars and streets. In South Tyrol, 87 litres of rain per square metre fell in one 24-hour period, causing a landslide in one instance.[17]

The Dutch military got involved too. In the summer of 2021, for instance, the Netherlands sent Chinook transport helicopters to Albania to help with firefighting efforts. The Dutch assistance is part of the European Union's RescEU programme, set up in 2017 to protect civilians from natural disasters. "Every day we flew, sometimes even before dawn, from the Albanian airbase to the deployment area", 26-old Jetze told the Defence staff magazine. She was working as a sergeant in the Dutch Royal Air Force at the time.[18] "In the distance, we could see the smoke rising, and we could smell the fire when we were still 15 minutes away. That smell stays with me." The sergeant also explained that the soldiers worked about three shifts a day. The flights were in mountainous terrain and in daytime temperatures of around 40 degrees, so these are tough conditions, even for the helicopter. "Once we arrived, everyone was on edge", says Jetze. "As loadmasters, we hook up the bambi bucket (a kind of inverted umbrella) and hit the button that opens the giant water bag and allows 8,000 to 10,000 litres of water to be dropped. Close coordination is needed with the pilots. They see the most as we fly towards the fire, and once above it we, lying on our bellies at the open hatch, have the best view. "Lastly", she added, "A nature reserve in the south was our first priority. When the fire there was under control, we carried on firefighting in the north. We saved a farmhouse just in the nick of time. From the air, we could see how grateful the residents were." In the end, we saw in the news reports reaching us here in the Netherlands that the deployment of the firefighting helicopters had been a crucial factor in mastering the fire.

On the other side of the Atlantic in 2021, the Canadian military was on standby to help evacuate towns and villages because of intense forest fires. Most of these had been caused by lightning strikes during intense thunderstorms (which in turn resulted from the extreme heat). Further south, wildfires were ravaging the western US, with tens of thousands more evacuated in California and elsewhere in the US. According to the Austrian Central Institute of Meteorology and Geodynamics, climate change was the underlying cause of the record temperatures.[19]

The wildfire season had only just begun in the US and would until November, but by the end of July the meter was already in the dark red zone: at that point, more than twice as much forest has already burnt down as in record year 2020. According to California governor Gavin Newsom, even more records are going to be broken in the coming years. "At the end of the day, we have to acknowledge this: the dry spells are getting drier and the heatwaves a lot hotter than they have been so far. We have to recognise that these forest fires are caused by climate change", Newsom said.[20]

"It is not even August yet", sighed Dutch firefighter Gert Zoutendijk, who was helping there in late July, "and already over 165,000 hectares of forest have burnt in the US state of Oregon." Zoutendijk normally worked in the Portland area, but at the time he was helping to fight the largest of more than 80 major active wildfires in America. In other years, he told a journalist, forest fires did not start here until late July at the earliest. But in southern Oregon, one of the largest wildfires ever had been raging for three weeks and had been dubbed the "Bootleg Fire".[21]

The Dutch firefighter also said he was surprised by the intensity, extreme behaviour and rapid spread of the fire. He had not seen this before in his time in the fire service. "In the first four days, the size of the fire doubled every day. The heat was so intense that pyrocumulus clouds formed (which form after air is heated by a wildfire or volcanic eruption and pushes up ash and smoke). Normally you might see that once or twice, now it has happened five days in a row. The fire thus created its own weather. We had lightning and a tornado. Really unprecedented", Zoutendijk said.

The firefighter explained that part of the problem was that people were building houses in forested areas. "Long ago, the forest took care of itself. There were occasional fires around dead wood and insect-infested trees, but that was not a problem, it burnt away and so the forest remained healthy. Now people build their houses in forested areas. For years, we firefighters put out fires there because they threatened houses. But as a result, the dead wood does not burn away and the forest remains full of combustible material. It is a national issue: how should we manage our forests? Should we use more controlled fires (to prevent uncontrolled fires), should we allow logging? The best thing is probably a combination of tactics."[22]

We have to assume that things will only get worse in Europe too as temperatures continue to rise. The rising heat means that the natural world is drying out faster in spring, especially in southern Europe. The change in climate then causes further drought around the Mediterranean Sea and with it a sharply increasing risk of forest fires. We saw the same in 2023. Southern Europe sweltered under a heatwave that summer and record temperatures were also registered elsewhere in the world. On the Greek island of Rhodes, some 20,000 people had to flee from forest fires. It was the biggest evacuation operation ever in Greece.[23]

Wildfires are having a major impact, and this is something we are going to face more frequently in more places around the world in the future. Furthermore, it is not only a direct threat to nature, people and animals, but also to the fragile economies in tourist areas and to the livelihoods and prosperity of local people. Tourists will be confronted by the reality of the situation and will hopefully reach the conclusion that we really need to adapt.

Notes

1. WWF (2021), Deforestation Fronts: drivers and responses in a changing world. Gland

2. European Commission (20201), JRC Technical Report: forest fires in Europe, Middle East and North Africa 2019. European Commission, Brussels

3. Mao, F. (2021, 22 October), "Climate change: why Australia refuses to give up coal", *BBC News*, see https://www.bbc.com/news/world-australia-57925798

4. Spratt, D. & Dunlop, I. (2019), "Existential climate-related security risk: A scenario approach", Breakthrough - National Centre for Climate Restoration, Melbourne

5. O'Malley, N. (2021, 20 April), "Military leaders, security chiefs demand action on climate threat", *The Sydney Morning Herald*, see https://www.smh.com.au/environment/climate-change/military-leaders-security-chiefs-demand-action-on-climate-threat-20210420-p57kve.html

6. Carey, A. (2020, 3 January), "Firefighter refuses to shake prime minister Scott Morrison's hand in Cobargo", *News.com.au*, see https://www.news.com.au/finance/work/leaders/firefighter-refuses-to-shake-prime-minister-scott-morrisons-hand-in-cobargo/news-story/beb7a2ef6f7f8efe90369d8aede75514

7. Noyes, J. (2019, 14 November), "'We saw it coming': former NSW fire chief says government was warned on bushfires", *The Sydney Morning Herald*, see https://www.smh.com.au/politics/federal/we-saw-it-coming-former-fire-commissioner-says-government-was-warned-on-bushfires-20191114-p53agj.html

8. *RTL News* (2020, 28 July), "Three billion animals hit by Australia wildfires", see https://www.rtlnieuws.nl/nieuws/buitenland/artikel/5173834/miljarden-dieren-bosbranden-australie-impact-natuur

9. Deems, A. (2019, 31 December), "Australia correspondent: 'It's an apocalyptic landscape, a wasteland'", *People's Newspaper*, see https://www.volkskrant.nl/nieuws-achtergrond/correspondent-vanuit-australie-het-is-een-apocalyptisch-landschap-een-woestenij-b318d221/

10. Gibbens, S. (2020, 6 January). "Intense 'firestorms' forming from Australia's deadly wildfires", *National Geographic*, see https://www.nationalgeographic.com/science/article/australian-wildfires-cause-firestorms

11. Albeck-Ripka, L. (2021, 4 January), "One year on from Australia's devastating wildfires", *National Geographic*, see https://www.nationalgeographic.nl/milieu/2021/01/een-jaar-na-de-verwoestende-bosbranden-in-australie

12. Schutterhelm, R. (2020, 6 January), "What is causing Australia's devastating wildfires?", *Nu.nl*, see https://www.nu.nl/klimaat/6022089/wat-is-de-oorzaak-van-de-verwoestende-bosbranden-in-australie.html

13. Quoted in Rossvan (2021, 20 April), "Climate change: former Australian secretary of defence asks government to investigate climate security risks", *Sydney News Today*

14. Mezahi, M. (2021, 22 August). Algeria's desperate wildfire fight: buckets and branches. *BBC News*, https://www.bbc.com/news/world-africa-58269789

15. Woudwijk, I. (2021, 9 August), "Angry Turks help put out many forest fires", *Nederlands Dagblad*

16. Legemaat, M. (2021, 3 August), "Heat sets Greece and Turkey alight", *Nederlands Dagblad*

17. Lange, P. (2021, 9 August), "Dozens more forest fires in Greece and Albania, downpours bring relief", *de Volkskrant*

18. *Stronger!*, December 2021, Ministry of Defence staff magazine.

19. ANP Productions (2021, 3 July), "Extreme forest fires in Canada and elsewhere in the world", *Noordhollands Dagblad*, see https://m.noordhollandsdagblad.nl/cnt/DMF20210703_3996506?origin=app&utm_source=google&utm_medium=organic

20. Butcher, S. (2021, 12 August), "All forest fire records about to tumble: trees in California drier than firewood", *Trouw*.

21-22. Houwelingen, K. (2021, 28 July). "Dutchman Gert helps fight wildfires 'I've never seen this intensity before'", *Algemeen Dagblad*

23. Walters, D., Derbali, N. & Van der Spek, B. (2023, 23 July). "Forest fires on Rhodes: never has Greece experienced such a huge evacuation", NRC, https://www.nrc.nl/nieuws/2023/07/23/evacuaties-op-rhodos-a4170397?t=1690976295

Chapter Eleven
On the run from climate change

"The flow [of migrants] will not stop if its causes are not addressed."

Sonja Wolf, German sociologist researching Central American migration

It is summer 1997. My family and I are living temporarily in Kansas, the "Sunflower State", in the American Midwest. There, I am attending the Army Command and General Staff College, a US college to prepare army officers for the rank of lieutenant colonel and colonel. For me, as a non-US participant, the first month is mainly about getting acquainted with the American way of life. A fair number of international students come from a completely different environment and culture, such as military personnel from Indonesia, Pakistan, Mozambique, Bangladesh, Senegal or Mongolia. Living in the US, many with partners and family, can be quite a culture shock for them.

For me, too, Kansas is a very different world. Here in the conservative heartland of the country, also called the beef-belt of America, I see almost nothing but vast grasslands of grazing cattle, huge granaries, cattle pens and large ranches. This is quite different from the densely populated cities and areas I know in the Netherlands and Germany. And there are cowboys here; not the type you see in Hollywood, but farmers who work hard outside in the sweltering heat. That is, unless a hurricane is raging across the country or there is flooding, in which case everyone runs for shelter, as fast as they can.

Climate is a fact of life

On the very first evening in Kansas, we suddenly get a tornado warning. At the time, I am having dinner at a local restaurant with my wife and two young children, and judging by the reaction of the staff, we cannot stay here. Get up, now! Within minutes, it turns jet black outside. You are very vulnerable with your family – and you know it – in a wooden restaurant that could blow away in an instant. Fortunately, most buildings have shelters. In our case, this turns out to be a large cold store where we and the other guests can take refuge among the ribeye steaks. It ends well, but for the first time I experience firsthand how powerful natural disasters can be, and how little you can do about them. The experience was pretty frightening.

The next day, life goes on, and I am in class. No-one is yet making the link to a changing climate, certainly not on my course. This deals primarily with conflicts and how to settle them. The news we are talking about at the time is mainly about NATO inviting the Czech Republic, Hungary and Poland to join the Alliance just under a decade after the fall of the Berlin Wall (1989). Later that year, we talk about Saddam Hussein, who is the leader of Iraq at the time and sparks a serious crisis when he denies two American UN inspectors access to his country, despite international pressure and the fact that he lost the Gulf War. That is pretty much the sum total of current events covered in my international military training here.

I understand from a young army major who recently spent two years studying in the US that climate change and the link to security are still not being covered in training. "Climate is just a fact of life for Americans, it seems. And it causes problems. Nothing more, nothing less", said the young soldier.

Checkpoint Charlie

Migration flows are of a different order. They are increasingly linked to climate change, which means that the changing climate is now also seen as a security issue by many in the US. The country, of course, is populated almost entirely by people who either migrated themselves or whose ancestors had settled there. It is a land of pioneers from all regions of the world, who left families behind to start over again. In addition, slavery caused a large, forced influx of people from Africa. This created a multicultural society in which the pioneer spirit and the drive for freedom is very palpable. It made the US great, but at the same time people became increasingly aware that the country could not become a global refuge.

The Cold War also put the brakes on the possibility of migrating to the US, and during my stay in 1997, I noticed what an important issue migration was to Americans, especially that of all the thousands of men, women and children from Central America seeking a better life and a safe haven. They are usually destitute, with at most a backpack and a few US dollars in their pockets. And even during my time in the US, Americans were trying to prevent those people from entering the country.

I clearly remember speaking to an air force colleague who was in the US at the time for a major international air defence exercise. It was taking place close to the Mexican border town of Ciudad Juárez, and some colleagues were going there to have a look. "It's like Checkpoint Charlie", my colleague tells me. For thirty years, that was the only border crossing between East and West Berlin. "In Ciudad Juárez you see high steel fences with wire mesh and barbed wire on top, just like in the Berlin of divided Germany back then." Even higher are the floodlights that illuminate the area in the evening and at night, not to mention the patrolling US border police. "Anyone who sees the fencing knows: there is no getting through." But both of us also know it won't stop people from trying to get across anyway.

Climate refugees

In the decades that follow, this proves to be true. Tens of thousands of people flee to the US every year, often to escape violence in their home country. Border control is tough, even for children. A low point was the Trump administration's deliberate child detention. Research by the journalistic Marshall Project shows that a total of half a million underage migrants were detained during this period. In many cases, children were separated from their parents and held longer than the 72 hours permitted by US law, which was traumatic for both the children and their parents.[1] Yet countless numbers of people still try to cross the border. They are often people from the "northern triangle", consisting of Guatemala, El Salvador and Honduras, which are often in the news because they are among the most violent countries in the world, where drug cartels rule and adults and children are recruited by violent gangs and therefore live in constant fear. Clearly, the spiral of violence, poverty and corruption drives many people to the north in search of a better life.[2]

As the previous chapters show, the changing climate serves to fuel the migration drive. In Central America, this has to do with geography and location, where both the frequency, intensity and impact of natural disasters have increased over the past 25 years.[3] Indeed, Central America is one of the most vulnerable regions when it comes to the impact of climate change.[4] Five of the top 10 countries in the Global Climate Risk Index most affected by climate change in the last two decades are in Central America or the Caribbean.[5]

Not surprisingly, therefore, floods, hurricanes, drought or long periods of extreme heat or cold can be the last straw that makes people decide to migrate, either within their own country or across the border.

Climate migration

"For five years it hardly ever rained", notes a journalist who is part of a major research project by a collective of *New York Times Magazine*, ProPublica and the Pulitzer Center.[6] In this project, researchers and journalists seek to better understand the forces and scale of climate migration. They hope to answer the question of which migrants are primarily driven by climate and where they go in search of a better life. One such migrant is Jorge from Guatemala. He was one of the many people who was very directly affected by the climate in 2019 and so decided to emigrate with his young son. According to the journalist, Jorge put his last grain seeds in the ground when it rained. The grain germinated into healthy green stalks and for a while there was hope. Until, without warning, the river flooded. Jorge waded deep into the fields with the water up to his chest, searching in vain for corn cobs he could still eat. To get any food at all, he struck a desperate deal with someone, offering the zinc-roofed hut – in which he lived with his wife and three children – in exchange for okra seed worth $1,500. Okra seeds can grow into a finger-shaped green fruit that is eaten as a vegetable. But that harvest too was destroyed after a period of drought that followed the earlier heavy flood.

Jorge knew that if he left Guatemala, his family behind could die of poverty and hunger. In March that year, Jorge and his seven-year-old son each put a pair of trousers, three T-shirts, underwear and a toothbrush into one thin, black, nylon drawstring bag. Jorge's father had pledged his last four goats to help pay for their trip. The man who arranged it called at 10 o'clock in the evening with the news that they could leave. At that point, Jorge and his son had no idea where they would end up, or what they would do when they reached their destination.[7]

As a father, I can hardly imagine how desperate you must be to undertake such a journey with your child of just seven years old. And Jorge is not the only one with a story like this. Hundreds of thousands of Guatemalans have attempted such a journey in recent years, within their own country, and to the US.[8] In 2021 alone, more than 153,000 people from Guatemala were apprehended at the border between Mexico and the US.[9] This figure does not include the many people who tried but failed to make it to the border, nor the many thousands of "lucky" people who managed to enter the US illegally. The number of migrants from Guatemala seeking a better life elsewhere is therefore actually much higher.

Research shows that, besides Jorge, many others are migrating because of natural disasters and climate change. On top of other factors, such as the unequal distribution of income in the country or fluctuations in coffee production prices, the places where people used to live in the mountains of Guatemala with thriving coffee plantations and dense forests, are now susceptible to a relentless mix of drought, flooding, volcanic eruptions and hurricanes that not only destroy homes, but also cause considerable damage to crops. In 2012 and 2013, Guatemala was hit by the coffee rust crisis (fungus) that swept across Central America. This affected 70 per cent of the total cultivated area and reduced yields in Guatemala by 20 to 25 per cent. The outbreak was partly caused by rising minimum temperatures and an early rainy season. As a result, people can run out of income and food overnight. In Alta Verapaz and Huehuetenango, for example, a mountainous region close to the Guatemala-Mexico border, 15% of families who have experienced a hurricane say that at least one family member has migrated or tried to migrate in the past five years. Among the top five reasons are natural disaster and climate change, according to the survey.[10]

The flight to the cities and the US

In the event of natural disasters and climate change, large cities become a haven for many people in Central America. Migration to the cities is something that has been happening for years, but almost three quarters of Central America's population now live in cities, and of these, a large proportion are living below the poverty line.[11] Many face violence and crime in those cities. One of the journalists collaborating on the research project mentioned earlier on the impact of climate change on Central America writes about meeting several men who were forced to leave their fields, only to go to work as security guards in Guatemala City or San Salvador, the capital of El Salvador. The journalist also describes an encounter with a 10-year-old boy who washes car windows at traffic lights in San Salvador for a pittance, in the belief that he will be able to buy back his parents' farmland with those few cents. That is virtually impossible given how little he earns every day. The journalist observes, "Cities offer choices and make people feel they can control their own destiny."

But the stories also reveal that cities are invariably traps, as challenges associated with rapid urbanisation mount up at an alarming rate. Those challenges include wholesale criminality, gang affiliation, water shortages, poor – if any – healthcare, and corruption. This is why migration to the city is called a "facade of order" in the research article, as the reality in the big cities is often very different from what many people from rural areas expect.

El Salvador, with 6.4 million people, is the most populous country in Central America. Since 2000, the population in the capital has grown by more than a third in size as migrants from rural areas have flocked to it.[12] Models show that much of the growth is concentrated in the city's slums and neighbouring municipalities, such as San Marcos, where people live in thousands of dilapidated buildings, many without electricity or water. Places where, even before the coronavirus pandemic, it was already very difficult to find work. And where there is widespread poverty, crime, domestic violence and unhygienic conditions. Because society in those cities is so weakened, crime is on the rise. It is estimated that the number of gang members in El Salvador is three times higher than the number of police officers. The gangs extort people, recruit new gang members and commit murder. The murder rate in El Salvador is one of the highest in the world.[13]

Against this background, it is not surprising that as many as one in six residents of El Salvador has fled to the US in recent decades. In 2019 alone, some 90,000 Salvadorans arrived at the US border.[14] People simply want a safer future for themselves and their children, with the prospect of a better life.

Crisis at the US border

The US is clearly the "promised land" for many thousands of people, especially for people from Central America, forced to leave loved ones behind to look for a better life elsewhere. Some, out of desperation, send their child alone on a perilous journey covering many kilometres. In the month of February 2021 alone, around 100,000 migrants were apprehended, including nearly 10,000 children travelling unaccompanied, children whose parents are so desperate that they entrust them to people smugglers. In such dire circumstances, it is clear that no fence or high wall or army of armed men can stop this flow. Not surprisingly, many Americans are talking about unmanageable conditions at the border.[15]

US President Joe Biden even called the situation at the southern border a "crisis" in 2021, although he had consistently avoided that word before. He was probably prompted not so much by the conditions at the southern border (and the US's actions), but rather by the dire conditions in Central America, which are forcing many – including many children – to migrate away (to the US).[16] Biden promised a billion-dollar aid package to neighbouring countries in exchange for help with the migration issue, aimed at improving living conditions in Central America.[17]

There is a vision behind this. After all, these problems are impossible to solve without looking at the root causes: food insecurity, malnutrition, poverty, corruption, crime, violence. That list should also include the implications of climate change, as global warming is a factor that can no longer be ignored. A New York Times Magazine research article states that if governments continue to take only "modest measures" to reduce emissions, some 680,000 climate migrants are expected to travel from Central America and Mexico to the US between now and 2050. But if we assume the most extreme climate scenarios over the next 30 years, this could exceed 30 million migrants.[18] This would be a massive influx, with all the implications it would entail.[19]

Making predictions is a dangerous science, especially when it comes to a complex issue like migration. There is a wide variety of reasons why people choose to leave their homes, and we should be wary of labelling all migration as climate migration. The link between migration and climate change is not only highly complex but often indirect. Yet there is indeed a strong relationship. Recent research by the Institute for Economics and Peace think tank has shown that there is a "cyclical link" between ecological degradation and conflict. To put it simply: when land becomes less habitable, it leads to conflict, and that conflict only exacerbates the situation further. People caught in that vicious circle eventually have no choice but to leave. The 30 countries most susceptible to this threat worldwide are currently home to 1.26 billion people. They will be increasingly exposed to deteriorating living conditions, conflict and failed governance in the coming years. In 2020, 34 million people were forced to leave their homelands due to violence and natural disasters. *Two-thirds* of those people were from the 30 most vulnerable countries.[20] It worries and saddens me that the same fate could eventually befall a large proportion of the population of these 30 countries. The World Bank recently stated in a report that there could be 216 million climate refugees worldwide by 2050. It is, of course, a forecast, and estimates vary. If the right measures are taken in time, the number of migrants could be limited to 44 million people.[21] I believe this uncertainty is an impetus for action. We must do everything we can to prevent the worst-case scenarios from becoming a reality.

We should also remember that by focusing only on climate factors, it is easy for countries to divert attention from their responsibility to fight corruption and crime. Vulnerable groups can be made more resilient to ecological setbacks through good governance.

It is undeniable that the changing climate is exacerbating the spiral of poverty, violence, corruption and unemployment. The misery suffered by many people in Central America due to a complex mix of causes is driving them away from their homes. They are seeking refuge elsewhere, heading mainly to the north, in search of a better life.

Notes

1. Flagg, A. & Calderon, A. (2020, 30 March). "500,000 kids, 30 million hours: Trump's vast expansion of child detention", *The Marshall Project*, https://www.themarshallproject.org/2020/10/30/500-000-kids-30-million-hours-trump-s-vast-expansion-of-child-detention

2. Cheatham, A. (2021, 1 July). Central America's turbulent northern triangle. *Council on Foreign Relations*, https://www.cfr.org/backgrounder/central-americas-turbulent-northern-triangle

3. OCHA (2019), Natural disasters in Latin America and the Caribbean 2000-2019, see https://reliefweb.int/sites/reliefweb.int/files/resources/20191203-ocha-desastres_naturales.pdf

4. Expert Group of the International Military Council on Climate (2020). The World Climate and Security Report 2020. Center for Climate and Security, Washington D.C. 88.

5. Eckstein, D., Hutfils, M., and Winges, M. (2018). "Global Climate Risk Index 2019: Who Suffers Most From Extreme Weather Events?" Weather-related Loss Events in 2017 and 1998 to 2017. Germanwatch. Bonn.

6-7. Lustgarten, A. (2019), "Where will everyone go?" Probublica, see https://features.propublica.org/climate-migration/model-how-climate-refugees-move-across-continents/

8. Babich, E. & Batalova, J. (2021), Central American Immigrants in the United States. Migration Policy Institute, Washington DC, see https://www.migrationpolicy.org/article/central-american-immigrants-united-states

9-10. Rodriguez, S. (2021, 19 July), "It's not a border crisis. It's a climate crisis", *Politico Magazine*, see https://www.politico.com/news/magazine/2021/07/19/guatemala-immigration-climate-change-499281

11. Augustin, M. et al. (2017), Central America Urbanization Review: Making cities work for Central America. World Bank, Washington DC

12-14. Lustgarten, A. (2019), "Where will everyone go?" Probublica, see https://features.propublica.org/climate-migration/model-how-climate-refugees-move-across-continents/

15. Daniel, F. & Hesson, T. (2021, 5 March), "U.S. detained nearly 100,000 migrants at Mexico border in February, sources say", *US News*, see https://www.usnews.com/news/world/articles/2021-03-05/us-detained-nearly-100-000-migrants-at-us-mexico-border-in-february-sources

16. Klein, B. (2021, 19 April). "White House backtracks after Biden calls border situation a 'crisis'". *CNN Politics*, https://edition.cnn.com/2021/04/19/politics/biden-border-crisis-unaccompanied-minors/index.html

17. Long-Garcia, J. (2021, 21 January), "Joe Biden's $4 billion plan to discourage Central American migration at its source", *America Magazine*, see https://www.americamagazine.org/politics-society/2021/01/21/joe-biden-four-billion-dollar-immigration-plan-central-america-239732

18. Lustgarten, A. (2020, 23 July), "The Great Climate Migration has Begun", *New York Times Magazine*, see https://www.nytimes.com/interactive/2020/07/23/magazine/climate-migration.html

19. Daniel, F. & Hesson, T. (2021, 5 March) "U.S. detained nearly 100,000 migrants at Mexico border in February, sources say", *US News*, see https://www.usnews.com/news/world/articles/2021-03-05/us-detained-nearly-100-000-migrants-at-us-mexico-border-in-february-sources

20. Institute for Economics & Peace. (2021) Ecological threat report 2021: understanding ecological threats, resilience and peace. IEP, Sydney. https://www.visionofhumanity.org/wp-content/uploads/2021/10/ETR-2021-web.pdf

21. Clement, V., Rigaud, K., de Sherbinin, A., Jones, B., Adamo, S., Schewe, J., Sadiq, N., Shabahat, E. (2021). Groundswell Part II: acting on international climate migration. World Bank, Washington D.C., https://openknowledge.worldbank.org/handle/10986/36248

Chapter Twelve
War in the granary

"I do not want my picture in your offices. The president is not an icon, an idol or a portrait. Hang your kids' photos instead, and look at them each time you are making a decision."

President Volodymyr Zelensky during his inauguration ceremony in Kyiv, Ukraine, May 20, 2019

Thursday, July 17, 2014, is a day I will never forget. It was a hot summer day that felt leaden in the late afternoon when news came in that a passenger plane had crashed over Ukraine. Large pieces of wreckage had hit the ground with an enormous bang and shattered into pieces and fire had broken out in several places. Local residents later told local media that chunks of debris had fallen from the sky onto their homes and fields and that remains and personal belongings of the occupants were also scattered over a large area.

As with any disaster, the first snippets eventually become a story, and a gruesome one at that. It turns out to be about flight MH17, a Malaysia Airways Boeing 777 flying from Amsterdam to Kuala Lumpur. Panic breaks out in the Netherlands when it emerges that many Dutch nationals were on board. Our prime minister, Mark Rutte, returns from holiday and it soon becomes clear; this is a major crisis.

More and more families start making their way to Schiphol, the national airport, desperate to find out about the fate of their loved ones. Professional support is available for them, but the exact passenger list is delayed. It turns out that there were 298 passengers on board, 196 of whom were Dutch.

There are no survivors. When news comes in about the identity of the Dutch passengers, heartbreaking scenes ensue.

Soon the first bouquets, cuddly toys and notes start appearing in front of Departure Hall 3 at Schiphol Airport. It soon grows into a huge sea of flowers, in stark contrast to the desolate disaster site in eastern Ukraine. Many people will remember the picture of a man in a camouflage cap holding up a child's small black-and-white toy monkey in a Ukrainian field full of debris. That image made it clear at a glance what was going on. There was chaos, there was war and there were 298 innocent victims, many of them children.

Military deployment?

In the days that followed, there was a great deal of disinformation. Russia, Ukraine and the separatists accused each other. I had to advise whether or not to send military personnel to the eastern part of Ukraine to secure the disaster site. The wreckage, victims and their personal belongings were in a disputed area occupied by separatists. The summer of 2014 thus became a traumatic time for all concerned, and my people were no exception.

I remember speaking to a member of our military police force. He was in the first team sent to the disaster site, unarmed. As a member of a special unit, he was no stranger to tough assignments, but for the first time in his life he was now saying goodbye to his family with the thought that he might not return, or only after a prolonged hostage situation. Imagine what it means to leave with that in mind and enter a disaster zone such as this one.

At the same time, there was no doubt in his mind about the necessity of the mission; not going was not an option. He went, as did many others. But when they arrived, the disaster site turned out to be inaccessible because of the danger and non-cooperative separatists in the area. Meanwhile, impatience was growing in the Netherlands. Everyone wanted the bodies of the Dutch victims to be brought back to the Netherlands as soon as possible. After a few days, Mark Rutte, the Dutch prime minister, asked me to work out military options as well, a sensible idea given the situation and circumstances at the disaster site.

To do this properly, we made contact with Australia, a country that had also lost many citizens. Work continued day and night on both sides and options were soon on the table. These ranged from doing nothing and waiting, to securing the disaster site by military means. The toughest option, that of a major military deployment, soon leaked out. This was to be expected. Military personnel were recalled from leave so they would be available in time should the need arise. Some had had to cut short their summer holidays and this was talked about on social media.

Explanation was required in order to avoid inadvertently hampering efforts in the disaster area, or worse: escalating the crisis. This was a potential deployment some 50 kilometres from the Russian border, where large numbers of Russian troops had been massing for some time, possibly waiting for an excuse to move into the eastern part of Ukraine. So we had to be very careful about what we said we were or were not going to do, and for what purpose.

Civilian mission

All options were carefully considered. The idea was that the repatriation would be a civil operation as far as possible. Military options were kept in reserve in case the civil plan did not succeed. A few days after the disaster, thanks in part to mediation by the Organisation for Security and Cooperation in Europe (OSCE), access to the area fortunately became possible. However, coordination was assigned to the Ministry of Defence, as was operational control over the execution of the mission. This was because of the multidisciplinary and international nature of the mission and the fact that it was taking place in a war zone with all the associated risks. There was also intensive cooperation with various Dutch government agencies, as well as with Malaysia, Australia, Ukraine and the OSCE. The latter was crucial because the Netherlands itself could not deal directly with the separatists as that might signify recognition of their territorial claims.

Before deployment, many hundreds of military personnel returned from leave without complaint. As soon as we were given the green light to enter the disaster area, the Dutch-led international mission got under way and an airlift was set up between Ukraine and the Netherlands. Military personnel and police officers performed their onerous task in eastern Ukraine, from the city of Kharkov and from a forward base in Soledar.

When fighting allowed, military personnel, forensic investigators, police officers and search dogs, as well as local miners, searched in and near the disaster site for human remains, personal belongings and wreckage. In a line, they combed forests, maize fields, allotments and meadows. With temperatures soaring above 40 degrees, they worked hard every day they could. Every minute counted, because the fighting could flare up again at any moment.

The search area was constantly on or near the front line. Fighting between Ukrainians and Russian-backed separatists was always nearby. Contact with the separatists was made through the OSCE for the political reasons referred to earlier. For the mission, this was an awkward and often dangerous situation. In such circumstances, as a military commander on the ground, and also as military and political leaders in the Netherlands, you face tough decisions. For instance, how long do you continue to search? What risks are acceptable for the rescue workers? When do you stop the mission? After all, the 298 casualties must not be allowed to become 299 or more.

In the Netherlands, everyone knows how it ended. The images of the ceremony receiving the victims' remains were broadcast all over the world. Again and again, we saw on television the deeply moving arrival at Eindhoven airbase and the long procession of hearses along an otherwise empty highway to the Korporaal van Oudheusden barracks in Hilversum, where the identification of the bodies took place. The highway was cleared each time out of respect for the victims and people lined the road and stood on the bridges to honour the victims. The whole of the country was in shock and in mourning.

Wake-up call

The downing of flight MH17 was a brutal reminder of how quickly things can go very wrong. To many, the conflict in eastern Ukraine had seemed very far away from their daily lives, but suddenly they were facing the harsh reality of a violent conflict in just under three hours' flight time from Amsterdam in which many innocent people had lost their lives. Almost everyone in the Netherlands knew someone on the plane, or someone who had family, friends or acquaintances on board. The war was suddenly very close to home. The shooting down of a passenger plane with a Buk missile also showed in no uncertain terms how insecurity abroad, in Europe, can also directly affect us in a safe country. And how the armed forces then suddenly become very closely involved.

Almost eight years after that fateful Thursday afternoon, the situation in Ukraine became even more dramatic. On the night of 23-24 February 2022, around 4 o'clock, Russia launched a violent attack on Ukraine across a broad front. Large areas in the east in particular were occupied. There was heavy fighting around the capital Kyiv, but the Russians failed to capture the city. For the first time since World War II, another major war was being fought on our continent. Much of the world was shocked and many leaders reacted in strong terms to Russia's unprecedented brutal attack on a sovereign nation.

The EU, the US and many other countries imposed even tougher sanctions than were already in force, and NATO decided to send troops to eastern Europe, strengthening the borders of the Baltic States, and thus NATO's own border. Fears of further escalation by the Russians were high, especially in the former Soviet states. There was a political landslide in Sweden and Finland, which had been neutral for decades. Suddenly, a large majority of the population was in favour of joining the NATO Alliance to protect their own security. Europe thus changed radically in a short space of time.

Immediately after the Russian attack, thousands and soon millions of people, especially women and children, fled Ukraine. Ukrainian President Zelensky called on all men in the country to take up arms against the enemy. There was talk of an all-out war, and reports of horrific war crimes by the Russian aggressor soon started coming in.

Putin even threatened on several occasions to deploy nuclear weapons. Despite this, the West continued to support Ukraine in many ways: with humanitarian aid, more and heavier weapons and ever more stringent sanctions packages against the Russian regime. In a short space of time, international and geopolitical relations were determined to an ever-greater extent by the war in Ukraine and attitudes towards Russia. These changes constituted a tipping point, the consequences and impact of which are still difficult to interpret.

What is clear is that a large number of countries condemned the Russian invasion. A small group voiced support for Russia, and a sizable group of countries was keeping a low profile. The United Nations seemed powerless. Russia is a permanent member of the Security Council and could paralyse it with its veto. Russia's ally, China, also a permanent member, did not condemn the invasion. Geopolitical relations were on a knife edge.

Disruption of food chains

Grain exports were also becoming part of the battle. Ukraine is one of the largest grain suppliers in the world, which is why it is also called the "granary" of Europe. Many countries worldwide depend on Ukraine's grain production, but since the invasion, there was hardly any grain leaving the country's ports. Partly because of this, global food prices rose to record levels in 2022.[1] After difficult and lengthy negotiations, Turkey managed to force a breakthrough, thus preventing hunger in many countries.

Fragile countries in North Africa and the Middle East are particularly sensitive to price increases.[2] A rise of just a few percent can be dramatic for many people on or below the poverty line and can have a major impact on food supplies. This in turn can have secondary effects such as rising tensions and uprisings. The Arab Spring was initially triggered by food price rises which, combined with other factors such as poverty, exacerbated the existing political instability.[3]

In short, a disruption in the food chain will lead to more famine and thus potentially rising tensions in much of the world. This is another tragic consequence of the Russian invasion.

Rising defence spending

The war was becoming more and more gruelling. Putin continued to attack Ukraine with missile strikes on power stations, railway stations, hospitals and even residential areas. The devastation in cities and villages was enormous.

Dire low points in the war followed one another in rapid succession. Russia abducted thousands of children, and tortured, raped, and executed many Ukrainians.[4] The Russian army was reinforced with mercenaries, mainly the Wagner Group, which actively recruits criminals in Russian prisons.[5] Yet the Ukrainian army continued to fight back bravely and tirelessly, still with unwavering support from the West.

In the wake of recent events, NATO has regained relevance and is expanding. Finland is now a member and Sweden's accession seems imminent. As a result, the border between Russia and NATO is growing enormously. NATO is reviewing its plans and NATO countries are investing in a strategy of deterrence and defence. The plans require more units that can be deployed quickly.

Countries are investing more heavily in their defence sector as a result. Whereas for years public opinion put defence at the top of the list when asked where cuts should be made, virtually all parties, both left and right on the political spectrum, are now calling for defence to be put in order. In 2022, defence spending therefore increased by 3.7% worldwide.[6] The war in Ukraine is leading to larger increases, especially among European countries. Finland, for instance, is scaling up its military budget by 36% and the

Netherlands by 12%. The years of taking peace for granted on the European continent suddenly seem like a distant memory, which will almost certainly lead to major, climate-unfriendly investments. More money for defence and thus more materiel also means higher emissions. The easiest way to invest quickly is to buy more of the same. However, it is also an opportunity to invest more heavily in innovative solutions that help reduce CO_2 emissions while improving the operational self-sufficiency of military units, for example. And that, in turn, can act as an accelerator for civil applications as I will explain in the next chapters.

Divisive China and the US

State conflicts were not high on the list of likely risks until recently.[7] We now know better. The war in Ukraine is looking more and more like a kind of shadow conflict between Russia, China and the West. Russia is increasingly isolated in its attack on Ukraine, making it more dependent on China, which is taking a fairly neutral stance on the Russian invasion. Hampered by Western sanctions, Russia is seeking new markets in countries such as China and India. Half of Russia's state budget is estimated to be dependent on the export of raw materials.[8] China, on the other hand, benefits economically from the sanctions imposed on Russia by Western countries after the invasion of Ukraine. Indeed, China can now buy commodities such as oil, gas and coal from Russia at a substantially reduced price.

The war in Ukraine also appears to be a welcome lightning rod for China, as there is now less focus on the tensions surrounding Taiwan. According to China, Taiwan is part of Chinese territory and is regarded as a renegade province. The US backs Taiwan and is the country's main arms supplier.

One of the main reasons why Taiwan is strategically important to both China and the US has to do with the fact that Taiwan controls most of the global production of computer chips. For the most technologically advanced chips, it accounts for as much as 90%.[9] These chips are in almost everything we use today: smartphones, computers, pacemakers, refrigerators, cars, coffee makers and weapons such as tanks, drones and rocket launchers. This is why some experts argue that computer chips will be the "oil of the 21st century"[10] and why, little by little, the Americans are now trying to cut China off from the world's most advanced technologies. For its part, China has been threatening to attack Taiwan militarily for years.

In short, the global economy depends on an island where security is not guaranteed. News reports have therefore cited Taiwan as a possible reason for the next major war. According to China expert Jonathan Holslag, China is particularly keen to look ahead to a potential military showdown in Eastern Asia. "If China ever attacks Taiwan, it will desperately need Russian help", he said.[11] In 2023, NATO Secretary-General Jens Stoltenberg said, "The world is at a historic turning point in the most serious and complex security environment since the end of World War II".[12]

Some go even further in their statements. "World War III has begun", argued renowned French historian Emmanuel Todd in 2023, who years before had predicted the collapse of the Soviet Union, and who sees the battle for Ukraine as the harbinger of a war over Taiwan. In Todd's tantalising but bleak analysis, a "limited territorial conflict" will grow into a "global economic confrontation" between a China-aligned Russia and the West.[13]

The "green heart"

The war in Ukraine is also having a dramatic impact on the environment. For instance, according to climate researchers, the Russian invasion led to at least 100 million tonnes of CO_2 emissions in the first seven months, about as much as the Netherlands' total emissions over the same period.[14] Half of the calculated greenhouse gases are thought to have been generated by the wholesale destruction of buildings and infrastructure. After that, most of the climate damage came from fires, and about 30% of the emissions were due to methane leaks. These leaks occurred after Nord Stream 1 and 2 gas pipelines were sabotaged in the Baltic Sea in an incident that environmental scientists call an outright "climate disaster".[15]

The destruction of the huge dam in the Cherson region in the summer of 2023 was a catastrophe on many fronts. Large areas downstream of the Dnieper river flooded when the giant reservoir behind the dam emptied. As a result, thousands of people had to be evacuated, but there was also extensive damage to the environment, agricultural land and infrastructure. The huge torrent of water dragged waste and pollutants from ports, industrial sites and gas stations, spread them over a large area and eventually deposited them in the soil. Many animals drowned and ecologists feared mass mortality of fish downstream and in the Black Sea.[16] It was a massive ecological disaster the consequences of which cannot yet be calculated.

There is also significant cause for concern with regard to the water supply in the area, as there is for Crimea, which, due to a canal link with the Dnieper, is largely dependent on freshwater behind the dam. The water is also important for cooling Europe's largest nuclear power plant near the city of Zaporizja. The International Atomic Energy Agency (IAEA) is closely monitoring the situation with concern. For now, the cooling water reservoir is well stocked, but the acts of war in the vicinity of the nuclear power plant and the destruction of the dam amount to more than just playing with fire. Whoever is responsible for the destruction, the dam has been used as a weapon of war.

Besides additional warming due to greenhouse gas emissions, the Russian invasion is also causing considerable damage to the local environment. For instance, at least 900 protected nature areas in Ukraine have been affected by military manoeuvres, with large numbers of tanks and armoured vehicles flattening the areas.[17] These actions are accompanied by rocket attacks, artillery shelling, aerial bombing and pollution from oil, fuels and metals. This has resulted in the loss of more than 20,000 square kilometres of forest landscape, an area that could otherwise have removed 10-25 million tonnes of CO_2 a year from the atmosphere.[18]

As a result, more and more pristine grasslands are also disappearing, as well as sections of old-growth forests. Ukraine used to be known as the green heart of Europe and was home to 35% of Europe's biodiversity, but now more and more habitats that used to be a natural carbon sink for CO_2 and home to thousands of plant species and animals are disappearing. Figures show, for example, that the Russian invasion has adversely affected 20% of protected areas, 600 animal species and 750 plant species.[19] That includes the thousands of dolphins that are now being washed up on Black Sea beaches due to explosions, sea mines and sonar.[20]

The war is also limiting other opportunities to reduce CO_2 emissions. For instance, Ukrainian NGO Ekodiya revealed that more than half of Ukraine's wind farms have been shut down, along with other renewable energy installations.[21] Solar panels and wind turbines have been damaged or destroyed, adversely affecting the necessary energy transition.

In addition, air quality is being diminished by shelling. For example, an attack on a chemical plant near Sumy in March 2023 released ammonia, and shortly afterwards an acid tank near Rubizhne exploded, releasing a toxic cloud of nitric acid.[22] Tons of chemicals have also been released into the environment by bombings of fuel depots, and explosions of bombs over farmland may lead to a build-up of heavy metals in the food chain, increasing the risk of diseases such as cancer.[23]

Finally, there are further threats looming at the time of writing. Ukraine's economy is largely built on heavy industry, especially in the east of the country. There, thousands of chemical plants, industrial sites, coal mines and other facilities produce and store toxic waste. If these sites are attacked, that will pose a direct threat to people's health and cause further damage to the environment. The destruction of the great Kachovka dam shows what the ecological consequences could be. Attacks on nuclear facilities also pose a risk, namely of radioactive contamination, both for Ukraine and Europe as a whole.

Faster energy transition

The war in Ukraine is leading directly to a rapid deterioration of the climate, but also to a variety of indirect climate developments. More than 40% of total EU gas imports, for example, came from Russia at the time of the invasion.[24] This caused gas prices to soar in countries like the Netherlands. The Central Planning Bureau estimates that 430,000 Dutch households will experience financial difficulties as a result.[25] Consequently, countries are keen to quickly gain independence from Russia and look for alternatives.

However, this is causing a spike in CO_2 emissions, as many countries, including the Netherlands, revert to polluting coal-fired power plants and oil and gas from other countries. According to the European Commission, 60% of around 101.5 billion cubic metres of Russian gas will be replaced by imports from other countries.[26]

At the same time, there is a positive side effect, as countries are suddenly being forced to speed up the energy transition. For instance, the International Energy Agency notes that countries are upping the pace of their investments in renewable energy and energy conservation.[27] This could eventually lead to a faster reduction of CO_2 emissions.

The only drawback is that China has been the biggest investor in greener alternatives to oil and gas in recent years. The country controls some 80% of global production of scarce raw materials that we need for our energy transition.[28] For example, lithium, nickel and cobalt for batteries in electric cars and silicon, indium and gallium for solar panels. In addition, those raw materials have to be processed into products, almost all of which are manufactured in China, giving the country a certain monopolistic position.

This advantage exists because China itself extracts the materials from the ground, but also because it has projects under way in other countries that provide the raw materials for green alternatives. Suppose one day China decides to embargo those rare raw materials? That would result in global shortages not only of wind turbines but also of raw materials for weapons materiel such as the F-35, computers, phones, cars and devices such as pacemakers and MRI scanners.

It is a worrying dependency, therefore, and the reason why both the US and Europe are now looking at ways to become more independent from China in this regard as soon as possible.

The cards are being shuffled

In short, the war in Ukraine is not only bringing untold suffering and triggering various chains of events, but it also shows that today's world could look very different tomorrow and freedom is anything but a given. What is also clear is that conflict makes finding solutions to global problems such as climate change even more complex.

The war has generated an unprecedented energy crisis in Europe, major disruptions in global food chains and significant regional environmental damage. Polluting coal-fired power plants are once again running at full capacity, albeit temporarily, and countries are quickly seeking to enable the energy transition and trying to become more independent from China when it comes to raw materials for renewable energy or products that are relevant today. At the same time, the polluting war industry is in full swing, and solar panels, wind turbines and heat pumps have now become a matter of national security.

All this is creating a new geopolitical situation in which major powers are shuffling the cards. It is clear that the West – like resource giant China that is seemingly doing so well – needs to think and act strategically, in terms of a hundred years or more. We must also realise that greater independence is a strategic necessity, but that everything in the world is interconnected and no single country can afford to cut itself off from the rest of the world.

It is precisely for this reason that we must continue to talk to each other, seek dialogue and work together to prevent conflict and damage to the environment. For the climate, for the economy and for the personal well-being of everyone on this fragile planet.

Notes

1. De La Hamaide, S. (2023, 6 January), "World food prices hit record high in 2022", Reuters, https://www.reuters.com/markets/world-food-prices-hit-record-high-2022-despite-december-fall-2023-01-06/

2. Byrd, W. (2022, 22 March), "Ukraine war fallout will damage fragile states and the poor", *United States Institute of Peace*, https://www.usip.org/publications/2022/03/ukraine-war-fallout-will-damage-fragile-states-and-poor

3. Kelley, C., Mohtadi, S., Cane, M., Seager, R. & Kushnir, Y. (2015). "Climate change and the recent Syrian drought", Proceedings of the National Academy of Sciences 112 (11), pp. 3241-3246. See also: Lieven, A. (2020). Climate change and the nation state: the realist case. Allen Lane, 25-26

4. UN Human Rights Council (2023, 15 March). Report of the Independent International Commission of Inquiry on Ukraine. A/HRC/52/62, https://www.ohchr.org/sites/default/files/documents/hrbodies/hrcouncil/coiukraine/A_HRC_52_62_AUV_EN.pdf

5. The Wagner Group has since indicated that it has stopped this activity, although this is difficult to verify. See Sauer, P. (2023, 15 February). "Wagner mercenary group will 'decrease' as prisoner recruitment ends, says boss". *The Guardian*. https://www.theguardian.com/world/2023/feb/15/wagner-mercenary-group-will-decrease-as-prisoner-recruitment-ends-says-boss

6. Scarazzato, L. et al (2023) "Trends in World Military Expenditure, 2022", Stockholm International Peace Research Institute. https://doi.org/10.55163/PNVP2622

7. The World Economic Forum's annual Global Risk Reports categorise risks by likelihood, and have identified and ranked 70 risks in order of likelihood in the period from 2007 to 2020. "Interstate conflict" is mentioned only twice during this period. See WEF (2020) "The Global Risks Report 2020". https://www3.weforum.org/docs/WEF_Global_Risk_Report_2020.pdf

8. Meinema, A. (2022, 24 February). "Can the Russian economy cope with such a war with Ukraine?" NOS, https://nos.nl/collectie/13888/artikel/2418752-kan-de-russische-economie-het-wel-hebben-zo-n-oorlog-met-oekraine

9. *The Economist* (2023, May 6). "Taiwan's dominance of the chip industry makes it more important", https://www.economist.com/special-report/2023/03/06/taiwans-dominance-of-the-chip-industry-makes-it-more-important

10. Chris Miller (2022) "Chip War: the fight for the world's most critical technology", Scribner: New York.

11. Quoted in Bosman, J. & Schelfaut, S. (2023, 20 March). "What do Putin and Xi want from each other?", *Algemeen Dagblad*, https://www.ad.nl/buitenland/wat-willen-poetin-en-xi-van-elkaar-als-china-taiwan-ooit-aanvalt-heeft-het-russische-hulp-hard-nodig~a5b5ec9c/?referrer=https%3A%2F%2Fwww.bing.com%2F

12. NOS News (2023, 31 January) "NATO and Japan strengthen ties over Russian and Chinese threat", NOS, https://nos.nl/artikel/2461946-navo-en-japan-halen-banden-aan-om-russische-en-chinese-dreiging

13. Quoted in Middelaar, L. (2023, 18 January). "We're living on the fault line of two eras", NRC, https://www.nrc.nl/nieuws/2023/01/18/we-leven-op-het-breukvlak-van-twee-tijdvakken-a4154480

14. De Klerk, L., et al (2022) "Climate Damage caused by Russia's war in Ukraine", by Initiative on GHG accounting of war https://en.ecoaction.org.ua/wp-content/uploads/2022/11/climate-damage-caused-by-rus-war_fin.pdf

15. Straver, F. (2022, 28 September). "Leak in Nord Stream gas pipe is the 'very last thing the climate needs'" *Trouw*.

16. Watts, J. (2023, 6 June). "Dam breach could be Ukraine's 'worst ecological disaster since Chernobyl'", *The Guardian*, https://www.theguardian.com/world/2023/jun/06/dam-breach-could-be-ukraines-worst-ecological-disaster-since-chornobyl

17. OSCE (2022, 1 July) "Environmental impacts of the war in Ukraine and prospects for a green reconstruction", *OECD Policy Responses to the war in Ukraine*, https://www.oecd.org/ukraine-hub/policy-responses/environmental-impacts-of-the-war-in-ukraine-and-prospects-for-a-green-reconstruction-9e86d691/#snotes-d4e99

18. Brown, O., et al (2023) "The impact of Russia's war against Ukraine on climate security and climate action", OSCE & Chatham House, 16, https://alpanalytica.org/wp-content/uploads/2023/02/Independent-Experts-Analysis-The-impact-of-Russias-war-against-Ukraine-on-climate-security-and-climate-action-9-Feb-23.pdf

19. Rannard, G. (2022, 14 November). "COP27: War causing huge release of climate warming gas, claims Ukraine". BBC News, https://www.bbc.com/news/science-environment-63625693

20. Georgiou, A. (2023, 4 May). "Russia-Ukraine war pushing dolphins to extinction in Black Sea", *Newsweek*, https://www.newsweek.com/dolphins-black-sea-face-extinction-russia-ukraine-war-1792786

21. Vykhor, B. & Beckmann, W. (2022, 16 June). "War in Ukraine hits Europe in the green heart too", *Global News*, https://www.mo.be/opinie/de-oorlog-oekra-ne-raakt-europa-ook-het-groene-hart

22. Vykhor, B. & Beckmann, W. (2022, 16 June). "War in Ukraine hits Europe in the green heart too", *Global News*, https://www.mo.be/opinie/de-oorlog-oekra-ne-raakt-europa-ook-het-groene-hart

23. Stein, J. & Birnhaum, M. (2023, 13 March). "The war in Ukraine is a human tragedy. It's also an environmental disaster", *Washington Post*, https://www.washingtonpost.com/world/2023/03/13/ukraine-war-environment-impact-disaster/

24. Thompson, E. (2022, 10 November). "These charts show Europe's reliance on gas before the war in Ukraine", WEF, https://www.weforum.org/agenda/2022/11/europe-gas-shortage-russia/

25. CPB (2022, 6 December). Energy price scenarios. https://www.cpb.nl/scenarios-energieprijzen

26. Merckx, V. (2022, 27 May). "Good and bad news: this is what the war in Ukraine means for the climate", VRT News, https://www.vrt.be/vrtnws/nl/2022/05/24/slecht-nieuws-op-de-korte-termijn-maar-ook-een-turbo-op-de-ener/#:~:text=So%20provides%20the%20European%20Commission,by%20renewable%20energy%20%C3%A9n%20energy-saving).

27. IEA (2022, 6 December). "Renewable power's growth is being turbocharged as countries seek to strengthen energy security", https://www.iea.org/news/renewable-power-s-growth-is-being-turbocharged-as-countries-seek-to-strengthen-energy-security

28. Keleman, B. & Stonor, A. (2022, 17 September). "Can the West shake its dependence on China's rare earths?", *The Diplomat*, https://thediplomat.com/2022/09/can-the-west-shake-its-dependence-on-chinas-rare-earths/

Part Two

From words to actions

Chapter Thirteen
War on climate disruption

"*The most defining photograph of our time is not that of the burning Twin Towers, nor that of the atomic bomb on Hiroshima or of the first mobile phone. What really overturned our world view was the photo, taken by Apollo 17, of that little blue planet in an inhospitable, deep black universe. For the first time, we became aware of our vulnerability, not just as individuals or nations, but as humanity.*"

Writer Louise O. Fresco in *NRC Handelsblad*, 20 September 2021

We need an astronaut's view, an *overview*, when looking at climate change. Only then do we realise how interconnected everything is, how vulnerable we are and how dependent all those billions of people are on this little blue dot. And when you consider that the world population will grow to some 11 billion this century, only then do you realise the magnitude of the challenge our children will face.

We will have to find answers to a great many questions and work on possible courses of action, because we cannot delay any longer.

That is the message I conveyed with Jeanine Hennis-Plasschaert, defence minister at the time, at the Future Force Conference (FFC) organised by the Ministry of Defence in The Hague in 2017 and attended by some 1,200 people from 50 countries and five continents. During the minister's opening speech, a picture from 1987 showing three men in blue and white spacesuits appears on the huge screen behind her in that large auditorium. The middle one, with a large dark moustache, is looking into the camera, smiling broadly. It is Muhammed Faris, the Syrian astronaut after whom a school, streets and even an airport were later named in Syria. To date, he is the only Syrian ever to have been in space and is referred to as the "Neil Armstrong of the Arab world".

Minister Hennis is showing this photo 30 years later because of Mr Faris' remarkable story. She explains that the photo of the Syrian astronaut was taken on his return to earth after a space voyage with two Russian astronauts with whom he had been conducting scientific research. That space voyage had such an effect on him that, once back in Syria, he wanted to teach people about science and especially astronomy. So that Faris could, as he himself would later say, pass on his privilege to others too.

Much to his disappointment, the air force officer and astronaut's ideas fell on deaf ears, as his superiors felt that training fighter pilots was 'much more important'. Faris did his job, but years later, in 2012, resolutely broke with the Assad regime. He could not stand by while his colleagues bombed innocent civilians at the behest of the government. He eventually even felt compelled to flee his homeland. Faris left Syria on foot to travel to Turkey, where he still lives as a refugee with his family. But that is not why Jeanine Hennis is showing that photo to all those people at the conference. She starts her speech with his story because of what Faris said in 1987, shortly after his return from space.

"Those seven days, 23 hours and five minutes changed my life", he said. "Because when you have seen the whole world through a tiny window, there is no more us and them, no more politics." This insightful observation clearly strikes a chord among the conference participants. Dutch astronaut André Kuipers enthusiastically shows me the photos he himself took from space. Those photos show a small, bright, blue ball with bits of green, floating in the endless darkness of space. He also shows me the different types of satellite image that can be produced these days. I see images of weather patterns, temperature fluctuations, soil erosion, air and water pollution, urbanisation and Earth's ever-shrinking "green lungs".

Looking at those satellite images over time reveals the shocking truth of how radically the world has changed over the past half century and how we are exhausting our planet. For example, the plumes of smoke from large tracts of burning rainforest are visible, as well as vast bare patches of logged areas in the Amazon: all because of the advance of agriculture for the sake of global prosperity. I also see images of the erosion of fertile land in Borneo and Madagascar, and of polluted air over the sprawling urbanised areas of China and India. Seeing all that and knowing what it means, I think those of us on earth can imagine how astronauts feel so far away from our planet and the effect it has on them. I understand how, for astronauts like André Kuipers and Mohamed Faris, the voyage to space was a turning point in their lives.

Spaceship Earth

It is not surprising that so many astronauts worldwide joined together in 2015 to record a video to deliver a powerful message for world leaders.[1] This video, entitled *A call to Earth*, makes it clear that everyone on Earth is like an astronaut, all using the same spaceship called "Earth". The message ahead of the Paris Climate Conference that year was that we need to take very good care of this fragile planet, our spaceship Earth.

US astronaut Dan Barry says in the video: "Our atmosphere connects us all. What happens in Africa affects North America. What happens in North America affects Asia." German astronaut Ernst Messerschmid says in his message: "We astronauts have witnessed the shrinking of the Aral Sea, the burning rainforest along the Amazon River, the polluted air over urbanised and industrial areas, and the polluted water in the great river deltas."

The first Dutch astronaut, Wubbo Ockels, was also featured in this video plea to world leaders, despite the fact that he was already terminally ill at the time. Lying in a hospital bed, he looks into the camera and says very clearly: "If you have the spirit, insight and attitude of an astronaut, you begin to love the earth in a way that other people do not. And if you really love something, you don't want to lose it..." He died a day later.

Ockels did not live to see the UN member states agree on a historic climate deal in Paris the same year, designed to reduce greenhouse gas emissions such as CO_2 and limit global warming to no more than two degrees Celsius, with one and a half degrees as a target. This should keep the planet largely habitable. However, it was agreed that countries would be allowed to set their own climate targets and that aviation and shipping would not be included. Countries also undertook in Paris to initiate a $100 billion fund intended for developing countries, which, despite the fact that they are not primarily responsible for the enormous climate damage caused by increasing prosperity, suffer disproportionately from the consequences.[2]

Cumbersome and sluggish super tanker

Since hearing the alarm bells of the 2015 Climate Conference and the call for drastic action, almost every country in the world has now set climate targets. The US and the EU claim they will be climate neutral by 2050, China by 2060 and India by 2070. Yet it is still not enough. For instance, climate scientists say that even if the major polluters deliver on their promises, the earth is still likely to warm by some 2.5 degrees this century.[3]

The alarmist tone also ensured that from then on, more and more oil and gas companies, including major multinational Shell, said they were aiming for net-zero emissions by the middle of this century. This refers to their "own emissions and those from purchased energy" and not those from products sold. So it may seem like a lot, but it is actually a fraction of total emissions.[4] The year 2021 also saw a report by the authoritative International Energy Agency (IEA), the organisation that publishes the World Energy Outlook every year, stating that there should be no more investment in prospecting for new fossil fuels worldwide. Existing fields can still be exploited for the coming decades, but new oil and gas fields are no longer needed, the IEA said.[5] This puts further pressure on governments and fossil fuel companies to come up with additional climate measures faster than originally envisaged.

Financial institutions also see the need to change. For instance, since the Paris Climate Agreement, the European Central Bank (ECB) has opened up the possibility of using the bank's €2,800 billion heavy procurement programme for the green transition.[6] And ahead of the Climate Summit in Glasgow at the end of October 2021, pension giant ABP announced its withdrawal from the oil and gas sector. This means that around €11 billion worth of fossil fuel shares will be sold. ABP will actively invest in sustainable energy companies and groups that are working to become climate-neutral.[7]

Also, in 2021, the court forced multinational Shell to reduce its CO_2 emissions faster and about 10 countries, including Vietnam, incorporated "ecocide" in some form in their legislation,[8] although enforcement is still very rare.[9] Ecocide is about protecting nature from large-scale destruction and depletion, such as logging in the Amazon, which is damaging not only to Brazil but to the world as a whole. Logging is destroying our common home. By making ecocide a crime, in the same way that genocide is a crime, we make top executives in business or government criminally liable for the environmental damage caused by their companies or governments. This is a good way to prevent companies from destroying ecosystems on a large scale for profit.

The EU also upped its target in early 2021 from 40% to 55% less greenhouse gas emissions by 2030. The new Dutch government is aiming as high as 60% by the end of 2021, according to the coalition agreement.[10] After taking office, US President Joe Biden said he wanted to make his country a leader in solving the climate problem, aiming to be CO_2-neutral by 2050.[11] Chinese leaders are also convinced that limiting global warming is an economic imperative. "To protect the environment is to protect productivity", said President Xi Jinping.[12] China therefore wants to be climate neutral by 2060.[13]

These developments are promising, as China and the US are the two largest emitters of CO_2. It is also promising that at the recent Climate

Conference in Glasgow, these two countries announced that they would work in the 2020s to accelerate methane emission cuts, call for stricter laws against deforestation and phase out the use of coal more quickly.[14] Definitive targets were not specified, however. The world has thus started to turn towards a more sustainable way of life, albeit like an cumbersome and sluggish super tanker. World leaders seem to have gained something of an astronaut's view, but they will have to start translating those fine words and targets into hard measures.

Climate disruption

All good intentions notwithstanding, 2021 also showed that fossil fuel use is still increasing and that the earth will be one and a half degrees warmer within a decade. Ten years earlier than expected. No part of the world will escape extreme climate events, according to the sixth report of the UN climate panel (IPCC). The report serves as the basis for climate policies of governments worldwide and is the result of years of research by hundreds of climate scientists. According to the IPCC, it has not been this warm in thousands of years and temperatures have never risen so rapidly. There is actually no doubt of a direct link, the report argues, between the current heatwaves and greenhouse gas emissions.

"Nowhere to run, nowhere to hide", says US climate scientist Linda Mearns. She is a researcher at the National Center for Atmospheric Research (NCAR) and co-author of the IPCC report.[15] The report also shows that global warming is already causing major changes in the atmosphere, on land and in the oceans. According to the IPCC, the evidence is stronger than that in the previous report, which at the time served as a prelude to the Paris Agreement.

This, according to UN chief António Guterres, indicates that we are destroying the earth with our use of fossil fuels. The report gives humanity a "code red" warning. Guterres points out that the very countries and communities that barely contribute to global warming are the first to become victims of climate change.

This became a key issue in 2022 at the climate summit in Egypt, where countries finally agreed on the establishment of a global fund for those countries vulnerable to the impacts of climate change. We will need to help vulnerable countries and communities and especially women and other vulnerable groups "on the front line of the climate crisis" to become more resilient to the impacts of climate change.[16] This will require investment in adaptation programmes.

Meanwhile, climate change is having an increasing disruptive effect on the global economy. Argentina, for example, which is kept afloat by the International Monetary Fund (IMF), suffered its worst ever drought in 2023, causing an economic slowdown.[17] Pakistan's national debt is at risk of becoming unsustainable, partly because of devastating floods in the country.[18]

In 2021, ahead of the publication of the UN's sixth climate report, 14,000 scientists from 150 countries were also sounding the alarm.[19] They were shocked by the number of natural disasters in the month of July 2021, with extreme heat, flooding and forest fires.[20] Greenland, for example, lost 8.5 billion tonnes of ice in one day due to the heat, enough to flood the entire state of Florida by 5 centimetres, according to US news channel CNN.[21] The changing conditions also explain why more and more climate migrants are arriving in the US. Fires along the west coast, rising sea levels in the Atlantic and the Gulf of Mexico and drought in the Midwest mean declining habitability in many places.[22]

In fact, according to some studies, 50% of Americans will face worsening living conditions due to drought and extreme heat in the coming decades. "Increasingly, the effects of climate change are becoming a factor that determines where people choose to live", argues Jesse Keenan, associate professor of real estate at Tulane University in New Orleans. "In addition to the affordability and availability of property, mobile well-educated people in particular are looking at which places are climate resilient", says Keenan.[23] Some scientists claim that with current warming trends from rising sea levels, as many as 13 million Americans will have to move. Some people will choose other states and cause the displacement of knowledge and income. Others will seek the better located parts of the city, a process already noticeable in Miami and elsewhere. Keenan talks about "climate gentrification".[24] The wealthy seek refuge in the safe parts of the city, driving up prices and displacing the lower classes and the less fortunate.

It is increasingly clear that climate change affects everything and everyone and puts further pressure on our basic services: water, food and energy security. Across the board, more and more organisations, groups and military leaders are therefore sounding the alarm. I myself receive more and more requests to comment on climate news in the media, and I am asked about the link between security and climate change. All this news and scientists' reports have led me to believe that "climate change" is actually too friendly a term for what we are facing; "climate disruption" would be more appropriate. This is also why much more action is needed.

Coronavirus crisis as a guide

We now need the same courage that some leaders showed during the coronavirus crisis. In other words, the courage to act quickly in an emergency. For example, many countries took unprecedented measures during the pandemic, and governments worldwide were making hundreds of billions of euros and dollars available to help people affected by the virus. It reminds me of the kind of leadership our parents and grandparents showed in the Netherlands in 1953 when the sea dikes broke and large parts of the province of Zeeland were flooded. After the *Watersnoodramp*, they chose to do more than patch up the existing dykes, despite the post-war hardships and the huge economic problems in our country at the time. They chose to invest in the long term – regardless of which party was in power – in the Delta Works, our future-proof water management system. A choice for which we are still grateful today, almost 70 years later. It is exactly such a mindset that the world needs today.

In many countries, people listened to the scientists and the experts during the coronavirus crisis. Schools, hairdressers and bars closed, and whole cohorts of people discovered in a very short space of time how their work could largely be performed online because of the no-contact ban: civil servants, teachers, students, general practitioners, psychologists and many other service providers. At the same time, we were investing in new technologies that allowed us to build solid, confidential relationships in the digital world without seeing each other in real life.

During the pandemic, cars and trucks stood idle for a long time, planes did not fly and factories shut down. In many places, temporary curfews were imposed and people were only allowed to leave their homes under strict conditions and with permission. The economic and social order was thus completely overturned. So much so that CO_2 emissions dropped to levels not seen since World War II. For a while, the blue sky had no vapour trails, the peaks of the Himalayas were visible again in northern India and, in the canals of Venice, clear water was flowing again in the absence of tourists.

Meanwhile, many companies were emerging as a force for good. For instance, new vaccines and new coronavirus tests were being developed in record time. The chemical group DSM produced 130,000 litres of disinfectant for hospitals at its own expense.[25] Beer giant Heineken made a million-dollar donation to the Red Cross, borrowing extra money to keep its own balance sheet healthy.[26] And Unilever, the multinational packaged goods company, allocated half a billion euros to support suppliers and retailers and donated 50 million euros worth of soap and hand gel.[27]

Leadership required

As the pandemic showed, we as humanity are thus capable of a great things in a crisis, even though in many cases it was nowhere near enough and not always in time. But unfortunately, we often only take action when we feel the need, or in other words when the consequences are already being felt, so it quickly becomes a case of treating the symptoms. The coronavirus crisis exposed our global vulnerability and taught us how important it was to be prepared, not to ignore signals and to act decisively where necessary. Military personnel have learned that lesson many times and know what price you can pay if you look the other way or are ill-prepared. That is why we should invest in a climate delta plan now, doing everything we can to stop the situation getting worse (mitigation) and to build resilience (adaptation) to the effects we cannot prevent.

This requires firm measures and substantial investments that will pay off in the long run, just as the Delta Works are still proving their worth decades later. Such choices are never easy, because they come at the expense of equally necessary short-term investments, for which there is greater public support at the time. That is difficult for some politicians, because such choices do not always score high in the popularity stakes.

When I think of the leadership that is required, one example that comes to mind is that of Theodor Roosevelt, the US president who held office from 1901 to 1909 and proved to be a born leader. During his presidency, Roosevelt founded 51 protected bird sanctuaries, doubled the number of national parks from five to ten, stipulated that millions of acres of publicly owned forest should become protected areas and used his power to establish National Monuments for 16 natural areas, including the Muir Redwoods in California, Mount Olympus in Washington state and the Grand Canyon.[28]

Roosevelt trod on many toes on the way, but that did not concern him. "Is there anything", he asked rhetorically, "that is stopping me from making Pelican Island a protected bird sanctuary? No? Well, then I hereby declare that it is." Partly because of his attitude and commitment, Roosevelt is now considered to be one of the most effective peacetime presidents the US has ever had. Historians consistently place him in the top five, alongside founding fathers such as Washington and Jefferson and alongside war presidents like Lincoln and the other Roosevelt.[29]

Roosevelt also pointed out the politician's struggle between "the urgent and the important". The "urgent" is about the crisis of the day, the daily hustle and bustle, on which all media attention is focused. The "important" is about preventing the crises of tomorrow, such as the climate crisis. In political reality, unfortunately, the urgent all too often wins out over the important.

I would therefore advocate a Roosevelt approach, where we keep "the important" in mind. We need convincing national leaders who stand up for the people at home as well as for common global interests. After all, everything and everyone has become interconnected, in terms of security, food and water security, economic development, prosperity, sustainability and migration, and climate change plays a defining role. It must therefore be addressed urgently and coherently in a global, concerted fight against global warming.

Waging "war" on climate change

In that fight, it is important not to leave climate adaptation and mitigation solely to one particular ministry, country or multilateral organisation. It is not the problem of a climate minister, for example, but a common problem that determines more and more policy development in almost all ministries. Like war, it is too important to "be left to the generals", as the French statesman Georges Clemenceau once so aptly put it. As I mentioned earlier, we all live on Spaceship Earth and we have not yet discovered any other habitable planet. We have to make do with that special little dot in space. It is the only home humanity has.

It is good, therefore, that the UN Security Council is increasingly linking a hotter world to conflict and instability. In a recent debate on 13 June 2023, the Security Council discussed the relationship between the climate crisis and security, in particular the effects of extreme weather conditions on peace missions in fragile regions.[30]

But it is nowhere near enough. To protect our home, we must now fight what is essentially a war. Not a battle between people or countries in the original sense of the word, nor a mobilisation in which the economy is transformed into a war economy aimed at producing military materiel, ammunition and equipment for the umpteen thousands of soldiers called up for duty. It is now about the battle we must wage together against the degradation of the planet.

The big issue of this century is how we are going to sustain a rapidly growing global population in the face of increasing resource scarcity and in a rapidly changing climate that is limiting the earth's habitability. It requires a radical change in the global economy and the way we live, for which a rapid, collective reduction of global CO_2 emissions is a crucial first step, but for which we also need to reduce our dependence on raw materials.

We need to move to an economy that is no longer relying on consumption only, but more on use and reuse. This will require massive adjustments to build resilience to the impacts of those changes.

I believe that the defence sector is an indispensable partner in countering that global disruption and building resilience. Not only because of its security role, but also because the defence sector is the biggest government polluter in almost every country. So how can this sector reduce its own emissions? How should defence organisations adapt to the impacts of climate change and what are the possible courses of action in this regard? What does it mean for future partnerships, for future operations, and for defence organisations' future configuration, equipment and training?

Only by ending the fossil-fuel era can we collectively stop the negative spiral of changing climate and thereby mitigate the more serious adverse impacts. We will also have to adapt to the irreversible changes in our climate that are undeniably already under way. We need to increase our resilience. In other words, climate mitigation and climate adaptation. That is what it is all about.

Notes

1. Planetary Collective (2015, 5 December), "Call to Earth – A message from the world's astronauts to COP21", YouTube, see https://www.youtube.com/watch?v=NN1eSMXI_6Y

2. Sengupta, S. (2021, 25 October), "The rich world's promise of $100 billion in climate aid inches forward", *New York Times*, see https://www.nytimes.com/2021/10/25/climate/100-billion-climate-aid-cop26.html

3. IPCC (2022). Sixth Assessment Report: Impacts, Adaptation and Vulnerability. https://www.ipcc.ch/report/ar6/wg2/

4. Shell products and operations account for 1% of total global CO_2 emissions. Boffey, D. (2021, 26 May), "Court orders Royal Dutch Shell to cut carbon emissions by 45% by 2030", *The Guardian*, see https://www.theguardian.com/business/2021/may/26/court-orders-royal-dutch-shell-to-cut-carbon-emissions-by-45-by-2030

5. IEA (2021), World Energy Outlook 2021. IEA, Paris, p. 20

6. Vansteenland, K. (2020), "Lagarde: 'We must use all our weapons against climate change'", *De Tijd*, see https://www.tijd.be/markten-live/nieuws/algemeen/lagarde-we-moeten-alle-wapens-inzetten-tegen-klimaatverandering/10237908.html

7. Waarloo, N. & Van de Weijer, B. (2021, 26 October), "ABP, Europe's largest pension fund, stops investing in fossil energy", *de Volkskrant*, see https://www.volkskrant.nl/nieuws-achtergrond/abp-het-grootste-pensioenfonds-van-europa-stopt-met-investeren-in-fossiele-energie~b17f0f87d/

8. Garcia, B. (2020, 27 February), "The history of ecocide, a new crime against humanity", *BBVA Open Minde*, see https://www.bbvaopenmind.com/en/science/environment/the-history-of-ecocide-a-new-crime-against-humanity/

9. Chin, S. (2021), "Ecocide law: the use of hard law to complement soft law", *Harvard International Law Journal blog post*, see https://harvardilj.org/2021/05/ecocide-law-the-use-of-hard-law-to-complement-soft-law/

10. VVD, D66, CDA, CU (2021, 15 December). Looking out for each other, looking forward to the future: Coalition Agreement 2021-2025. See Coalition agreement "Looking out for each other, looking ahead to the future" | Publication | Government.nl

11. Newburger, E. (2021, 22 April), "Biden pledges to slash greenhouse gas emissions in half by 2030", *CNBC*, see https://www.cnbc.com/2021/04/22/biden-pledges-to-slash-greenhouse-gas-emissions-in-half-by-2030.html

12. Xi, quoted in Wagendorp, B. (2021, 22 April), "As far as Biden is concerned, the war on global warming has begun", *de Volkskrant*, see https://www.volkskrant.nl/columns-opinie/wat-biden-betreft-is-de-oorlog-tegen-de-opwarming-van-de-aarde-begonnen~ba57dc14/

13. Lee Meyers, S. (2020, 23 September), "China's pledge to be carbon neutral by 2060: what it means", *New York Times*, see https://www.nytimes.com/2020/09/23/world/asia/china-climate-change.html

14. Dennis, B., Kaplan, S., Mufson, S. & Birnbaum, M. (2021, 10 November), "U.S. and China issue joint pledge to slow climate change", *Washington Post*, see https://www.washingtonpost.com/climate-environment/2021/11/10/us-china-declaration-climate/

15-16. Havermans, O. (2021, 10 August), "Everyone will be affected by climate change", *Trouw*

17. Sigal, L. & Raszewski, E. (2023, 9 March), "Argentina's 'unprecedented' drought pummels farmers and economy", Reuters, https://www.reuters.com/business/environment/argentinas-unprecedented-drought-pummels-farmers-economy-2023-03-09/

18. Parkin, B. (2022, 23 September), "Flood-hit Pakistan should suspend debt repayments, says UN policy paper", *Financial Times*, https://www.ft.com/content/31061741-16a1-49fe-a495-6d7dbd3c886a

19. Ripple, W.J., Wolf, C., Newsome, T.M., Gregg, J.W., Lenton, T.M., Palomo, I., Eikelboom, J.A., Law, B.E., Huq, S., Duffy, P.B., Rockström, J. (2021), "World scientists' warning of a climate emergency 2021", *BioScience* 71(9), 894-898, see https://doi.org/10.1093/biosci/biab079

20. Hook, L., Shepherd, C., Astrasheuskaya, N. (2021, 24 July), "Extreme weather takes climate change models 'off the scale'", *Financial times*, see https://www.ft.com/content/9a647a51-ede8-480e-ba78-cbf14ad878b7

21. Ramirez, R. (2021, 30 July), "The amount of Greenland ice that melted on Tuesday could cover Florida in 2 inches of water", CNN, see https://edition.cnn.com/2021/07/29/us/greenland-ice-melting-climate-change/index.html?utm_source=InsideClimate+News&utm_campaign=b778970285-&utm_medium=email&utm_term=0_29c928ffb5-b778970285-328164402

22-23. Thomas, C. (2021, 23 November). "Fleeing fire and smoke", *Het Financieele Dagblad*, see https://fd.nl/samenleving/1418854/op-de-vlucht-voor-vuur-en-rook-pdl1cakKuKlc

24. Calculations by Michael Hauer, a sociologist at Florida State University, show that with current warming trends, 13 million Americans will have to move due to rising sea levels alone, see Thomas, C. (2021, 23 November), "Fleeing fire and smoke", *Het Financieele Dagblad*, see https://fd.nl/samenleving/1418854/op-de-vlucht-voor-vuur-en-rook-pdl1cakKuKlc

25. DSM (2020, 21 March), "DSM helps Dutch government with disinfectants for healthcare workers", *DSM press release*, see https://www.dsm.com/nederland/nl_NL/nieuws/2020/2020-03-20-dsm-helpt-nederlandse-overheid-met-desinfectiemiddelen-voor-zorgmedewerkers.html

26. Hermanides, E. (2020, 22 April), "Heineken: help hospitality trade by briefly eliminating VAT on beer," *Trouw*, see https://www.trouw.nl/economie/heineken-help-horeca-door-even-geen-btw-meer-te-heffen-op-bier-b5a35298/

27. Schelfaut, S. (2020, 24 March), "Unilever puts up cash in fight against coronavirus", *Algemeen Dagblad*, see https://www.ad.nl/koken-en-eten/unilever-trekt-portemonnee-in-strijd-tegen-coronavirus-a1d5da60/

28. National Park Service (2021, 14 January), "Theodore Roosevelt and the National Park System", https://www.nps.gov/thrb/learn/historyculture/trandthenpsystem.htm, accessed 8 December 2021

29. Casado, L. (2020, 2 July), "These are the top 25 US presidents, according to historians and biographers", *Business Insider*, see https://www.businessinsider.nl/the-top-20-presidents-in-us-history-according-to-historians-2017-2?international=true&r=US

30. Immongault, H., quoted in the Security Council debate (2023, 13 June). "With Climate Crisis Generating Growing Threats to Global Peace, Security Council Must Ramp up Efforts, lessen Risk of Conflicts, Speakers Stress in Open Debate", SC/15318, https://press.un.org/en/2023/sc15318.doc.htm

Chapter Fourteen
Action-based and climate-conscious collaboration

"How much climate-related violence 2021 will see is uncertain, but the broader trend is clear enough: without urgent action, the danger of climate-related conflict will rise in the years ahead."

Robert Malley (former President of the International Crisis Group) in "Ten Conflicts to Watch in 2021"

In my final year as Chief of Defence in 2017, I visit the Baltic states. There, the population is acutely aware of the threat from Russia. The three small former Soviet states with a Russian population minority are sandwiched between the Baltic Sea and the larger, increasingly assertive Russia. Every day – without fail – there is Russian influence *via* the media and the sound of gunfire in regular major exercises off Russia's coasts and just across its borders. The siting of missiles capable of carrying nuclear warheads in the nearby Russian enclave of Kaliningrad in 2016 has certainly done nothing to reduce the sense of insecurity. Russia's annexation of Crimea and its invasion of Ukraine are horror scenarios that have become a reality. That is why in Lithuania, every home has the government-issue, 75-page handbook entitled *What to do if the Russians come?* It is full of tips such as "How do I recognise a Russian tank?" and "How to move in the dark and survive in the woods".[1]

The perceived Russian threat is also the reason why NATO, our transatlantic Alliance, sends troops to Poland, Estonia, Latvia and Lithuania. Since 2016, Dutch military personnel have been stationed in Lithuania as part of a NATO unit training there as the enhanced Forward Presence (eFP), making their presence felt to the Russians, and of course to the population. This is important for the actual protection of our NATO allies, but above all for sending a signal to Russia that we take the protection of our NATO allies seriously.

Existing and emerging threats

This renewed focus on protecting eastern borders during my tenure makes perfect sense at the time. The military alliance must always be mindful of military superpowers that pose a potential danger to its member countries. For instance, there is the threat of Russian nuclear cruise missiles and we are experiencing the direct consequences of Russia's increased assertiveness and aggression. Then in the case of the Netherlands, there is, for example, the downing of the Malaysia Airlines passenger plane, flight MH17, and the Russian intelligence agents caught at the multilateral Organisation for the Prohibition of Chemical Weapons (OPCW) in The Hague.

War changes so much. Oil and gas prices are being forced up and solar panels, wind turbines and heat pumps have become a matter of national security. At the same time, coal-fired power plants are running at full capacity again, partly due to the loss of much of the supply of Russian gas.

Only after the invasion did we fully realise just how vulnerable and dependent we were in Europe. For instance, we depend on the US for our security, on Asia for the sophisticated chips we need to develop new technologies, and on Africa and China for the raw materials needed to produce renewable energy.

Finally, the focus on the military is growing. Even the militaries themselves are now viewing the threat from a different angle. There is a widespread realisation that we must be ready to fight at any moment. Ready to fight tonight, as the Americans would say. NATO stresses the importance of "boots on the ground". "The world is at a historic inflection point in the most severe and complex security environment since the end of World War II", according to NATO's secretary-general.[2]

NATO and the EU are now looking at China through different eyes and with greater caution. Not only because China supports Russia in the conflict and wants to present a united front against Western influence, but also because China has the third-largest defence budget in the world and an increasingly sophisticated arsenal of weapons. China also has an increasingly obvious global repressive effect on access to raw materials, and the development of a heavy Western dependence on those makes us vulnerable. Geopolitical competition for access to scarce raw materials is increasing, and after the conflict in Ukraine, Europe wants to be able to operate more autonomously and end its vulnerability in this regard. This involves ensuring the availability of scarce raw materials for batteries, computer chips and solar panels, for example, but access to markets is also crucial. The Chinese are chess players who look generations ahead and have been working on this for decades, while we are only now really waking up. For NATO, therefore, it is not just about the Chinese military threat, but also about the competition for raw materials, market influence and the protection of supply routes; a competition that is increasingly being waged with terrifying military means and which could lead to new conflict situations.

Focus on climate security

The increasing diversity of threats and security risks is nothing new for either NATO or the EU, but the disruptive influence and driving effect of climate change on all these security concerns is still underestimated. While we see increasing focus in both organisations on the impact of climate change on our security, concrete action is urgently needed. Climate change, as argued earlier, is a driver of security risks and conflicts, and is placing increasing demands on our militaries.

The disruptive effect of climate change thus indirectly poses perhaps the greatest threat to peace and stability in virtually all parts of the world. It is therefore hugely important that NATO make climate change a key element in its strategy and policy development in order to anticipate what lies ahead, and also to show leadership and responsibility in emission reduction. After all, the 30 member states together account for about half the value of the global economy and represent almost a billion people. Together, they produce a very large amount of CO_2.

In order to draw more attention to climate security, together with my IMCCS colleagues and partners such as Luxembourg's defence minister and deputy prime minister François Bausch, I have raised the relationship between climate and security on regular occasions within NATO and the EU in recent years. Time and time again, in an attempt to make politicians, administrators and senior military officers aware of the need to put this issue on the agenda and place greater emphasis on making armed forces more sustainable.

That is why I am also relieved that, since June 2021, NATO has made the fight against climate change a priority, has also translated this into its planning and strategy development, and is increasingly integrating climate-related considerations into the Alliance's full work spectrum.[3] NATO now recognises that climate change is becoming an increasingly prominent feature of political instability, conflict and migration, and thus directly affects our allies' interests.

An action plan has now been drawn up too, outlining how NATO intends to cope with climate change and how it sees its role in mitigating it,[4] for example by raising awareness among allies through an annual climate change impact assessment on security, and by integrating climate change considerations into NATO'S many work areas, such as defence planning, exercises and disaster response. In addition, NATO aims to reduce its environmental and logistic footprint and has introduced a method to measure its own emissions in 2023. Further laudable ambitions include a desire to strengthen collaboration with the UN, the EU, scientists and industry to reduce emissions, and plans to establish a centre of excellence on climate security.

One reason why NATO is now making this about-turn has much to do with US President Biden taking office. This has made the issue negotiable within the Alliance. What also helps is that NATO's secretary-general, Jens Stoltenberg, is a former climate envoy and, partly because of this, is more aware of the relationship between climate change and security. In the German newspaper *Die Welt* – and in rather more detail in a speech – he said in September 2020, well before NATO'S action plan was ratified: "Some may ask if NATO, a military alliance, should be concerned about climate change. My answer to that is yes, we should. And for three reasons. Because climate change is making the world more dangerous. Because it makes it harder for our military forces to keep our people safe. And because we all have a responsibility to do more to combat climate change."[5]

Increasing climate resilience

Stoltenberg also cites examples of how NATO allies can take more account of climate change. One example is to ensure that energy and telecommunications networks can withstand more extreme weather conditions. He also wants to enhance the ability of NATO forces to respond to natural disasters, basically in an approach similar to that used in the COVID-19 pandemic. According to Stoltenberg, NATO's disaster coordination cell, the Euro-Atlantic Disaster Response Coordination Centre, has brought many countries together in the face of COVID-19. "Hundreds of tonnes of essential supplies were jointly distributed around the world, nearly 100 field hospitals were set up and we transported medical staff and patients." He added: "Just as we supported national governments during the COVID-19 crisis, we must also be prepared to do more in relation to climate-related disasters."[6]

Finally, Stoltenberg believes it is the responsibility of NATO to help military forces reduce emissions without sacrificing effectiveness. That expertise, he says, can in turn be shared with partners around the world. Calculating the CO_2 emissions of military forces and reporting on them would be a first step. Targets could then be set to reduce emissions.[7]

Walking the walk!

It is heartening to see that a new wind is blowing through NATO, that climate change is being recognised as a security risk, and that the secretary-general is calling on NATO allies to act. Yet for now, many intentions are on paper only, still quite general and non-committal. Ultimately, it is the member states that have to make the change, and not all of them are eager to do so. Many fear the costs, some do not see the need and many would rather invest in other defence priorities. I believe the momentum should be stepped up, given the scientific warnings. Fortunately, some countries are taking the lead on this, namely the more western member states such as the US, the UK, France, the Scandinavian countries and now the Netherlands.

In my work for IMCCS, I have learned that awareness is the first step towards recognition. It is not a question of unwillingness, but for many military personnel, climate change has little to do with their work. Once they are familiar with the operational examples in the first part of this book, however, realisation starts to dawn.

That is also what makes a NATO centre of excellence so important. It deepens military knowledge and the understanding of the relationship between climate and security, and thus makes the need for action palpable. A centre of expertise could also play a pivotal role in collaboration with external knowledge institutes and networks such as IMCCS, and it could help in sharing experiences and lessons learned so that the wheel does not have to be reinvented country by country.

NATO is the only organisation that connects the countries of Europe and North America on many levels. This makes it the perfect hub for sharing information, expertise and ideas, and means that it is ideally placed to become a pioneer on the topic of climate and security.

Greater collaboration between the EU and NATO

The EU is having a similar change of mind and so, in addition to the Green Deal, the roadmap intended to make the EU climate neutral by 2050, it has developed a climate change and defence roadmap.[8] This roadmap should integrate climate change into EU defence actions and it emphasises the need to reduce the ecological footprint of EU armed forces. Even more so than in NATO, in the EU the issue remains somewhat stuck at the level of fine objectives and intentions. Little is happening in terms of an actual translation into security and defence policy. In June 2023, the Commission and the High Representative for Foreign Affairs and Security Policy presented a joint communiqué on the link between climate and security. They announced concrete actions to incorporate climate change impacts into policy-making, conflict analysis and operational planning. Like NATO, the EU also wants to reduce its carbon footprint and strengthen international collaboration.

So we see many parallels here with the NATO Action Plan. Both organisations recognise the need for further collaboration on this issue and this offers opportunities for more integrated action.

Indeed, NATO and the EU have a long history of collaboration. From institutional cooperation and staff exchanges to planning and executing of joint military exercises and missions. In addition, the majority of EU member states are also NATO allies. With both NATO and the EU putting climate security on the agenda and setting out ambitions and actions for the future, these roadmaps can boost existing collaboration.

This is extremely important because the EU has more tools than the military Alliance to combat climate change or adapt societies accordingly. For instance, the EU has partnerships with many countries in fragile regions, as well as with regional organisations. This enables, for instance, the sharing of knowledge and experience and the acceleration of measures to counter the effects of climate change. The EU also has the European Defence Agency, which plays a driving role in European defence cooperation on the development of future defence capabilities. This agency is also increasingly involved in the development of more sustainable defence capabilities.

In addition, the EU is seeking greater autonomy in the pursuit of its security interests and also wants to strengthen its own industrial base. It is for this purpose that the European Defence Fund (EDF) has been set up, focusing on European collaboration in the research and development of future equipment and other systems for the security sector.[9] This fund could also boost the development of technologies that contribute to the necessary sustainability of future capabilities, such as military camps, vehicles, ships and aircraft, thus indirectly contributing to sustainability in the civilian sector. This dovetails neatly with NATO's plan when it comes to helping armed forces to reduce emissions without sacrificing effectiveness.

The EU is thus the ideal organisation to take a more integrated look at climate security and to combine diplomatic, economic and military efforts in public-private partnership programmes within the ring of instability around us. It would therefore be logical to strengthen cooperation between the two organisations on this issue in particular.

Climate-heavy cooperation

A more integrated approach and response requires military units in NATO and EU countries to be able to collaborate much more with civil bodies, such as police, fire services and organisations such as the Red Cross. Only by working together can we cope with natural disasters and refugee flows, and only by working together can we prevent the fragile countries around us from descending into conflict. The future requires us to make our collaboration more professional and adapt it to the likely scenarios.

In a NATO or EU context, in coalitions or under the UN flag, military forces can also work to develop partnerships with the many vulnerable countries around us, where climate change could lead to further disruption and to conflict. In those partnerships, we can set up resilience programmes to help local security forces to cope with the impact of climate change, set up regional coordination mechanisms for disaster response, help to develop local contingency plans and – where necessary – create a safe environment for the implementation of civil relief programmes in that area.

Military engagement should always be part of a broader, comprehensive approach. My British former colleague and friend, Lieutenant General Richard Nugee, suggested, for instance, the idea of setting up a special NATO staff focused on working with African countries and supporting civil efforts in those countries, to help make them more resilient to the negative climate spiral these countries increasingly find themselves in. Somewhat similar to the US's African Command (AFRICOM), I believe it is an interesting idea that would offer possibilities for streamlining and strengthening cooperation with the EU, the UN and other organisations.

It is all very well talking the talk; we also need to walk the walk. We need to take action. And anyone who thinks that this will come at the expense of focusing on existing threats and security risks should just think of US President Eisenhower, who once received advice from his economic advisers at the height of the Cold War. They informed him of the possible impact of a nuclear war on the exchange rate of the US dollar. Eisenhower is said to have replied at the time: "Wait a minute, boys. We're not going to be reconstructing the dollar. We're going to be grubbing for worms", making it clear that the exchange rate of the US currency was less relevant when faced with the threat of nuclear war.[10]

This is exactly what we should keep in mind when talking about the necessary adaptation to climate change. Climate change does not make existing threats less important, it actually reinforces and changes them. All those threats are directly or indirectly influenced and driven by the disruptive effects of our changing climate. So if we do not adapt now to the new reality that climate change brings, and do not make climate security an integral part of the strategy, doctrines, and organisational development of NATO, EU and UN missions, then our economies and our well-trained and equipped militaries will soon be of little use to us.

Then the world will be engulfed by a tsunami of effects of climate change and we will be playing catch-up, with all the costs and repercussions that would entail.

Notes

1. Payton, M. (2016, 29 October), "Lithuania issues booklets to citizens about how to deal with Russian invasion", *The Independent*, see https://www.independent.co.uk/news/world/europe/lithuania-booklets-citizens-russian-invasion-civil-defence-a7386246.html

2. Stoltenberg, J & Kishida, F. (2023, 31 January) "Joint statement issued on the occasion of the meeting beweteen H.E. Mr Jens Stoltenberg, NATO Secretary General and H.E. Mr Kishida Fumio, Prime Minister of Japan", *NATO*, https://www.nato.int/cps/en/natohq/opinions_211294.htm

3-4. NATO (2021, 14 June), "NATO climate change and security action plan", NATO press release, see https://www.nato.int/cps/en/natohq/official_texts_185174.htm

5-6-7. Stoltenberg, J. (2020, 28 September), NATO and the security implications of climate change. Virtual speech by NATO Secretary General, see https://www.nato.int/cps/en/natohq/opinions_178355.htm

8. European External Action Service (2020). Climate change and defence roadmap. EEAS (2020) 1251, Brussels. https://data.consilium.europa.eu/doc/document/ST-12741-2020-INIT/en/pdf

9. Csernatoni, R. (2021). The EU's defence ambitions: understanding the emergence of a European defence technological industrial complex. Carnegie Europe, Brussels. https://carnegieeurope.eu/2021/12/06/eu-s-defense-ambitions-understanding-emergence-of-european-defense-technological-and-industrial-complex-pub-85884

10. Quoted in Pasca Palmer, C. (2019, 16 January), "Why a healthy planet and a healthy economy go hand-in-hand", *World Economic Forum 2019*, see https://www.weforum.org/agenda/2019/01/save-the-planet-save-the-economy-cristiana-pasca-palmer/

Chapter Fifteen
Defence should and could be more sustainable

"Many of them [armed forces] talk the talk, but none of them really walk the walk."

Anatol Lieven, professor of international relations, in his book *Climate Change and the Nation State*

In the summer of 2020, a couple of years after I retired, I get an email from Ronald van der Bij.[1] He is a major in the air force and asks my advice on what he can do achieve more sustainability within the defence organisation. Ronald writes that he is an aerospace engineering graduate from Delft University of Technology and is currently on secondment for the Ministry of Defence in the US in the international team responsible for setting up maintenance for the new fighter aircraft, the F-35. Given the role of this aircraft in the coming decades and the interests of the countries flying it, it is a highly responsible job.

In the first two years, Ronald travels somewhere in the world every fortnight for consultations. He makes 34 international official trips in less than two years. "I'm in the air more than I'm in the office," he writes in that email to me. "Makes you feel very important and I like the air miles I earn," he explains, but eventually it starts to get to you. He wonders about what he is doing and whether it is efficient to travel to the other side of the world for a meeting. "It's quite a big deal. I have two small children, aged nine and seven. How do I explain that to them?"

This leads Ronald to the idea of starting a tree-planting campaign *via* social media with the idea that everyone who takes a flight compensates by planting a tree and tagging two people to do the same. That initiative soon starts to mushroom, I gather from his story, although he does get teased about it by his colleagues. Then comes the coronavirus pandemic, which brings the world to a standstill and prevents Ronald from flying. Nevertheless, he decides to continue planting cuttings. Some 350 in his own garden just outside the city of Washington. "Because why should I only plant trees when I travel," Ronald asks himself.

Soon he is giving away all the young saplings free to people to plant in their own gardens. More and more people come to get cuttings from Ronald; five hundred trees are planted. Then comes the idea of planting a thousand trees through his children's school. "Because," says Ronald, "even if only one tree makes it to a mature tree in thirty years' time, that's still a bonus." What matters most to him is his position as a role model. "Not only within Defence, but also for the people around me and for my children." And, he says: "Because of my actions, my children are now much more involved with nature and have a good understanding of the impact we as humans have on it."

Military emissions

Ronald's concerns are legitimate and touch on a much broader problem. Everyone should be much more aware of the impact of climate change and what we can do about it. This also applies to military forces worldwide. In 2019, for example, the greenhouse gas emissions from the US military alone were more than the total emissions of several medium-sized European countries combined. If the US military was a country, researchers from Brown University concluded, it would rank 55th among countries with the highest emissions, with 5,270 million tonnes of CO_2.[2] It is a similar story for military forces within the EU. In 2021, annual greenhouse gas emissions from EU military activities were equivalent to that of 14 million cars: 25 million tonnes of CO$_2$.[3] Given the need to drastically reduce global emissions, it is clear that the military sector cannot be left out of the discussion on climate action. Especially when military forces themselves report that climate change is a threat to national and international security. The defence organisation itself must therefore become more sustainable, as stated in our IMCCS World Climate Security Report in March 2021.[4]

It would obviously have been better if military forces had started large-scale sustainability efforts years ago, but actually the opposite was true. In many countries, defence was the balancing item for the national budget for decades. In the Netherlands, one round of cuts followed another. Support units in particular were subject to major cuts, as was the maintenance of buildings and sites. When I took office as CDS in 2012, I had to cut another 12,000 jobs, even though at that time we were fully deployed as a military force; conducting 20 to 25 different missions simultaneously worldwide was quite normal at that time.

This meant that all units and weapons systems were deployed and we were on our knees as a result, leaving the military short of deployable units, strategic transport to move people and equipment over long distances, support for special forces, intelligence and medical support; this is still the case at the time of writing (2023). A wide range of shortages meant that in the fight against ISIS, for example, we were often unable to deploy F-16s for a period of time and had to withdraw. There were simply too few support units to be able to continue the mission safely. The painful truth is that the Dutch armed forces, in that condition, were not able to perform their constitutional tasks satisfactorily.

In a situation like this, investing in sustainable solutions is frankly the last thing on a soldier's mind. Apart from the lack of a sense of urgency, there is little or no money available. It would mean even deeper cuts in the organisation, thus making further concessions in terms of combat power and deployability. In other words, a smaller contribution to NATO, EU or UN missions, as well as fewer aircraft, fewer ships and fewer battalions.

This is hard to sell when you consider that until recently, the Netherlands was already contributing far below the European average to the NATO Alliance and was something of a free rider in the international context.

The conflict in Ukraine acted as a political wake-up call that prompted many member states to start investing in their security again. The Netherlands also decided to start spending 2% of gross domestic product (GDP) on the military. This increase means that military deployability can be brought back up to the required level, taking into account the need to incorporate sustainability improvements.

Political demand

Until recently, hardly any Western military force felt much of a need for sustainability. Individuals and groups did try to develop initiatives, but there was only a trickle of money available from the organisation for the purpose.

Now that the relationship between climate and security is becoming increasingly recognised, that picture is changing. The Netherlands' ambitions, for instance, are fortunately offering a better outlook, as the country aims to become a frontrunner in Europe in terms of combating climate change. A sum of €35 billion has been made available for this for the next 10 years.

In addition, the defence budget is increasing to 2%. These are promising and necessary steps that should enable Defence to make up for a lot of lost ground, not only to get its house in order and contribute proportionately in an international context, but also to prepare the armed forces for the future and make them climate-proof.

This means, however, that the required sustainability objectives need to be integrated in the restoration and renewal of the defence organisation, thus investing in both security and the climate.

Positive developments

Fortunately, the reduction of emissions in particular is beginning to take shape in the Dutch armed forces. The aim is to be 70% less dependent on fossil fuels by 2050 as compared to 2010, and to make camps completely self-sufficient in terms of energy by that year.[5] In effect, this means that all equipment currently being developed and all the defence infrastructure and capabilities that are to be replaced in the coming years must be as emission-free as possible. Defence must also start using alternative, more sustainable fuels.

One important step that can be taken in the short term is to make all real estate more sustainable. The defence organisation wants to concentrate and renovate all real estate, with a greater involvement of ecological values through the use of circular materials and by making defence complexes energy-neutral. For example, by using heat pumps, cladding buildings with (flexible) solar panels, CO_2 storage or using geothermal energy – in other words, sustainable heat from underground that can be used to heat houses, buildings and greenhouses.

There are also interesting collaboration opportunities here with surrounding municipalities that are also becoming more sustainable. For instance, the Dutch defence organisation could make space available at former defence sites for energy conversion and storage as part of a regional energy system in return for something else.

Making the property more sustainable and the way the energy transition takes shape must obviously be in keeping with the use of that energy. For instance, Defence is procuring electric cars for passenger transport and conducting a range of experiments with hydrogen cars, hydrogen-powered tugboats and electric firefighting vehicles.

The same goes for the "flower turbine", a kind of vertical wind turbine without rotating blades that produces clean energy even at low wind speeds (1.2 mtr/s) and from any wind direction. It is only a small contribution to the total energy requirement, but it shows that no opportunity is left unexploited. Wind energy at airports was taboo for a long time, but Woensdrecht airbase in the Netherlands is now home to five such special wind turbines. The blades are perpendicular to the wind and the wind turbine is three metres high, so the structures pose no danger to air traffic.

Also promising is the Fieldlab Smart Base used by the Dutch military as a platform for innovation. Here, Defence is seeking collaboration with technology companies, universities and research institutes to establish a self-sufficient compound that can generate its own energy, produce water and can print 3D parts for vehicles. It sounds futuristic, but the technology is developing rapidly and it offers major operational advantages for the defence sector. Self-sufficient military units thereby gain much greater logistical independence, and a smaller logistical footprint generates significant savings and is good for the environment, making it a highly worthwhile development.

Pace too slow

While these are positive developments, they are only the first hesitant steps. Like in most other Western countries, the Dutch Ministry of Defence is still clearly struggling with the question of how it will achieve the sustainability goals on a large scale. Many see it as an additional cost or worry about the impact on operational deployability. An electric tank simply does not get very far. It is therefore important to harness the potential of new, green technologies in a way that does not compromise operational deployability, as in the earlier example of the Fieldlab Smart Base.

Just going through the motions will not achieve climate targets. At present, the Dutch Ministry of Defence still uses some 55 million litres of kerosene a year for aircraft, 30 million litres of diesel for ships and 22 million litres of diesel for wheeled vehicles and other systems. Moreover, the news that the old diesel generators are being replaced by new ones that should last for another few decades clearly indicates that we are still not on the right track.

The new diesel generators are "fortunately" suitable for biofuel blends, but even so...

In this way, the defence organisation will remain dependent on fossil fuels for years to come, while civilian sectors in the EU are speeding up their transition. For instance, EU targets show that the automotive sector should be at net zero by 2035, trucks should be 90% net zero by 2040 and the maritime sector should complete the energy transition by 2050. Defence must keep up with this acceleration to avoid becoming the West's "Cuba".

Meanwhile, the defence organisation's fuel consumption is only likely to increase. After all, new and modern military equipment tends to be heavier, bigger and faster and thus consumes more fuel; the growth to a 2% defence budget also leads to a greater energy requirement. The four new multipurpose frigates (M-frigates), for example, which the Netherlands is building with Belgium and which are due to be ready in 2027 for anti-submarine warfare, among other things, are powered by fossil fuels. They are much larger than the current M-class frigates: 5,500 tonnes as opposed to 3,300 tonnes.

Even the new F-35 Lightning II, best known as the JSF (Joint Strike Fighter), which Defence plans to use over the next 30 years, uses kerosene and consumes more than the F-16. Although biokerosene for aircraft is a cleaner solution, it cannot be used on a large scale at present, because most NATO military bases are connected to a NATO pipeline system. This does not cater for biodiesel for the time being.

All the more reason to make international agreements and organise things differently. In my opinion, this approach should also apply to the way we deal with surplus equipment. It is usual practice to sell obsolete frigates, aircraft, tanks and other vehicles to other countries; assets have in the past been sold to Chile, Turkey, Jordan and African countries, for example. While it is understandable that some countries benefit from buying second-hand equipment and that we also get something out of it, we should be aware that by selling obsolete and polluting equipment, we are not helping to reduce CO_2 emissions.

Low-hanging fruit

The question facing all Western militaries is, of course, how to address and, if possible, accelerate the transition. What needs to happen to make militaries more self-sufficient and reduce their footprint, while continuing to safeguard their core tasks and ensuring that our military personnel still have everything they need to fight successfully?

Sustainability must not come at the expense of deployability or combat power. That would automatically put us at a disadvantage in a conflict. It is therefore important to shape sustainability in a way that enhances the effectiveness of military units, for instance, by developing future naval ships that, with the help of green technologies, not only reduce emissions, but also have a longer range and can therefore be deployed operationally for longer without having to refuel in port.

A pragmatic approach is to start with the non-operational capabilities for which good, technological, green alternatives are already available: the low-hanging fruit. For example, the first step can be taken relatively easily by making all hopelessly outdated barracks more sustainable and using part of the available space on defence sites for the generation, storage and conversion of clean energy. The ordinary service vehicles used in peacetime for surveillance, supplies and passenger transport can easily be replaced by electric vehicles or by another form of sustainable transport without any operational implications.

This is where Defence can hitch a ride in the energy transition as it takes shape in civil society and the commercial sector, driven by the new government's plans and available budgets. New, clean technologies are becoming increasingly available and can be used without any adverse impact on the way units perform their tasks. Various smaller-scale measures could also be implemented, such as training closer to home wherever and whenever possible. In the case of international exercises, equipment could in principle be transported by train or ship instead of in columns by road. Staff could be given a public transport card instead of a travel allowance if the workplace is easily accessible by public transport. Ships could be made to travel slower en route to an exercise, thus using less fuel, or sailing routes could be planned more smartly, taking more account of favourable winds and/or currents.

Furthermore, there could be a very different approach to mobility. Why move by car when you could use an electric scooter to go from one location to another if it is nearby? You could even question whether you need to move at all. The COVID-19 crisis showed that virtual meetings can be held in many cases, and this can be encouraged by employers. It is also possible to drive, sail and fly with cleaner and more sustainable fuels by adding biofuel blends, as is already common practice in the case of some military vehicles and ships.

Many defence employees very much want the organisation to change and think that it should. As Bas, a captain and the commander of a training platoon at the Royal Military Academy (KMA) says in 2021 in *Stronger!*, the Ministry of Defence's staff magazine. Bas is someone who very much wants to help to making Defence more sustainable, but is infuriated by inflexible business processes. Given that big companies are taking a leading role in making the world a better place, he wonders why the military is lagging behind. The Ministry of Defence only started to address the energy transition last summer, Bas laments in his report. "That really infuriates me. For 75% of young people, sustainability is a key issue, and that's our target group. If you don't connect with them in your communication and recruitment, you exclude three quarters. Change is not super complicated, but it does require courage and nerve. I have two young children, and that makes you think about the kind of world you are leaving behind," he writes.

Other colleagues feel the same way. Like Bas Stegmann, who is head of the Integrated Business Operations Department at Woensdrecht airbase in 2023. He says in staff magazine *Sterker!*: "At Woensdrecht airbase, we saved 500,000 cubic metres of gas in one year. A gigantic amount! Five years ago, I set up a green team to make our airbase more sustainable. We laid roofs full of solar panels, carried out campaigns at barracks: 'turn off your heating when you go home', and we looked, together with the Government Real Estate Agency, at what actually makes up our energy consumption. The settings on some installations turned out to be incorrect, so they were using a lot of gas at night and at weekends, and outdated boilers turned out to be energy guzzlers. Thanks to all kinds of minor adjustments, we were able to make substantial savings."

Bas Stegmann also says: "Now that the low-hanging fruit has been picked, we want to take the next step by installing intermediate meters in the main buildings, so that we know exactly how much gas is being consumed where, allowing us to address issues in a more targeted way. Everyone is enthusiastic, right up to the heads of department. Defence also has a budget for sustainability, but although I have been trying to get money for our plan since February, and we've heard nothing so far. I have filled in a form, sent reminders... We need two hundred grand, which may sound a lot. But when you consider that we've saved two million euros in terms of civil prices, it's nothing. What's more, it is estimated that we will recoup the money within a year".

He's annoyed about that. "What frustrates me is that the urgency we all feel when it comes to sustainability is not being translated into action. The EU target was for households to use at least 15% less gas compared to recent years. Defence has extended that to its own organisation. You should reward departmental initiatives that save a lot of money. Give the money saved back to the unit. By doing that, you're saying: 'Well done, keep it up!'"[6]

Higher-hanging fruit

The second round in sustainability should focus on the fruit that hangs that little bit higher. I am referring to the smaller operational vehicles and systems which are necessary for military deployment, but which can be greened in the short term with existing technology. Examples are small all-terrain vehicles, quads, drones or systems that provide power (generators). This does mean joining forces with companies that have extensive knowledge in this field. It is also important that all that equipment can run on locally generated power or hydrogen wherever possible, for instance by using biogas machines which, in a major international mission, can turn all fruit and vegetable waste at the camps into biogas and use it to generate electricity and to heat buildings. Not all military equipment is deployed globally and depends on the supply or local generation of renewable energy in mission areas for greening. Vehicles, ships and aircraft deployed on and around permanent defence complexes, such as tugs, forklifts and training aircraft, can be greened relatively easily and will then serve as an example of and driver for the greening of other military equipment.

Furthermore, an organisation such as Defence can impose sustainability requirements on the equipment it buys on the civil market. It should, therefore, be a condition of purchase that items such as office supplies or parts for ships, vehicles and aircraft are produced sustainably and/or are circular wherever possible.

Among the higher-hanging fruit are more sophisticated simulators, so that fewer ships, vehicles or aircraft are needed for training and practice. Thanks to rapidly advancing technology, simulators are improving all the time and are highly realistic. You can also link different simulators together to create an even more lifelike setting. For instance, personnel can simulate shooting exercises in complex environments with a virtual enemy, but they can also practise what to do if an aircraft engine fails or carry out complex missions with multiple aircraft against a variety of ground and air threats.

In addition, simulators and virtual reality allow military personnel to create conditions that do not exist in real life: a night movement at sea in an autumn storm in the middle of summer, for example. Simulation also allows instructors to closely monitor exactly what happens when weapons are used in manoeuvres by different units in the field or in virtual combat training in urbanised areas. This allows everyone to look back afterwards and discuss what went well and what went wrong, thus making the evaluation more valuable.

There are numerous advantages when it comes to simulation. Commanders should therefore – ideally in association with the commercial sector – look at other potential uses of simulation in training and exercises, focusing specifically at what can be done, rather than pointing out what cannot.

Highest-hanging fruit

Then there is the fruit that is most difficult to reach: the aircraft, ships and heavier vehicles that need to be deployable anywhere in the world and for which no good alternative, clean or sustainable technologies or energy supply lines are yet available. To make this happen, the Ministry of Defence needs to team up with knowledge institutes and defence firms and focus fully on developing the next generation of aircraft, ships, heavy vehicles and energy systems without harmful emissions.

For example, the Dutch armed forces now face the task of replacing all the navy's support vessels, as they are technically and operationally obsolete. The least sustainable and now probably the cheapest and fastest option is to replace them with modern ships that still run on fossil fuels or, better still, on biofuel blends. Ideally, the first step is to look at how to achieve the desired effect and then work out what resources are needed. So rather than start from a new ship, look at what is needed to achieve the same goal. That is obviously something for the longer term, but the requirement for the purchase of zero-emission ships could be set now and then developed accordingly in association with the industry and knowledge institutes.

However, this also means that armed forces cannot buy 'off the shelf', but that they join forces with the business sector and research institutes as early as the development phase to initiate and implement new concepts for ships, aircraft and vehicles that are more self-sufficient in terms of energy. This should be possible, as industry is leading the way in many areas when it comes to sustainability.

This represents an ideal opportunity to work with companies and knowledge institutes to develop a modern naval ship or land vehicle that is more self-sufficient and cleaner, without compromising on operational effectiveness. Moreover, this approach also offers economic opportunities. For example, if a maritime country like the Netherlands can develop a new naval ship powered by clean energy and has a long range, it will open up opportunities for the shipping industry as a whole. The maritime industry can thus become a forerunner in the field of alternatively propelled vessels. The Maritime Master Plan, for example, is one such partnership for energy transition in the maritime sector in which the Dutch Ministry of Defence is also participating with the development of zero-emission support ships.[7]

To make that happen, however, upfront investment is needed for innovation, even before the ships go into production. The European Defence Fund (EDF) offers opportunities for this. Through this fund, the European Commission provides billions of euros for the development of future military capabilities, as long as countries also contribute to this themselves and collaborate in a European context. The Dutch national climate fund also provides opportunities for funding sustainability, for example in the case of Ministry of Defence real estate.

In the collaboration to modernise and make the military more sustainable, armed forces can provide a platform for renewal and innovation. There are many existing examples of technologies that have been developed in the defence sector and subsequently found their way to consumers, for example the zip fastener or the microwave oven, or jet engines for aircraft, or GPS systems. Who knows what else we can discover and develop together?

This does mean that the military needs to clarify at an early stage what requirements future defence equipment has to meet so that innovation can be focused accordingly. These requirements are not only operational, but also relate to sustainability, self-sufficiency and circularity. A period of 20 years or so could easily elapse between the development and commissioning of complex weapon systems, and the idea is that they will then be used for many decades. In order to be independent of fossil fuels by 2050, therefore, most equipment will have to meet different requirements by then, and that will only be possible if those requirements are included in the needs assessment for that equipment now. This is driving industry to develop concepts that meet these requirements.

A role for the EU

Companies will therefore need to shift the focus of their research and development to sustainable weapon systems and invest accordingly. So far, the EU does not appear to be heading in this direction. The Green Deal by former EU commissioner Frans Timmermans does offer a comprehensive package of EU proposals to adapt all sectors of the economy to make Europe the first climate-neutral continent in the world by 2050, and it contains a variety of measures on sustainable transport, a clean and efficient energy system, green housing for all and nature conservation. But the translation to the defence sector has not yet been made, even though it is such a major polluter.

Meanwhile, the EU has set up the aforementioned European Defence Fund to increase the combined clout of European defence industries in the research and development of future military capabilities. Little by little, sustainability goals are starting to trickle through into the programmes here too, but companies should only claim money from the fund if the weapon systems they are developing actually meet the sustainability requirements.

The European Commission should therefore look more closely at how the various European investment programmes, such as the Green Deal and EDF, can complement each other. Sustainability requirements could, for example, be imposed on the plans submitted by companies. In this way, defence projects from the EDF can contribute to the common climate goals and, in reverse, investments from climate programmes can help to make the defence sector more sustainable, thus ensuring greater synergy and coherence in European efforts.

Attracting inspired individuals

Finally, military forces should also develop their own knowledge and identify inspired and qualified people within their own organisation who are willing and able to make a difference. People like Ronald and Bas represent a growing group of young leaders with clear ideas on how Defence can become more sustainable. Use this enthusiasm and give them space to make a difference on this issue. Create testing grounds within units and let them collaborate with knowledge institutes and companies to develop and test new innovations to drive sustainability. That has great appeal to many people and, more importantly, it creates opportunities to speed up the necessary sustainability and makes the organisation more attractive to new personnel. After all, many young people want to contribute directly to issues like these.

In short, there are numerous opportunities to get rid of the military's expensive, fragile and polluting logistic footprint. It is important, however, that the military does not perceive this as an extra obligation that comes at the expense of their effectiveness, but rather as an opportunity to use green technology to both reduce emissions and increase combat power.

It is obviously not the primary mission of a military force to combat climate change, but it should not be actively contributing to the destruction of our planet, our only spacecraft. Solidarity is part and parcel of Defence and that, by definition, also extends to future generations.

Notes

1. Ronald left the Dutch Armed Forces in mid-2023 to join the NGO Justdiggit. This organisation is engaged in connecting and mobilising people worldwide to bring back nature.

2. Watson Institute (2019), "Fuel use, climate change, and the costs of war". Watson Institute, Brown University

3. Conflict and Environment Observatory (2021). "The EU military sector's carbon footprint", CEOBS, Mytholmroyd, see https://ceobs.org/the-eu-military-sectors-carbon-footprint/

4. International Military Council on Climate and Security (2021), The World Climate and Security Report 2021. IMCCS

5. Letter from State Secretary of Defence to Parliament, Stronger Netherlands, Safer Europe, Sustainability Implementation Agenda, 36124-25, 31 Jan 2023

6. *Stronger!*, July 2023, Ministry of Defence staff magazine.

7. https://maritiemmasterplan.nl/

Chapter Sixteen
Towards clean energy

"When we are no longer able to change a situation, we are challenged to change ourselves."

Viktor Frankl, Austrian neurologist and psychiatrist

For me, it is clear that developing technology in relation to the energy transition is the key to taking significant steps towards becoming climate neutral. That requires more than the modernisation of existing infrastructure and equipment; it requires entirely new approaches and new innovative concepts. For example, suppose you could use a modular energy system locally, where you could choose between different forms of clean energy generation, with all excess energy in peak hours being buffered in batteries or converted into hydrogen, which is easier to store, so that the energy could be used again in off-peak hours? That would indeed be an important option for Defence to become more self-sufficient at its sites in the Netherlands and – where possible – also when deployed in mission areas. However, that would require an entirely different energy supply concept and entirely new forms of collaboration between industry, local authorities and Defence. But where do you start?

A former Defence colleague, who now helps financial institutions become more sustainable, knows that I am looking for ways to make the military sector more sustainable. He puts me in touch with climate entrepreneur Robert Colijn, who "knows better than anyone else how to make a difference in the energy transition". He should have a good vision on "cash flows and sustainable energy" and be the right person to help me further. A little while later, we have a meeting and I realise that Robert could indeed be extremely helpful with his knowledge, although we are not quite each other's type at first. Robert, a conscientious objector from the Cold War era, and in his own words someone with a "moralistic streak", is a mechanical engineer who went on to study environmental sciences. After a job with the province of Overijssel, he started as an independent entrepreneur to make a greater contribution towards renewable energy sources. Now he tries to bring companies, residents and governments along with him in his plans and ideas, inspiring them to participate and take action.

Technology, energy and autonomy

Visiting Robert, I notice that he has a talent for visualising complicated issues and processes. As the energy transition is a complex issue, this is a valuable skill. Robert shows a picture that highlights how the availability of energy and technology are related to a society's place in the hierarchy of needs in Maslow's pyramid. He also talks about how living things are in fact "living technology" powered by solar energy. Indeed, he believes that the nourishment of all life comes indirectly from solar energy.

Robert explains that our ability to manufacture tools and thus tap into energy sources allows us to make energy work for us. "This allows us to create the path of least resistance for ourselves." Technology and energy thus help us climb Maslow's pyramid, starting at the bottom with physical basic needs, such as shelter, water and food, followed by safety and security, to self-actualisation at the top of the pyramid. The latter means being able to see yourself as part of the bigger picture of this planet. "So that you can help other people move forward", Robert explains about Maslow's theory of motivation.

People facing the extreme impacts of climate change, he argues, end up at the bottom of the pyramid. "Because they are affected by the often disastrous effects of floods, hurricanes or severe drought. As a result, harvests fail, farmland is destroyed or people have no access to clean drinking water."

He too recognises that this is a direct source of conflict. "But if you manage to unlock energy through technology locally in such a way that it becomes accessible to everyone, people are then able to improve their own situation. By working together, they can look after themselves better in emergency situations and thus end up higher on the pyramid. So it is the combination of technology and energy that gives people autonomy", Robert concludes.

Self-sufficient military camps

Robert appears very enthusiastic and keeps talking, also clearly managing to place the energy transition in a broader context and naming new connections within it. For instance, he gives the example of a military camp that would ideally be completely self-sufficient through solar and wind energy, as well as soil energy. "If you know you will be settling down somewhere for a military mission lasting a few years, you might consider using geothermal energy and drilling a small hole a few kilometres into the earth. It's about 100 degrees there and then you can use the production of steam *via* a turbine and a generator to make electricity and thus hydrogen. And when the mission ends, you can leave the power supply technology behind for the local population." A military camp, as well as a base or barracks, is really nothing more than an extended version of a housing estate or industrial estate, he explains. He looks at me questioningly, to see if I am still following him. Then he says: "It's all about the mindset, do you see?"

Robert keeps insisting that we should harvest energy locally and invest our money in that rather than the fossil-fuel industry. That way, we can keep those cash flows local and regional and contribute positively to the regional economy and energy autonomy. "By doing so, you avoid dependence and therefore potential tensions or conflicts", he says. "Look at the dependence on Russian gas, for example. If you organise it differently, you create a very different situation."

Robert now raises his arms in the air and shouts enthusiastically: "Tell people and businesses, 'Look, we're going to build our own energy supply here in the province or municipality, which will make us all self-sufficient, we'll spend less money on energy bills and no longer depend on fossil fuels or the associated industrial energy giants or dubious regimes in other countries.' In my experience, this is when they get really excited and start looking at local energy generation options through different eyes. The social component of the energy transition, community involvement and empowerment, is often forgotten. So this is about the importance and necessity of bottom-up cooperation, not based on a hierarchy, but on equality among public and private partners. And we also need to step up the pace: for my daughter, for your children, for all generations to come."

WeSustain

After his presentation, we quickly get onto the subject of how to pool our knowledge and experience. It is clear that Robert has the knowledge and I have the network. So we decide, together with my former colleague from Defence, to first develop a concept we call "WeSustain" for application in the Netherlands. Here, we consider an area, such as a village, city or region, a residential area or a business park, as a local power plant. After all, every citizen and every entrepreneur will soon not only be a consumer but also a producer of energy. This creates local networks of buyers and producers in which everyone is a kind of shareholder. The more energy you put in, the more you get in return. Energy is also becoming increasingly exchangeable; from electricity to hydrogen and vice versa, with reuse of the released heat and oxygen. These are all benefits which make communities more independent and which could be of interest to Defence in more ways than one.

The trick is to develop a coherent and modular concept that can flexibly accommodate the peaks and troughs in local energy supply, but also respond to new innovations. Experiments are already being conducted in many locations at home and abroad, but it is still proving difficult to make this kind of innovative cooperation concept really work and to scale it up.

Zwolle

Again, as I often say: "Think big, act small, start somewhere." We began with that "start small" in Zwolle, a town of 130,000 inhabitants in the north-east of the Netherlands. We started building electrolysers that use solar and wind energy to produce hydrogen, oxygen and heat. The last two turned out to be very useful for local sewage treatment, which is a great way to create a local cycle. But above all, this also provides an alternative sales route for sustainable energy and, on the other hand, an opportunity to store that energy in the form of hydrogen. This creates more space in the area for wind and solar energy projects and prevents overloading of existing energy networks.

Meanwhile, the Netherlands has been experiencing two types of congestion in its power grid. First of all the networks can't keep up with the developing peaks in the energy demand. That demand is increasing rapidly as businesses and households become more sustainable. At the same time, more and more energy is being produced at the local level through all kinds of energy projects. The networks find it hard to deal with that local production because they are set up for the top-down distribution of energy that we generate or import centrally, and like the veins in a leaf, become more and more finely meshed towards the user. However, as more and more energy is produced at the user end and there is a surplus of energy during peak hours when there is plenty of sun and wind, those grids get overloaded quickly and individuals and businesses cannot dispose of the power they have generated. This problem is occurring with increasing frequency and in more and more places in the Netherlands.

An expensive – multi-billion-dollar – solution is to beef up all power grids to handle those peaks and dispose of the surplus power during those peak times. The problem is that you are building an expensive six-lane highway that you only use to a limited extent. The alternative we are looking at with WeSustain is an integrated solution in which we do not dispose of surplus power, but store it in batteries or convert it into hydrogen, for example.

The hydrogen produced can be stored, marketed and distributed locally, *via* a pipeline to a hydrogen filling point and *via* buffer containers to local entrepreneurs who are switching to hydrogen-electric powered vehicles and tools. If necessary, the hydrogen can be converted back into electricity. The oxygen and heat released in the production of hydrogen help to substantially lower electricity consumption for the sewage treatment plant. And after the next treatment stage, the cycle is complete and the water can be used again to produce hydrogen, oxygen and heat. In this way, all green energy stays within the region and does not have to be transported *via* the overloaded energy networks. In principle, this solution could be applied anywhere and tailored to local needs.

The project in Zwolle is still in its infancy, but is a great opportunity for the region. It is developing rapidly, with more than 60 companies creating their own energy cooperation in close association with local and regional authorities, with the energy supplier and other regional initiatives. The more energy we generate and use locally, the less money will be swallowed up by the multinationals *via* energy bills. For the residents and businesses of a city like Zwolle, this quickly adds up to several hundred million euros a year, which is then preserved for the local economy and helps it become more resilient.

The project shows that energy transition is not only a technical task, but also an economic and collaborative one. New, decentralised forms of collaboration are emerging between local authorities, companies and residents. The collaboration benefits everyone. In effect, a local ecosystem is emerging that is increasingly self-sufficient in terms of its own energy needs. And the great thing is that all investments in that energy system also benefit the regional economy.

Meanwhile, the provinces of Overijssel and Gelderland have joined forces in OostNL, the East Netherlands Development Agency, with the aim of becoming a pioneering region in the development of these Smart Energy Hubs.

Hydrogen as an alternative

Hydrogen is, of course, not new and is already being used in many places. It has huge potential that we are so far only exploiting to a limited extent. The technology is there, but its application is still very much under development. Until now, we had enough gas and electricity, and hydrogen was not an attractive alternative. Hydrogen is made *via* electrolysis, and this can also be CO_2-neutral, making use of wind or solar energy. This green hydrogen can then be converted back into electricity *via* a fuel cell. Hydrogen can also be used to fuel larger power sources, making it increasingly attractive for trucks and other heavier vehicles, or typically the range in which Defence equipment operates.

Hydrogen can also be used as an alternative to natural gas, all without CO_2 emissions. The only residual product is water. The heat generated in the conversion process to hydrogen and back to electricity can be put to good use by making smart location choices, just like the oxygen that is released. The hydrogen gas can be transported through our gas pipelines and stored and used when needed. With the Netherlands' long and extensive experience with natural gas, we can take a further leap by exploiting it for hydrogen applications.

By using hydrogen as an emission-free fuel for vehicles, we can again contribute to improving air quality to solve the nitrogen issue in the Netherlands. This is extremely important, as the nitrogen problem is causing stagnation in many areas, such as housing construction and numerous infrastructure works. Finally, hydrogen is also a good solution for businesses. Local hydrogen chains and hubs like the project in Zwolle can grow into a larger network. It has huge potential, therefore, and represents one of the few possibilities for storing energy locally, thus enabling the closure of local cycles and chains.

Opportunities for the Ministry of Defence

Local concepts, such as WeSustain, also present interesting opportunities for Defence. They enable the organisation to drastically reduce its energy-dependency and the environmental and logistic footprint of deployed military units. The aforementioned Defence's Fieldlab Smart Base – an outcome of the 2017 Future Force Conference – is exploring those possibilities, providing scope for technology companies, universities and research centres to trial new technologies with the overarching goal of achieving camps that are self-sufficient in their energy, water and perhaps even food supply. The experiences gained are of course broadly useful for applications in civil society. A win-win situation, with Defence as a platform for renewal and innovation.

Special opportunities for cooperation between the Defence organisation and municipalities are also arising in the Netherlands. For example, for real estate at various sites, organisation can fully connect to the energy transition that takes shape all over the Netherlands. Ministry of Defence airbases, barracks and ports are located in various Dutch municipalities, where lack of space is often a problem. The organisation could offer co-use of its sites for the regional generation, conversion and/or storage of energy.

Defence sites are spacious, secure and also have broader licensing options. This means the organisation has something to offer, for which it can expect something in return. This creates some interesting "business cases" at local level that can help both the Defence organisation and municipalities meet local sustainability goals. These are just a few ideas, but it is clear that there is already a range of possible courses of action. We need to get started, and we can do so now.

Working together on discovery and development

Although the subject matter is complex, the gist is in fact simple. We all face the enormous challenge of transforming our energy system from centralised to decentralised generation and use, and from separate supply systems for power, gas and heat to an integrated system in which power, hydrogen and heat are interchangeable. There also needs to be a shift towards a system in which all private individuals and businesses are not only consumers of energy, but are themselves producers. Energy technology, collaboration and regional economy come together in this system.

The WeSustain concept is just one example of how we as a society can look for new strategies to reduce our CO_2 emissions and our energy dependence. After all, the current energy supply is no longer sustainable in many respects. Climate change and its effects are forcing us to change, as is our dependence on Russian gas and Middle Eastern oil. The price explosions in autumn 2021 and following Russia's invasion of Ukraine are a bad omen. Whichever way you look at it, it is an undesirable situation that could lead to tension and conflict. Reducing energy dependence in any way, whether civil or military, is therefore a smart strategic choice in many respects.

The need for an interim solution

The World Energy Outlook 2023, published by the International Energy Agency, shows how investment in clean energy has risen by 40% since 2020, not just to bring down emissions but also to improve energy security. According to this report, the share of coal, oil and natural gas in global energy supply – stuck for decades at around 80% – is starting to edge downwards and will reach 73% by 2030. This is an important shift, but nowhere near enough to reach global climate goals. There is a strong push to further accelerate the deployment of renewables.

At the same time we need to be realistic in our expectations; it takes time to replace a fossil fuel system that has been developed and optimised over more than a century, especially when taking into account the huge global population increase, particularly in Africa, Asia, and other BRICS nations. These regions are witnessing rapid urbanization and development, which is inevitably leading to an escalating energy demand. However, many of these nations have fragile economies, making it imperative to find a balanced mix of energy sources that can cater to their growing needs without causing economic upheavals.

We also need to take into account that the production of renewable technologies is not without its challenges. We are currently witnessing constraints in the manufacturing of renewables due to the scarcity of essential raw materials. China's dominant position in the supply chains for these materials further complicates the scenario. Their near-monopoly can lead to potential disruptions in production chains, which in turn can impact the scalability and affordability of renewable technologies on a global scale.

All of this affects the speed of the energy transition. Scenarios show that it will probably take 30 to 50 years, during which period fossil fuels will still be needed to sustain our economies unless we can complement the energy transition with other, interim solutions that provide cleaner alternatives to the current coal and gas power plants.

Nuclear energy

In the inevitable energy transition, we have to consider all options. In parallel with the deployment of cleaner solutions, therefore, we should be looking at nuclear energy as an interim solution, as it can be used to generate energy without CO_2 emissions. In fact, according to proponents of nuclear power, such as ex-NASA chief and prominent climate scientist James Hansen (one of the first scientists who warned about climate change and managed to put nuclear power on the political agenda in the US), nuclear power is the next logical step in our energy supply. Hansen states in an interview with the Volkskrant: "We started with wood to stoke fires. Then we found coal: it was so condensed that you needed much less of it to get much more energy. Then came petroleum and then natural gas: each time a step further, each time with lower CO_2 emissions. And then came the much cleaner nuclear energy with even higher energy density: a ping-pong-ball-sized amount of uranium is enough to meet all energy needs of an average American lifestyle for a hundred years. And we Americans are not nearly as frugal or smart as you are in Europe! Meanwhile, there is more than enough uranium in the earth, and otherwise there is thorium, a ubiquitous resource that can also be used if we further develop nuclear power plants."[1]

Fukushima

It seems a valid argument from Hansen, were it not for the fact that many people still feel enormous resistance because of the fear of nuclear disasters and radiation. "Don't forget Fukushima", cries one person. "Remember Chernobyl", says another. On the one hand, this reaction is understandable. On the other, we have to realise that we are comparing apples to oranges if we let disasters like Chernobyl and Fukushima be the yardstick for judging nuclear power.

Take Fukushima. The 2011 earthquake off the coast of Japan caused a 14-metre-high tsunami, was the fifth strongest earthquake ever measured (9.0 on the Richter scale) and claimed the lives of nearly 19,000 people.[2] What we remember, however, is the story of Fukushima's ageing nuclear power plant going into meltdown due to the tsunami and a hydrogen explosion. It was terrifying, of course, and hugely disruptive to the lives of many in the region. But the extraordinary thing is that 19,000 people in Japan were killed by the quake, and one single person – most likely – by radiation from the nuclear reactor. Someone who was tasked with measuring the radiation after the explosion and subsequently died of lung cancer.[3]

Two years later, in 2013, a UN commission (UNSCEAR) reported that no adverse health effects had been identified as a result of radiation exposure following the Fukushima nuclear disaster.[4] Not among the workers, nor in the rest of the population. UN experts also consider it unlikely that there will be any in the future. So Fukushima should not actually be an argument against nuclear power, but rather for it.

But it is not usually seen that way. Sentiment is downright negative. Since the Fukushima disaster, for instance, Germany has chosen to get rid of nuclear power altogether – in a country that is not even in an earthquake zone, let alone one as violent as Japan's. Professor Rob de Meijer, a nuclear geophysicist in Cape Town and Groningen, calculated, for instance, that 17,500 nuclear bombs would have to explode to match the energy of the earthquake in Japan.[5] A slim chance, therefore, that this would happen again. However, the consequence of the disaster itself is that while Germany is among the international forerunners when it comes to using renewable energy, in the meantime it is emitting more CO_2 than before. This is because Germany simply cannot generate enough solar and wind power to meet the country's energy needs, and so falls back on power plants running on natural gas, coal and even lignite. And the latter is really the biggest polluter of all. As a result, Germany, a country that was initially reasonably well on its way to reducing greenhouse gas emissions, is now set to fail to meet the goals of the Paris Climate Agreement.[6]

Chernobyl

And then, of course, there is that other disaster involving an ageing nuclear power plant, the biggest disaster ever: Chernobyl. In northern Ukraine, not far from the border with Belarus, a reactor in a nuclear power plant exploded in the middle of the night on 26 April 1986. Investigating the disaster, UNSCEAR concluded that 134 people had been exposed to so much radiation in this disaster that they were suffering from radiation sickness. Twenty-eight people died instantly, and more than six thousand cases of thyroid cancer in children were diagnosed; a result of contaminated milk.[7]

The consequences are incredibly sad, especially as children were also affected. It is also true, however, that 7 million people now die every year as a direct result of air pollution.[8] Ten thousand people also die every day from pollution caused by fossil fuels.[9] That too is incredibly sad.

Radioactive waste

So we are probably not afraid of nuclear power because of the numbers, as Dutch programme maker Arjen Lubach aptly put it in his 2018 programme, but because of the feeling. "Oil and coal, we get that. It's dirty, but you can understand it", Lubach said. "Nuclear power and radiation we don't. That's scary." And what sounds even scarier, the programme maker said, 'is nuclear waste, as that can remain active for 100,000 years."[10] In his programme, Lubach shows where we in the Netherlands store our highly radioactive waste, namely in a huge container located next to the nuclear power plant in Borssele, the only one we still have. A container that can withstand earthquakes, floods, hurricanes, aircraft impacts and gas explosions. A woman appears on screen holding an apple and saying that if you use nuclear power for a lifetime, you will be left with about an apple-sized amount of nuclear waste. That does not seem very much. Yet many people find storing nuclear waste a frightening thought, because it remains active for 100,000 years.

However, if you dig a little deeper, you will discover that various countries have already investigated suitable locations for geological disposal of nuclear energy. The Finns and Swedes, for instance, are already far advanced: they want to store waste in granite rocks.[11] And in the Netherlands, 225-metre-deep clay layers in the Kempen region of Brabant are being considered.[12] That sounds like a pretty safe solution. Also, current nuclear reactors in the Netherlands and surrounding countries are much better and safer than those in Chernobyl and Fukushima, and the safety culture at and around nuclear plants is extremely high. At the slightest alarm, nuclear reactors are shut down immediately, which is one reason why there has never been a fatal accident at any of our nuclear power plants.

It also shows that reactors of fourth-generation nuclear power plants (the latest version) produce less long-term radioactive waste. They are considered safer because the new plants use new coolants, such as sodium, lead, helium or molten salt. So what exactly is the argument "against" storing nuclear waste? That you don't know who will be using it in two hundred or a thousand years? Then would you really prefer those coal-fired power plants that are now spewing mercury, sulphur and particulates into the air? Those CO_2 emissions and nitrogen oxides from gas power plants? The air that we breathe causing hundreds of thousands of deaths as people get cancer and lung problems? In fact, shouldn't we all be scratching our heads when NASA states that if we were using nuclear power now instead of all those fossil fuels, we could have prevented nearly 2 million people from dying?[13]

And yes, of course there is that – very important – argument that the risk of proliferation of nuclear weapons increases as a result of using nuclear power. But it is still the case that the vast majority of countries that produce nuclear energy do not themselves have the technology to produce weapons. Besides, the UN's International Atomic Energy Agency (IAEA) also maintains global oversight when it comes to all activities relating to nuclear energy.

This is not to say that knowledge about nuclear technology cannot fall into the wrong hands. After all, that has happened before with Pakistan's nuclear weapons. But that argument could apply to other areas too, argues Behnam Taebi in a 2019 interview. Taebi is an associate professor of philosophy of technology at Delft University of Technology and is considered a co-founder of the research field on the ethics of nuclear energy. He wonders in that interview whether we should then also stop biotechnology, "because that knowledge could be used to make biological weapons". Besides, he adds, "a country that is determined to produce nuclear weapons does not even have to go down the path of nuclear energy. Nuclear energy and nuclear weapons are two different things that you have to see separately."[14]

When the interviewer then inquires about the risk of an attack on a nuclear power plant, and the possibility of terrorists gaining access to a reactor or using radioactive waste to make a "dirty bomb", the engineer philosopher replies: "You can make a dirty bomb more easily with radioactive hospital waste than with highly radioactive nuclear waste. A nuclear power plant – however well guarded – is dangerous because of the high radiation sources, for example the spent fuel rods that in many reactors are immersed in large baths to cool down. But you can't just steal a super-hot fuel rod."[15]

So the only problem we are left with, in my view, is the time it takes to build a nuclear reactor and the financing. For instance, a global survey shows that building a new nuclear reactor can easily take up to 10 years due to stringent safety requirements and other factors. In France, China, the US and Russia: it is slow everywhere. And, of course, it costs a great deal of money. Already, according to the energy research centre ECN, the latest nuclear power plants cost around €3 billion per 1,600 megawatts.[16] The lifespan of a power plant is, however, considerably longer than that of wind farms, the current scalability and environmental impact of which are still being addressed.

Ideally sustainable, but how?

The fact remains, of course, that ideally we would much rather combat climate change through the generation of renewable energy. The good news is that the energy transition is picking up speed. We are also witnessing a high innovation rate in the development of new technologies to produce, store, convert, distribute and use clean energies. The advantages are enormous. They not only reduce emissions, but they also run on free wind, solar and geothermal energy, and they can help countries to lower the energy bill and improve energy security. But it will take time before renewable energy is able to power a country, which is one of the reasons why, as I said earlier, Germany is now switching back to fossil fuels. Precious time, during which we also remain dependent on fossil fuels.

All this explains why many scientists have been convinced of the usefulness of nuclear power for years now. For example, the aforementioned scientist James Hansen, together with Ken Caldeira (atmospheric scientist working in the Global Ecology Department of the Carnegie Institute for Science), Kerry Emanuel (professor of meteorology) and Tom Wigley (climate scientist) wrote an open letter in 2013 in which they sought to open up the debate in the US on nuclear power. The letter stated that "innovative energy sources such as wind, solar and biomass certainly have a role to play in a future energy economy, but those energy sources do not provide the cheap and reliable power required by the global economy fast enough". The scientists therefore called on everyone to "demonstrate real concern about climate change and damage, by calling for the development and implementation of advanced nuclear power".[17] A voice we are now hearing much more often.

And then there is the scientist James Lovelock, now over 100 years old (born 1919), a chemist, environmentalist and inventor. Long considered the icon of the environmental movement, he was showered with scientific awards for many years. For instance, it was Lovelock who established the presence of atoms and molecules in the air, which suddenly made it possible to show very low concentrations of gases in the atmosphere. In his most recent book *Novacene: The Coming Age of Hyperintelligence*, he states: "We may be the only source of high intelligence in the cosmos, but avoiding nuclear power generation is tantamount to autogenocide. Nothing shows the limits of our intelligence more clearly."[18]

Time for action

Putting all the facts together, I reach the conclusion that nuclear power is a necessary additional part of the solution that could replace fossil fuel use on a large scale. That conclusion seems to be gaining ground. Worldwide, nuclear energy is on the rise. Indeed, there are many applications outside electricity production for which nuclear energy can be used. For instance, seawater desalination, hydrogen production, district heating and process heating for industry (glass and cement production, metal production), refining and the production of synthesis gas.

Unsurprisingly, numerous countries such as China, Russia, Poland, the UK, Finland and many others are starting to use nuclear power or expanding their capacity.[19] The new government in the Netherlands wants to build two large nuclear power plants and keep the existing Borssele plant open.[20] This is because life extension of existing nuclear power plants is a very cost-efficient and emission-free "construction method".[21]

The US and Canada are also on the brink of a revival. Besides maintaining and increasing the energy yields of existing power plants for longer through technological developments, they are also looking at mini-reactors and nuclear batteries.[22] Because of their relatively small size, they can be built in a ready-made module form in a factory and linked together on site as well as to the electricity grid and heating network. Production lines are thus standardised and products can be manufactured internationally and under licence in a short time, as in the case of parts for the aircraft industry. Construction quality, safety and efficiency are guaranteed and production costs are lower than is currently the case for construction of nuclear power plants.

This development is certainly as interesting for the security sector as it is for the energy transition in civil society. Not only because nuclear energy takes up relatively little space, but also because it reduces dependence on other countries.

The Pentagon, the US Department of Defense, is therefore also investigating how nuclear energy could be applied to the deployment of military units in the field. Consider, for example, small modular reactors (SMRs), instead of long rows of polluting diesel generators that require a continuous supply of fuel, with all the risks that involves.

Such facilities can operate remotely to meet a local shortage of nuclear expertise without compromising nuclear safeguards. The small footprint (just four shipping containers for a military base) and energy reliability of a small nuclear reactor or mobile nuclear battery are definite advantages, and those who can make such modifications can also make large military sites, such as national air bases, barracks complexes, seaports like Den Helder and large military camps in deployment areas safer and less dependent on energy sources that accelerate climate change.

Small nuclear reactors such as these can thus serve both as energy sources for on-site heat and power production and as local energy sources for synthetic fuel production, which is a sustainable alternative when carbon emissions are difficult to avoid, as in specific applications such as military aviation, while jumpstarting civil synfuel production. They can also be used for hydrogen production, radar/communications/data centres and drinking water production, including desalination. These newer generations of nuclear power plants use air cooling.

Large ships can also be provided with clean and safe propulsion using nuclear power as the energy source in this way. Applications of uranium-fission-based nuclear power plants have been in use for decades. A future alternative to this would be nuclear power plants based on the omnipresent thorium, molten salt reactors (MSRs),[23] where, in addition to thorium, stored long-life uranium-fission products serve as fuel.

All these developments are highly relevant for a country like the Netherlands, where the application of these mobile and static variants of nuclear power sources for barracks and platforms is thus improving all the time, partly because of the perfect match between increasing military electrification in transport and heating, lack of space and the energy density of nuclear power.

The nuclear energy sources being researched by the US could just be the solution for the future energy supply of many countries and their military units, given that they are small, safe, cost-efficient, proliferation-proof, energy diverse, reliable, mobile and CO_2-neutral.

In the ongoing debate in many countries on the subject of energy sources, there is a heated political divide between proponents of nuclear energy and advocates for renewables and the central issue we should address is the opposition between the two. The truth is, these two options do not necessarily represent an either/or choice, but rather they could work in tandem to address our energy needs and combat climate change. Rather than pitting them against each other, we should view them as allies in our battle against common enemies like oil, coal, and fossil gas. To replace fossil fuels entirely, we must recognize that both renewables and nuclear energy are essential components of the solution. They are two sides of the same fossil-free coin. Our electricity production needs to be multiplied on a massive scale and it is impossible for a single source to address the issue. In the short term, it is essential to invest in both renewables and nuclear energy, as neither one in isolation possesses the necessary capacity to meet our energy demands. The effect of the continuing standoff between the two camps is to place a stranglehold on further investment in any of the technologies, which, in view of the increasing urgency of the climate crisis, is the worst possible situation. It is time to set aside the divisive debate and find a balance between the two types of energy source to ensure that we have a sustainable and reliable source of power for future generations.

It is clear that a significant shift in our energy profile is required to make a real impact on reducing greenhouse gas emissions. The reality is that not only do we need both research and development in new forms of energy, but we also need a more conservative approach to energy consumption. The goal should be to avoid relying on coal at all costs.

In conclusion, while the allure of a world powered entirely by renewables is undeniably compelling, the road to achieving this vision is riddled with complexities. Incorporating nuclear energy, at least in the transitional phase, seems not just practical, but essential to meeting our global energy demands while ensuring environmental sustainability.

Notes

1. "He was one of the first to warn about climate change and now he is embracing nuclear power", 18 Nov 2017, *de Volkskrant*

2. McCurry, J. (2021, 11 March), "Japan marks 10 years since triple disaster killed 18,500 people", *The Guardian*, see https://www.theguardian.com/world/2021/mar/11/japan-marks-ten-years-since-triple-disaster-killed-18500-people

3. BBC News (2018, 5 September), Japan confirms first Fukushima worker death from radiation. *BBC News*, see https://www.bbc.com/news/world-asia-45423575

4. UNSCEAR (2013), Sources, effects and risks of ionising radiation. UNSCEAR, Vienna, see report http://www.unscear.org/unscear/en/about_us.html

5. Gelt Dekker, J. (2011, 16 March), "Nuclear power: yes please!", *Follow the Money*, see https://www.ftm.nl/artikelen/kernenergie-ja-graag?share=xBwMWMhNqtbbs%2BjApdm1Qe7Vucn5T1sYRnia8q9lr3%2FhP2KPrl94c6ZeenT5

6. Oltermann, P. (2021, 22 July), "Merkel: Germany has not done enough to hit Paris climate targets", *The Guardian*, see https://www.theguardian.com/world/2021/jul/22/merkel-germany-not-done-enough-hit-paris-climate-target

7. UNSCEAR (2021, 6 April). "The Chernobyl accident", https://www.unscear.org/unscear/en/chernobyl.html, accessed 9 December 2021

8. World Health Organization (2021, 22 September). New WHO global air quality guidelines aim to save millions of lives from air pollution. *WHO press release*. https://www.who.int/news/item/22-09-2021-new-who-global-air-quality-guidelines-aim-to-save-millions-of-lives-from-air-pollution

9. Pielke, R. (2020, 10 March). "Every day 10,000 people die due to air pollution from fossil fuels", *Forbes*, see https://www.forbes.com/sites/rogerpielke/2020/03/10/every-day-10000-people-die-due-to-air-pollution-from-fossil-fuels/

10. Can be seen on YouTube: https://www.youtube.com/watch?v=YjFWiMJdotM&t=2s

11. Gordon, H. (2017, 24 April), "Journey deep into the Finnish caverns where nuclear waste will be buried for millenia", *Wired*, https://www.wired.co.uk/article/olkiluoto-island-finland-nuclear-waste-onkalo

12. Van Dijk, M. (2020, 23 July). Will there be a nuclear waste repository near the Brabant clay? *Eindhovens Dagblad*. https://www.ed.nl/kempen/komt-er-een-kernafvalberging-nabij-de-brabantse-klei~ab809caf/?referrer=https%3A%2F%2Fwww.google.com%2F&auth_rd=1

13. Kharecha, P.A. & Hansen, J.E. (2013), "Prevented mortality and greenhouse gas emissions from historical and Projected Nuclear Power", *Environmental Science & Technology*, 47(9), pp. 4889-4895, see https://doi.org/10.1021/es3051197

14-15. Quoted in Visscher, M. (2019, 16 March), "Closing nuclear power plants is like sticking your head in the sand", *Trouw*, https://www.trouw.nl/duurzaamheid-natuur/kerncentrales-sluiten-is-je-kop-in-het-zand-steken~b4f740e7/

16. Gamboa Palacios, S. & Jansen, J. (2018), Nuclear energy economics: an update to fact finding nuclear energy. TNO technology factsheet, https://energy.nl/wp-content/uploads/2019/06/TNO-2018-P11577.pdf

17. "Top climate change scientists' letter to policy influencers", 3 November 2013, CNN World https://www.cnn.com/2013/11/03/world/nuclear-energy-climate-change-scientists-letter/index.html

18. Quoted in Lange, R. (2020, 29 February), "Without intuitive intelligence and nuclear power, we die", *Het Financieele Dagblad*, https://fd.nl/futures/1334390/zonder-intuitieve-intelligentie-en-kernenergie-sterven-we

19. Ichford, R.F. (2021, 10 November), "Nuclear power and the energy transition in non-OECD countries", *Atlantic Council's EnergySource*, https://www.atlanticcouncil.org/blogs/energysource/nuclear-power-and-the-energy-transition-in-non-oecd-countries/

20. VVD, D66, CDA, CU (2021, 15 December). Looking out for each other, looking forward to the future: Coalition agreement 2021-2025. Coalition agreement "Looking out for each other, looking ahead to the future" | Publication | Government.nl

21. A. Fratto-Oyler and J. Parsons, The Climate and Economic Rationale for Investment in Life Extension of Spanish Nuclear Plants, MIT Center for Energy and Environmental Policy Research Working Paper 2018-016, November 19, 2018. http://ssrn.com/abstract=3290828

22. Buongiorno, J., Freda, R., Aumeier, S., Chilton, K. (2021), "A strategy to unlock the potential of nuclear energy for a new and resilient global energy-industrial paradigm", *The Bridge* 51(2), 48-56, https://www.nae.edu/255810/A-Strategy-to-Unlock-the-Potential-of-Nuclear-Energy-for-a-New-and-Resilient-Global-EnergyIndustrial-Paradigm

23. https://www.thorizon.com/press-release-thorizon-raises-e125-million-to-turn-nuclear-waste-into-co2-free-energy/

Chapter Seventeen
Forecasting and warning

"This is not like an asteroid that permanently changes the weather instantaneously for a million years. It's not like that; it's slow moving. It's like cancer. If you catch most forms of cancer early enough with the current state of medical knowledge, most cancer patients will live a very good, long life. But if you wait until it's stage four and it's all over the body, well, all bets are off."

Robert Tucker, futurologist and president of the Innovation Resource Consulting Group

The climate crisis is drawing increasing attention. Many people, especially young people, are concerned and are demanding change. The scientists who are expressing their fact-based concerns with increasing emphasis and the growing social unrest are combining to put climate change high on the political agenda. It is also clear from the many requests and questions I receive on the topic. I think climate change will remain a regular agenda item for the foreseeable future. Climate change is a fact, and so, therefore, is global warming. Its impact is so extensive that it is directly affecting our security. We need to adapt to those circumstances.

To do that, it is important to have a clear picture of the potential impact of climate change. For instance, to be able to predict where climate change will lead to instability and where migration flows will occur. Those analyses are crucial to create reaction time and for the ability to respond swiftly to what is coming our way. So when, in autumn 2020, I am asked by Dr Hinrich Thoelken, diplomat at the German Ministry of Foreign Affairs, to join a key advisory board, I am not surprised. He explains that the German foreign minister, Heiko Maas, considers it important to examine the risks to international peace and security. He therefore announced at a UN meeting in July that year that Germany was starting a Global Climate Security Risk and Foresight Assessment: a broad, holistic analysis with a security perspective, conducted by well-known research institutes. Led by the German think tank Adelphi and the Potsdam Institute for Climate Impact Research (PIK), the researchers will define climate risks based on data, analysis and the latest climate models.

According to the e-mail he sends to me, the Germans hope that in this way policymakers, NGOs, companies and a wide range of organisations at local and national level will be helped by better analyses of climate risks, and that countries and international institutions will thus find it easier to gain a better understanding of the greatest risks with regard to climate change. It will also create more opportunities to take timely action.

Looking to the future

The group's advisory board at the time consists of a number of experts, including Federica Mogherini (former EU foreign affairs chief), Robert Malley (CEO, International Crisis Group, ICG) and Shenggen Fan (former director of International Food Policy Research in China). For a moment, I hesitate to commit to another forum, but when I think about the impact of climate change and the importance of a better understanding and management of climate risks, I decide I'm in. The question has long since ceased to be *whether* we will be affected by climate change, but *when* and to what extent. Those who then make science-based assumptions based on the extrapolation of data and trends have a better picture of what the future holds for us, what we should take into account, and more importantly what measures we should take.

On the basis of current data, therefore, we can be certain that we will experience more weather extremes: more intense rainfall, higher sea levels, more salinized land, more and more intense wildfires, more severe hurricanes and greater temperature fluctuations. Not only will there be very long dry spells in many places, but we could also see widespread and severe freezing, as experienced in February 2021 in the usually warm state of Texas. There, the extreme cold left nearly 4.5 million homes and businesses without power and 57 people died.[1]

In such conditions, we will also start to see reservoirs run dry due to prolonged heat and drought, causing dams to stop producing electricity. Power plants may also shut down more frequently due to prolonged heat and lack of cooling capacity, putting pressure on energy supplies. Looking at Europe, this applies not only to countries around the Mediterranean (such as Spain, Italy, Greece and France), but also to countries along Europe's major rivers.

Leiden scientists argued in 2017 in the *Nature Energy* journal that by 2030, the number of regions with vulnerable energy supplies "will have greatly increased" because of the huge amounts of freshwater needed for cooling. For example, a large gas power plant consumes about one Olympic-sized swimming pool of water per minute to cool.[2] And if there is too little water, or if the available water is too hot, then energy production has to be scaled back or plants even shut down completely. This happened in the long hot summer of 2015 in Poland, for example.[3] If this happens on a large scale and several power plants shut down simultaneously, there is a potential for major social upheaval, and social unrest due to prolonged power cuts is not inconceivable.

Here, it is important to realise that energy supply is crucial in our modern society. Think of the increasing number of data centres that also need cooling water, and of our dependence on ICT. If there is a prolonged period of heat, both our energy supply and ICT services could come under pressure at the same time. If electricity and the internet are down, people will be unable to do their shopping, run their fridge, store food, charge their car or pay electronically. Hospitals will have to switch to emergency generators in the event of power outages.

Unforeseen circumstances

There are other consequences of climate change that are going to impact our way of life if we do not see them coming in time and take action. For example, rising water temperatures affect fish stocks and cause the growth of more blue-green algae. Changing climate means that the hay fever season lasts longer and that the effects of hay fever are intensifying, and thus rising healthcare costs. Heat stress puts the elderly, the chronically ill and other vulnerable people at significant risk of premature death. Extreme rainfall can cause serious traffic and transport problems, floods can cause traffic lights and streetlights to fail. In windstorms, the underground infrastructure of water and gas pipes can be damaged by the disturbance of tree roots. And in many countries, people will soon be unable to work outside at the hottest time of the day, or in some cases at any time of the day.

We must also take into account the outbreak of new animal diseases resulting in large-scale culls, as well as the arrival of "exotic" insects. For example, the increase in the number of ticks and the presence of the oak processionary caterpillar in the Netherlands are a direct consequence of a warmer climate. Another worrying development is the rise of the West Nile virus, an infectious tropical disease. Southern Europe experienced a major outbreak of this virus in 2018, spread by a common mosquito. The virus claimed a total of 181 lives that year.[4] Finally, it is also likely that insurance companies will go bankrupt if extreme weather events continue to occur. In California, for instance, an insurance company went into liquidation because of a major wildfire.[5]

There is also a growing number of reports, from the IPCC, McKinsey, BlackRock, the US Commodities Future Trading Council and others, warning of the collapse of insurance companies, banks and other financial institutions when businesses and houses with mortgages are destroyed by storms or floods.[6] Many insurance companies may soon be unwilling to insure properties in high-risk areas for this reason. In 2022, for instance, natural disasters caused about $270 billion of damage worldwide, of which about $120 billion was insured.[7] Similarly, the damage caused by Hurricane Ian, which swept through the US state of Florida in October 2023 and claimed more than 100 lives, was insured for $60 billion while it actually amounted to $100 billion.

An individual who narrowly survives a natural disaster is likely to be left empty-handed and that is what local and national governments, as well as international companies, need to prepare for and plan for. In short, identification of the risks associated with climatic developments is an absolute necessity.

Water, Peace and Security

Not everyone agrees that there is a need to combine data on climate trends with risks in conflict zones. Some are apprehensive about militarising the issue of climate change, or involving the security sector in an issue that is already complex enough. But it is precisely in those locations, where many are so vulnerable to the effects of climate change, that we should be combining data to look for ways to mitigate the impacts of natural disasters.

One promising forecasting initiative that I am involved in through the HCSS think tank is the Water, Peace and Security partnership (WPS), which received the prestigious Luxembourg Peace Prize for Outstanding Environmental Peace from the Schengen Peace Foundation in 2020 and 2021 (a year after biologist and anthropologist Jane Goodall received the same award for her work).[8]

The partnership uses quantitative and qualitative research to help policymakers, diplomats, crisis managers and many others to formulate faster and smarter interventions in high-risk hotspots, in other words countries and regions where water-related risks could lead to instability or even conflict. The partnership derives its predictive power from machine learning and large public data files that are gathered into an interactive web-based tool called the "WPS Global Early Warning Tool", based on the ACLED database (Armed Conflict Location and Event Database).[9]

Many water-related indicators, such as the severity of drought and access to clean water, are added to this database, along with social, political, economic and demographic data to predict what conflicts may occur in the next 12 months.[10] Reliable news sources and satellite images are used for verification, given that everything is interrelated. For instance, too much, too little or excessively dirty water is not only caused by climate-related factors, but is also linked to social and political unrest in many cases.

Consider the Sahel, where researchers can see where tensions are rising due to crop failures or polluted rivers. They can also see where residents have recently abandoned their homes following a natural disaster, and where there is violence and terror inflicted by armed militias, such as Boko Haram or groups affiliated with ISIS.

The researchers claim that when that array of information is combined with all available past and present data, and analysed by machine learning algorithms, the contours of the future come into view. This will give international organisations an increasingly sophisticated tool to spot water-related conflicts. Indeed, according to the researchers, it will allow them to predict as many as 86% of these conflicts. They focus not only on hotspot regions where conflicts may break out, but also on regions which are becoming more stable and calm.

These developments are excellent in their own right, especially as the WPS early warning system is linked to a broader integrated approach that focuses on building capacity and facilitating dialogues in identified hotspots to prevent possible conflict. WPS tools and services are also designed to enable many more people and organisations to make use of the data and then link their own data back to it. Depending on the outcomes and the political and governmental goodwill of local, regional or national authorities and/or leaders, this will then show what is actually needed to increase the resilience of citizens and countries to numerous risks.

The findings also help to increase the focus on international efforts in those fragile regions which target the sources of potential problems and tensions that could lead to conflict. For example, if it turns out that the distribution of scarce water might lead to problems, efforts could focus on issues such as funding for irrigation techniques, encouraging the import of agricultural products that require less water, making the use of groundwater more sustainable, or establishing agreements on the distribution of water from transboundary rivers and aquifers (an underground layer of rock or sediment that contains water).

A forecasting tool that combines multiple types of data could therefore, in theory, be a powerful tool to enable administrators to anticipate problems that will arise partly as a result of climate change. However, it is important that a tool such as the WPS does not become bogged down in bureaucracy or die a quiet death after a few years to make way for yet another initiative. Such an early warning system is only useful if it is broadly supported and widely used.

Satellite data

In tools that enhance predictive capability based on objective data and trend analysis, modern satellites can play an important role. After all, from space you can see more and more precisely what is happening on Earth, such as changes in ice caps, glaciers, forest fires or air quality. Launched in 2020, the Copernicus Sentinel-6 Michael Freilich satellite, named after the former director of NASA's Earth Science Division, can measure sea level changes and obtain data on Earth's humidity. This allows scientists to make more accurate predictions regarding the nature and development of hurricanes and improve the accuracy of climate models.

The ongoing development of more sophisticated satellites allows for better and continuous observation worldwide, and this is combined with increasingly powerful computers for researchers and analysts, as well as improved models of regional climate conditions. This is also why the HCSS think tank is working with both datasets and satellites to identify causal links between climate change and instability and/or conflict. With models using thousands of data points from satellite data, graphs can be visualised geographically, which in turn makes it much easier for users such as policymakers to interpret the models. Forecasts can thus be more detailed and reliable so that more targeted action can be taken.

In terms of data, no amount of collaboration is ever enough, even with Russia and China. I have in mind a database of raw data and (trend) analyses that is available to every country. With that data, a large-scale, common warning system could be created, allowing every country, every region and also every large city to see at an early stage what climate risks exist for its own inhabitants, allowing politicians, government officials, businesses, organisations and individuals to prepare a timely response to whatever lies ahead.

These tools will provide answers to questions such as "is it safe for people to live here?" Or "is this an area about to experience an extremely dry season?" If people know in advance, they can prepare, for instance by providing an allowance to farmers that enables them to buy other (usually more expensive) seeds in good time that are more resistant to drought. Or by helping farmers finance alternative methods of irrigation, such as drip irrigation, so that they need much less water and agriculture becomes less dependent on rainfall.

Also interesting in this context is Google's Earth Engine. With this, and together with the researchers involved, the internet giant is making an important contribution to climate science. Huge amounts of data from open satellite sources are analysed with special analysis software and made available free of charge to conservationists, urban planners, researchers and activists. Answers to specific questions are provided within seconds or minutes, rather than after years of research.[11]

Security-proofing

The good news is that these data-driven methods have the necessary added value for climate adaptation. Security and adaptation were separate worlds until recently, but there is now growing recognition that they are in fact two sides of the same coin; there is no adaptation without security, just as security is not sustainable without structural adaptation. It is therefore important to implement adaptation programmes in fragile regions in a security-conscious manner so that they contribute to enhanced stability rather than greater instability.

That recognition resulted in my contribution to the 2022 State and Trends in Adaptation report by the Global Center on Adaptation. In the security chapter, I worked with researchers from the US Center for Climate and Security and HCSS to set out a roadmap on how to "security-proof" projects and programmes aimed at adaptation.[12] This is essential, especially in conflict zones, where adaptation can be difficult to implement.

Inspiring examples

In other sectors too, there is interest in security-proofing adaptation projects, for example where investment risks for large-scale and long-term projects are concerned.

I am involved in a project by the Dutch organisation The Weather Makers, who have developed an ecosystem planning and management strategy to break and reverse the vicious circle of drought and desertification. They are currently working on a major project to restore the ecology of Sinai, thereby reactivating the local water cycle and eventually bringing back rainfall. The initiators know that the Sinai desert in Egypt was once a green place full of water and life and are determined to restore it to its former glory by creating large-scale ecosystems that repair the water cycle.

An ecosystem consists of many different organisms, such as plants, animals, fungi and bacteria, and if you know how to build this, you can create a green and healthy landscape that also provides more clouds and more rain, a landscape where plants provide shade and coolness, just as moisture, twigs, leaves and roots make the soil richer, thus holding water more effectively when it rains.

And where more rain falls on healthy soil, plants have a greater chance to grow. Plants that in turn will provide more water. The idea is that nature will thus return to the arid and searingly hot Sinai desert, and that new evaporation patterns will emerge, leading to the restoration of the water cycle.

Solutions like this have the potential to make a major positive impact when it comes to challenges such as water security, biodiversity, climate change and food security. The extensive underlying scientific research is also favourable in terms of the Weather Makers initiative's chance of success and the Egyptian government is therefore happy to cooperate.

Warning systems

With modern instrumentation and intensive collaboration, scientists are better able to predict the near future, something that is crucial in order to be able to give advance warning. But we need to be in a position to do so. This can be done by placing warning systems – alarm systems – in numerous locations, especially in developing countries, that are susceptible to the effects of drought, storms, floods or extreme temperatures. If people know 24 hours in advance that extreme and dangerous weather is on the way, damage can be reduced by 30%, according to the Global Center on Adaptation (GCA).[13] This could obviously save many lives too, which is no doubt why the US has set up sophisticated warning systems in certain parts of the country where tornadoes are common: radar systems that can detect thunderstorms before a tornado develops below them and, in very severe instances, can issue the warning before the tornado touches the ground.

This saves lives, and thanks in part to such systems, the death toll from natural disasters has fallen worldwide.[14] The internet and mobile phones can also be useful ways of alerting people, but for this to work, it is important to enhance internet access in remote rural areas, especially in areas vulnerable to climate change.

Weather stations

Warning systems work with computer models, which means that in the Netherlands, for example, we can calculate and predict water levels and river water runoff, and evacuate people and livestock in time. Computer models can calculate how much rain will fall where, what the soil's absorption capacity is, what the possibilities are for draining the water and thus determine the impact of the coming rainfall. This is crucial information for residents of areas with deep valleys where rivers flow, as in many places in Western Europe. There, floods pose a real danger as soon as precipitation becomes heavier than normal.

You have to measure to manage. But you also need weather radar that can accurately determine the amount of rainfall, as well as the expertise needed to use the data to make predictions. Then people living in a particular area need to be given timely warning. This can be done through media announcements, loudspeakers, sirens and push messages to phones. But even then, there is no guarantee that people will leave. Not everyone will feel compelled to leave their home after a text message, for example. It is difficult for anyone to imagine that their house will be under water within a short space of time. A clear message therefore needs to be formulated in advance. German Christian Kuhlicke of the Helmholtz Center for Environmental Research (UFZ) gives an example in an interview. He advises using clear communication in such situations, for example with a text message along the lines of: "It is 80% certain that your house will flood. We expect water levels to reach a height of 2 metres. Please leave your home as soon as possible."[15]

Artificial intelligence can automatically create consistent and clear warning messages that are easy for residents in a given area to understand. All active mobile phones within the risk areas can be identified and reached. Linked to a geographic information system, this can also be used to guide a rescue operation. It makes cooperation much more effective in an evacuation and when emergency assistance is being provided.

Vulnerable countries

We actually need to set up a natural disaster risk centre, in which specialists have all the data and analytical tools to enable optimal preparation, protection and assistance for people worldwide. The UN will be able to take the lead in this as an independent international organisation, but warning systems would have to be set up in a great many locations. Unfortunately, it is currently the case that many developing countries do not have base stations for the ground and balloon soundings needed to make warning systems reliable. So it is precisely those countries that are particularly vulnerable to climate change, including countries in Africa, Central America, in the Pacific and Caribbean island nations, which currently have no capabilities for collecting high-quality weather, climate, hydrological and related data needed to make warning systems reliable.

This puts great numbers of people at unnecessary risk and also makes data collection more costly. For example, the World Bank, the UN World Meteorological Organization (WMO) and the Met Office in the UK estimated in 2021 that improving the collection and international sharing of observational data would generate additional socioeconomic benefits, such as less damage and higher prosperity through improved water management, worth more than $5 billion a year.[16] And that is still a conservative estimate that does not take into account lives saved and welfare for developing countries.

In Bangladesh, where warning systems are in place, cyclone deaths have been reduced by as much as 98%. As recently as 1970, cyclones killed half a million people in Bangladesh, compared to 130,000 in 1991.[17] By contrast, in 2016, cyclone Roanu – which wiped out tens of thousands of homes, fisheries and roads – killed "only" twenty-three people in Bangladesh.[18] This significant reduction in the death toll is due to the warning system, whereby thousands of specially trained volunteers in coastal areas warn locals when a storm is approaching, using simple means such as flag signals, megaphones, hand sirens or large drums. As a result, the authorities managed to get half a million people to shelter in time in thousands of specially built, higher-lying concrete bunkers.[19]

Nevertheless, it is often the case that people in Bangladesh cannot return to their homes or neighbourhoods if a natural disaster has occurred. They have to rebuild livelihoods again or elsewhere, for which they usually lack the resources. The spread of infectious diseases, such as cholera, as a result of climate change must also be taken into account, so healthcare remains a concern.

Forecast-based financing

The measures which enable to take action before a natural disaster occurs make the biggest difference. In July 2017, for example, heavy rains caused severe flooding along the Jamuna River in Bangladesh. Five days before these floods were at their worst, the Bengal Red Crescent and the German Red Cross activated a forecasting and funding mechanism based on meteorological information from the Red Cross Climate Centre. This enabled the aid agencies to warn people and also give cash to 1,000 vulnerable households, with which they could buy what they needed to get themselves to safety and survive.[20]

The UN is also experimenting with data analysis and forecasting on the basis of which money is donated even before a crisis occurs. For example, in July 2020, nearly 20,000 households in Bangladesh received $53 in aid even before the monsoon rains peaked. It was one of the fastest funding allocations ever. Hygiene kits were also distributed to some 15,000 women, girls and transgender people, and water-tight storage containers were given to about 15,000 families to keep valuables such as seeds and agricultural tools dry.[21] These examples show that warning mechanisms are essential; but they are only effective if there is maximum cooperation and real action.

Role of the security sector

Warning mechanisms are therefore effective if the subsequent actions are right. If we want to be able to move from crisis management to risk management and keep our world habitable, global data, observational data, warning mechanisms and specific policies are indispensable. Ideally, all these elements should be interconnected because of the specific relationship between climate change and security, which is what I wish to emphasise in this book.

For now, those hardest hit by climate change are in fragile states and regions. Because events there also affect other countries, Western intelligence services have been monitoring these worrying developments for some time. The growing awareness that climate change directly affects security requires these services to investigate and include the impact of climate change in their analyses. Climate change should be an integral part of intelligence analyses as a basis for planning the military contribution to missions.

This will give us more insight into the root causes of conflict and allow us to identify the problem much more precisely in order to prevent conflict and to do more than merely treat the symptoms, as in the case of counter-piracy missions. Where will drought or flooding occur, for instance? Where is there a greater risk of major landslides, cyclones or extreme heat? What does this mean for sea-level rise and for people who are persuaded to flee as a result? What migration flows might this lead to? Where could this cause local tensions and instability? To what extent does this provide a breeding ground for terrorism or organised crime? How can we act more quickly in collaboration with other countries and NGOs? And once that information has been analysed, how do we proceed? Is it every man for himself, or do we act collectively? Or do we leave it to a designated conflict prevention unit?

These are all questions which countries and organisations should be asking themselves when it comes to climate change, and which would be answered more effectively if we had a common database. The added value of intelligence services lies in the fact that they can use the same data to make targeted analyses and assessments of potential security impacts. This allows us to anticipate tensions and security issues and prevents us from having to deal with the aftermath when we are too late.

No-one can predict exactly what is going to happen. At least within our IMCCS organisation, the Hague-based think tank HCSS is now developing a Climate Security Risk Matrix, in which researchers can link the available databases of the World Bank, the UN and other organisations. This will allow the Dutch think tank to identify the likelihood of climate-related risks, such as floods, drought or other natural disasters, per country and even down to provincial level.

The EU member states have now also set up a model where think tanks from across the union provide information.[22] In my opinion, NATO could be part of this, by sharing information and working with EU experts to collate and analyse all available data from countries and organisations. This would not only enhance understanding and predictive capability regarding climate threats, but would also improve the ability to detect disruptive effects in time. In this way, NATO could help vulnerable countries make their security organisations more resilient to the effects of climate change. However, all these dreams of the future require much more intensive civil-military cooperation than we have today, which would allow us to get away from the functional pillars and be more collaborative. Only then can the security sector play a valuable role in wider international knowledge sharing, technology development and the implementation of adaptation programmes, all with one common goal: to prevent and, where necessary, mitigate the impact of climate change.

Notes

1. Busby, J.W., Baker, K., Bazilian, M.D., Gilbert, A.Q., Grubert, E., Rai, V., Rhodes, J.D., Shidore, S., Smith, C.A., Webber, M.E. (2021), "Cascading risks: Understanding the 2021 Winter Blackout in Texas", *Energy Research & Social Science* 77, 102106, https://doi.org/10.1016/j.erss.2021.102106

2. Behrens, P., Van Vliet, M.T., Nanninga, T., Walsh, B., Rodrigues, J.F. (2017), "Climate change and the vulnerability of electricity generation to water stress in the European Union", *Nature Energy*, 2(8), https://doi.org/10.1038/nenergy.2017.114

3. Reuters (2015, Aug10), "Polish heatwave cuts power supply to industry", Reuters, https://www.reuters.com/article/poland-energy-heatwave-idUSL5N10L2QJ20150810

4. Camp, J.V. & Nowotny, N. (2020), "The knowns and unknowns of West Nile virus in Europe: What did we learn from the 2018 outbreak?", *Expert Review of Anti-Infective Therapy*, 18(2), pp. 145-154, https://doi.org/10.1080/14787210.2020.1713751

5. Yan, H. & Boyette, C. (2018, 4 December), "Insurance company goes under after California's most destructive wildfire". *CNN*, https://edition.cnn.com/2018/12/04/us/camp-fire-insurance-company-liquidation/index.html

6. Subcommittee on Climate-Related Market Risk of the Market Risk Advisory Committee of the U.S. Commodity Futures Trading Commission (2020). Managing climate risk in the U.S. financial system. *U.S. Commodity Futures Trading Commission*, Washington D.C.

7. Inventory of German insurer Munich Re, January 2023

8. Press release HCSS (2021, 19 May): Water, Peace & Security wins Outstanding Environmental Peace Prize, https://hcss.nl/news/water-peace-security-wps-wins-outstanding-environmental-peace-prize/

9. https://waterpeacesecurity.org/map

10. For more info: see https://files.wri.org/d8/s3fs-public/leveraging-water-data-in-machine-learning-based-model-for-forecasting-violent-conflict.pdf

11. *Het Financiële Dagblad*, 19-11-2021, "Researchers scour Google's data for climate disasters"

12. GCA State and Trends in Adaptation Report 2022, July 2022, Section 3 - Cross Sectoral Themes: Security, 438-457. https://hcss.nl/wp-content/uploads/2022/11/GCA_State-and-Trends-in-Adaptation-2022_Fullreport.pdf

13. Global Center on Adaptation (2020), *GCA business plan 2020-2025*. GCA, Rotterdam, p.24

14. World Meteorological Organization (2021), *WMO atlas of mortality and economic losses from weather, climate and water extremes (1970-2019.)*. WMO, Geneva

15. Quoted in Dane, K. (2021, 23 July), "The alarm went off, but the Germans went to bed", *Trouw*

16. Kull, D., Riishojgaard, L., Eyre, J., Varley, R. (2021), "The value of surface-based metereological observation data", World Bank, WMO & Met Office, https://openknowledge.worldbank.org/handle/10986/35178

17. Haque, U., Hashizume, M., Kolivras, K.N., Overgaard, H.J., Das, B., Yamamoto, T. (2011), "Reduced death rates from cyclones in Bangladesh: what more needs to be done?", *Bulletin of the World Health Organization*, 90(2), pp. 150-156, https://doi.org/10.2471/blt.11.088302

18. Al Jazeera (2016, 21 May), "Half a million flee as Cyclone Roanu hits Bangladesh", Al Jazeera, https://www.aljazeera.com/news/2016/5/21/half-a-million-flee-as-cyclone-roanu-hits-bangladesh

19. Rohmensen, G. (2007, 20 November), "Warning system prevented more deaths in Bangladesh", *Trouw*, https://www.trouw.nl/nieuws/waarschuwingsysteem-voorkwam-nog-meer-doden-in-bangladesh~b653f094/

20. Red Cross (2018, 7 May). "Future of disaster relief: funding based on predictions". Red Cross press release, https://www.rodekruis.nl/nieuwsbericht/toekomst-van-noodhulp-forecast-based-financing/

21. FAO (2020, 15 July), "Bangladesh: UN helps monsoon-affected river communities before peak flooding hits". World Food and Agriculture Organisation press release, https://www.fao.org/resilience/news-events/detail/en/c/1298316/

22. The European Think Tanks Group (ETTG). See https://ettg.eu/about/doi.org/10.1080/14787210.2020.1713751

Chapter Eighteen
Think big, act small, start somewhere

"I wish it need not have happened in my time, said Frodo. So do I, said Gandalf, and so do all who live to see such times. But that is not for them to decide. All we have to decide is what to do with the time that is given to us."

J.R.R. Tolkien, *The Fellowship of the Ring*

During the coffee break at the Future Force Conference in February 2017, a man wearing glasses walks up to me. He asks if he can have a word with me and introduces himself as Ap Verheggen. Then he says: "General, what if I were able to extract water from the air in the Sahara desert? So in the driest, hottest place on earth. By just using the sun." Then he falls silent and looks at me with a twinkle in his eye, waiting for my response. I smile at him and say in all honesty, "Sir, that sounds fantastic. Hope it works out." And actually I wanted to wish him luck and leave it at that, but I realise that I have just called on all 1,200 conference participants to share their ideas and, above all, to listen to everyone else's ideas, no matter how far-fetched they may seem at first. Who knows what collaborative possibilities and opportunities might emerge? I turn to the man again and ask him to explain to me what he means.

Water from desert air

Enthusiastically, he explains that he is a Dutch inventor and artist. He is working with a friend who knows a great deal about renewable energy to make a device that works on solar energy to extract water from the air.

He pauses for a moment and then goes on to say that he calls his invention SunGlacier. It looks like a work of art because he does not want to "fill Africa – the place for which it is primarily intended – with ugly things". But he says it is certainly not just meant as art. No, he truly believes his technology could be a solution to the water scarcity in many parts of the world. Ap says: "General, many people believe that the desert is the driest place on earth. But desert air can be very humid. The hotter it gets, the more water the air can hold. Normally, higher temperatures also mean more sunshine. So why not focus on extracting water from the air, just by using renewable solar energy?"

"The principle is quite simple", explains Ap. "If you take a can of soda out of the fridge on a hot summer day, water droplets will appear on the outside, right? In the desert, it can be 50 degrees Celsius, but even there, drops will appear on the can. That's how I want it to work: using water vapour in the air, and then letting it condense. To do this, I use a simple plate that costs no more than 3 euros. This is called a Peltier element and it is normally used to cool computer chips. However, if this plate receives power from, say, a solar panel, the underside becomes ice-cold and the top red hot. The trick is to use it to cool air so much that condensation drops form on a cone. I can then collect these in a glass. And then I have water." He beams. "What a discovery it would be if people living in hot, dry areas could soon produce their own water with this. They could use it to water their fields every day. All I need now", says Ap, "is to be able to test my theory under extreme conditions. So by trial and error. Again and again, until it works."

His concept seems too good to be true. How do you extract water from desert air of over 45 degrees Celsius and less than 5% humidity? Surely all the water would evaporate immediately? At the same time, I also know that technological developments are rapid and solar energy generation has made huge progress in recent years. Besides, I am obviously no expert on extracting water from the air. But just the thought that it could work is particularly tantalising. That this man, Ap, could one day make a contribution with his SunGlacier and his technology could be a forerunner to the technical solution to the growing water problem. And that we would thus be able to prevent crop failures, or people fleeing their homes or children dying. How could anyone not want that? How could I not want that?

On to Mali

Before I know it, I say something rather unusual to this innovator. I offer him the opportunity to test his technology at our military camp in Mali, Camp Castor. At 40, 50 degrees Celsius, Mali is one of the hottest and driest places on earth. Living there feels like living in an oven. I know it is not a safe place, but experimenting at a military camp means working in relatively safe conditions. "Besides", I say, "my people can make sure you get there and arrange a place for you to sleep. So let's try to give this idea a chance to work." Ap looks at me, perplexed. He nods, hands me his business card. It doesn't seem to have sunk in; he doesn't believe me. But a few weeks later, it is really happening and he and his team are on a military plane to Mali in Africa.

Ap is not the only one to get such an opportunity. I offer another Future Force Conference participant the opportunity to test an invention in Mali. That is Emad, who fled from Iran and is now studying at The Hague University of Applied Sciences where he is currently working, under the guidance of former Defence Minister Professor Joris Voorhoeve, to invent a water purification device the size of a coffee machine. He wants to develop it to one day purify and desalinate brackish and salt water, as much as 20 litres per hour. Initially using 70 watts of energy, which is the equivalent to watching less than an hour of television.

His ambition? To provide a solution to drinking water shortages in refugee camps in the Middle East and elsewhere in the world. So I hope for his sake that he too can develop his prototype further in Mali. I know that current devices able to convert seawater or brackish water to freshwater are huge and very expensive, and they also consume enormous amounts of electricity.

So what if you had a portable device that is user-friendly, complete with a manual for dummies and, once working, produced 20 litres of desalinated water per hour? That's a pretty good result. And even better: suppose you can then perfect the device so that it also runs on solar power? Such an invention would also have enormous potential. Not only for families around the world, but also for military units, which increasingly have to operate in arid regions and take water from the environment where it is often already in short supply.

In short, both Ap the inventor and Emad the young social innovator are going to Mali, accompanied by an enthusiastic reservist from the National Reserve, who was himself a regular soldier and is currently working as a lecturer at The Hague University of Applied Sciences. He will help the group get a place to sleep, food and drink, and make sure they can get to work as soon as possible. The other military personnel at the camp will not have time to show a bunch of inventors the ropes, tell them what the rules are and where they can and cannot go. That is a perfect job for the reservist as special project leader.

Successful field trials

This remarkable team of people eventually manage to get off to a great start. At the Dutch camp, for instance, student engineer Emad tests river water from the Niger by purifying it using electrodialysis and UV filtration. Using a pilot plant, he conducts numerous field tests and concludes that the device works well in Mali's extreme weather conditions. He collects the samples for subsequent analysis in the Netherlands. In the searing heat of the Malian desert, inventor Ap's team creates a shaded area against the fence of the Dutch UN camp using a large canvas sheet. Beneath it is the SunGlacier headquarters for the week. Using a bulldozer, they then level a stretch of desert sand, after which testing can begin. They do this by installing what they call the desert twins in the blazing sun: solar panel devices specially developed for Mali which have the appearance of a small lunar module and which contain the Peltier element Ap told me about in The Hague.

Unfortunately, for the first four days, there is not a drop of water to be seen. The condensation droplets are evidently evaporating even before they reach the collection tray. This is because the temperature inside the cabinets is initially too high to keep it below the dew point. But when Ap cools the containers by other means, it is successful. The water from the desert air actually condenses. With help from technical engineer Peter van Geloven, Ap perseveres until he finds the ideal configuration and the water drops fall one after the other into the tray. The energy they use comes from the two small solar panels installed on the desert twins. In the end, Ap manages to produce half a glass of water in six hours. It is certainly not much at this stage, but an excellent first step. This proves he can do it, that he can actually extract water from the hot desert air.

Collaboration with Defence

Back in the Netherlands, we organise a press conference to present the success story. HUGE BREAKTHROUGH: DUTCHMAN MAKES WATER IN THE DESERT, a newspaper headline proclaims. NOS News talks about a "dream come true". Ap, meanwhile, is more motivated than ever to carry on developing the technology. To help him further, I put him in touch with the military personnel who are currently setting up a Fieldlab Smart Base (a result of the Future Force Conference), a site at the barracks in Amersfoort where army personnel test sustainable innovations for the military camp of the future. At Woensdrecht air force base, at the Meteorological Centre's Climatic Test Facility, a climatic chamber in the form of a gigantic hangar large enough for an aircraft is quickly made available for Ap to continue his testing and development. There, he develops a completely new condensation technique whereby extracted water can no longer evaporate. I have seen it myself. It is like a waterfall that swells and is then collected in a reservoir.

Ap has now reached the point where he can produce an average of 20 litres of water a day. He even managed to make 40 litres of water in one day in the climate chamber, using only a very small amount of energy. It also works in areas with a bone-dry climate and thus very low relative humidity. Ap was able to run many tests over several days, producing quite a few buckets of water. Besides quantity, the quality of the water is obviously important as well. The meter indicates that there are only four parts per million (ppm) of undissolved particles in the water, so the water Ap extracts from the air is extremely good quality and can also be enriched with minerals if required.

That is also the reason why the Dutch army has now built two units with Ap that will be tested over an extended period, one of them on Curaçao. These units are plug-and-play, so ready for immediate use. They are packed in a mobile flight case the size of a dustbin, so military personnel can take them anywhere. Now it is a matter of testing by trial and error to see if this innovation can be applied in practice. The Ministry of Defence hopes to use one installation to extract about 20 litres in 24 hours in bone-dry areas where there is little or no clean water.

Sharing knowledge

Since the field test in Mali, Ap has also been trying to whip up enthusiasm for his invention among students around the world so that they can contribute to its further development. He is holding a SunGlacier Challenge in Oman, where 15 student teams from eight different countries are trying to solve the evaporation problem, because Ap still wonders whether he could condense water vapour with a much cheaper cooled surface after all. "I really hope others will pick this up and do something amazing with it", he says. So the Peltier plate technique is on the internet as open source (the falling water technique is patented). "After all, it's really cheap technology, with no moving parts that can break. There's a future in that."

It is great to see that the Dutch Ministry of Foreign Affairs has also embraced Ap's expertise. The ministry was asked to contribute to the Dutch pavilion at the World Expo in Dubai in 2020, and Ap demonstrated the SunGlacier invention in practice there. The system blows warm air through a cold shower whereby the water vapour from the air condenses against the falling water droplets, thus expanding the volume of the water. Peter calls it the "growing waterfall".

In this closed system, evaporation of the extracted water has now become impossible, which was still a major problem in the earlier test in Mali. On the roof of the Dutch pavilion in Dubai, at around 50 degrees Celsius, was a SunGlacier that made more than 1,000 litres of water a day from the hot desert air, powered by solar panels. The SunGlacier supplied water to a huge plant-covered structure, in the shape of a pyramid, while also helping to cool the pavilion. An impressive presentation of how to grow plants in the middle of the hottest desert.

Global impact

Many companies around the world are looking for ways to extract water from the air. Almost all of them require a great deal of energy to make this possible. Ap and his team have succeeded in making this happen more efficiently and with relatively cheap technology, making it more widely applicable. This also eliminates the need to drill deeper and deeper for groundwater, which only increases dehydration of the earth.

Furthermore, air is an almost unlimited source of water and Ap's concept is fully circular. All the energy needed comes from the air and all the water is extracted from the air, but also goes back into the air over time. Also, the water is pure which can reduce health problems associated with the use of polluted water. An entirely new concept for local water supply is thus emerging in places that are increasingly at risk of becoming uninhabitable due to drought and heat.

So wouldn't it be fantastic if we could use Ap's invention in refugee camps? Or turn it into products that could provide water for entire families and communities in the driest regions of the world? That we can use to contribute to climate change resilience and, if possible, help prevent migration flows?

Wouldn't it also be fantastic if we could use this invention to make the cultivation of greenhouse crops circular and self-sufficient? And also reduce the use of plastic? Consider, for example, all those military forces who, with the help of this invention, will soon be able to supply their units with drinking water, eliminating the need for the expensive supply of hundreds of thousands of bottles of drinking water as well as the mountain of plastic waste.

I want to continue to believe in this and that is why I have also used my network outside the Defence organisation to help Ap to get his invention to market. Together with several Dutch captains of industry, I looked at how we could accelerate the further development of his innovation and scale it up with one or more Dutch companies, so that the devices could eventually be produced on a large scale and at an affordable price. I also put Ap and his team in touch with a former classmate with extensive experience in guiding companies through scale-up and growth processes.

We have since found a company that can develop Ap's invention further into a market-ready product and can quickly put the device into production. This company is now busy detailing and documenting the design, after which a prototype can be built and tested that should lead to eventual large-scale production, hopefully in 2024.

Just start somewhere

The collaboration with Ap, and also with Emad, illustrates my maxim of "think big, act small, start somewhere". I believe this should be the guiding principle if we want to be able to work together in security ecosystems. For inventor Ap, "thinking big" means solving the issue of water scarcity. The remarkable thing about this collaboration, starting with the field test in Mali, is that it has actually been developed much further than that, with a practical result.

For engineer Emad, "thinking big" means producing drinking water around the world. He started with a small, low-cost device that transforms brackish and salt water into drinking water. He too did a field test in Mali. It was partly on the back of this that the start-up Water Future was created soon afterwards; he is currently developing a membrane technology to extract substances from water for small-scale applications in agriculture. With this, Emad wants to help people in developing countries.

Both experiments in Mali yielded valuable field test results. Emad's water treatment project turned out to be much easier and more energy-efficient than initially thought, and Ap is now well on the way to large-scale production. Obviously, you cannot always expect an idea or a test to produce immediate results. But that does not mean you shouldn't try. Indeed, we should all try. Testing new technologies and concepts together so that we learn whether proposed solutions actually work. Simply improving the well-trodden paths is not going to get us there. That much is clear.

The examples illustrate the enormous strides we can make if we dare to veer from the beaten track, if we dare to make mistakes in order to arrive at entirely new concepts. Furthermore, people like Emad and Ap show that we can all make a difference. Generally speaking, it is not governments or multinationals that come up with ground-breaking solutions. It is mainly the young innovators, dissenting loners who look at problems from an entirely different angle and see solutions that no one else had thought of. But then we need governments and multinationals to quickly scale up successful innovations. Above all, let's give those innovators space and help them. Not everything will be successful, of course, but even if only 1% of the initiatives succeed, that 1% can make a difference worldwide. We must continue to believe in that.

Chapter Nineteen
People make the difference

"If you want to change the world, start off by making your bed."
Admiral William McCraven in his speech at the University of Austin

Many people want to help to mitigate climate change or learn how to cope with its effects, but the problem is huge and highly complex. For me, however, it is abundantly clear that individual choices and actions can have a huge impact, even though individuals may only be a small cog in a wider whole. In this chapter, I would like to share some examples showing that people who dare to think big and start small can make a huge difference. And yes, this is often a matter of trial and error; many initiatives turn out not to be feasible or do not receive any support. But that too is part of change and innovation. There will inevitably be mistakes on the road to success. That requires perseverance and patience.

There are inspiring stories from all over the world showing how one or a few individuals are successfully combating the causes and consequences of climate change. During my research work, for example, I read about the Indian region of Ladakh, a plateau in the northern tip of India and home to people who build "ice stupas".[1] These are tall ice cones that provide water when they melt in spring. They were invented by Sonam Wangchuk, a mechanical engineer and founder of a free school in Ladakh. In 2013, he discovered that in the shadow of a bridge, ice remained frozen until mid-summer. At that point, he came up with the idea of helping villages in the area by freezing water in winter and storing it for use in spring. This is crucial in the area where he lives, as the region relies on winter snow and melt water from glaciers. However, snow is increasingly irregular and has usually melted by the time farmers start planting in spring.

So together with students, and with money obtained through crowdfunding, Wangchuk makes a tall ice mound with steep sides, shading its own interior. He does this by diverting some of the water from a stream down the mountain through a pipe, after which the water is forced up through a vertical pipe to a nozzle. As soon as the mercury drops below freezing, the nozzle is opened, causing small drops of water to freeze as they fall. An ice mound of frozen water droplets thus rises slowly around the pipe. That first "ice stupa" is 6 metres high, contains 150,000 litres of water and will last until May.

The next step is to teach other people in the area how to build ice stupas themselves. In 2019, twelve stupas were built using this technique, two of them more than 30 metres high. By 2020, 26 had already been built. Now Wangchuk hopes that the irrigation water from the stupas will also help to revegetate the slopes, so that winter rains can be utilised locally. "If a stupa's size and location are right, it could survive the summer", he claims.[2] This would create an ice cone as resistant as a mini glacier.

I hope it succeeds; at least the results look promising. Students at a nearby school – where Wangchuk is considered a hero – are making an ice cone 22 metres high. In the shadow of the mountain peak, it will last until August, allowing farmers to irrigate their fields all that time. In 2020, students built an even taller ice cone. "One day", the head of the school says, "we will build an ice stupa that keeps growing."[3] Meanwhile, ice stupas seem to be taking the world by storm. They are being built in the Karakoram mountains in Pakistan and there are also plans to build them in South America.

Indigenous knowledge

On the other side of the world, too, individuals are making a big difference. Like the sisters of the Quechua community in Costa Rica, Marcela and Magdalena Machaca. Both women are agricultural engineers and, thanks to the knowledge inherited from their ancestors, have managed to build reservoirs high in the mountains near the city of Ayacucho to collect rainwater. They started building their first reservoir in 1995 and have since built more than 120.[4] The women choose sites in natural landscapes that already have the shape of reservoirs, so that less digging is required. They seal any leaks with soil and plant native ferns that cling firmly to the soil, naturally filter the water and provide shelter for birds. Then they create small channels to drain excess water, preventing the reservoir from overflowing or the dam from breaking. The existing reservoirs are up to 600 metres in diameter and fill up quickly in the rainy season.

One reservoir costs a million dollars, an amount the two sisters pay largely from their own foundation.[5] The reservoirs have been such a great success that the sisters managed to raise the money they needed. Indeed, reservoirs are now also being built – under the sisters' supervision – in northern Costa Rica. Currently, five small-scale reservoirs into which three rivers flow have already been built there in the mountains. Farmland in the dry areas downstream can now be easily irrigated to grow crops.[6]

Clean air conditioners

Anyone who can harness the vast amounts of knowledge and experience of inspired people will be able to move mountains. The story of Moluccan-Dutch entrepreneur Ton Letwory is another striking illustration of this. Fifteen years ago, he attended an international conference discussing, amongst other things, the impact of air conditioners on the environment. Not only did he discover that air conditioners are big energy guzzlers, but also that current models use refrigerants that contain huge amounts of harmful greenhouse gases, namely CFCs, HFCs and HCFCs. These are fluorinated chemicals that have a greenhouse effect up to 1,000-9,000 times greater than CO_2. These super greenhouse gases thus form a chemical bomb for the climate. It is also clear that the more we use air conditioners, the more the earth warms up and we then need more cooling to function normally.

A vicious circle from which it is difficult to escape and which has major repercussions.

This is where Ton's journey begins. He has a clear vision that at first glance seems impossible: to develop an air conditioner that consumes hardly any energy and contains no harmful refrigerants.

The first step is to invest in an idea: using the evaporation of water for cooling. He does not yet know what he will encounter on his path, but like a true explorer, Ton charts a course. Many steps are needed to turn an idea into a product, such as figuring out principles of physics, making test set-ups and building prototypes. And just like a journey of discovery, sometimes you have to go back to the beginning and choose a different path. After many years of hard work, using all his personal financial resources and sometimes going against the tide, Ton arrives at a workable final product.

He has now developed a ventilation and cooling system that does not work on the basis of harmful chemicals, but uses H_2O; water, in other words. He manages to obtain numerous patents, even a unique "concept patent". "I want to do something good for the world", says Ton. It is then time to call on Vincent Trip. He is related to friends of Ton, and very high up at Philips, where he manages thousands of people. He plays in the champions league of plastics manufacturers, so to speak, and is responsible for the production of many tens of millions of products a year. At Ton's request, he is working on making his device out of plastic instead of stainless steel, and on making it modular. This means it will be lighter, cheaper, will last longer and be easily recycled.

Pooling knowledge and experience

Further research and the conducting of pilots and field tests takes roughly two years, after which the dry-to-cool technology is firmly in place. They have made an air conditioner from recycled plastic that can be used in any building worldwide with 80% energy savings on cooling and without using greenhouse gases. Ton then tries to get funding to ramp up production, but his invention is apparently so revolutionary that he has no joy at all. For a while, it looks as if his pioneering innovation is going to die in its prime.

That is, until Ton and Vincent bump into Dutch sustainability entrepreneur Maurits Groen (creator of such products as the WakaWaka lamp and Kipster). "This can't be true", says Maurits when he hears that no investment money can be found. Immediately, he mobilises his network and, as he puts it himself, "keeps nagging" philanthropists until they put in a total of about 1.5 million euros. Now the real work can begin. Through Ton's adopted son, who works as a marketer, he manages to pull in contracts and his company can move to large premises in Nieuwleusen. There, large-scale production of the ICECUBE, as the system is now called, can start, with the help of a large robot.

Warming caused by harmful refrigerants

The trio assumes that rapid global developments are going to help them get production going. Indeed, in October 2016, representatives from more than 170 countries agreed to find a solution to the use of the highly damaging chemicals. They agreed that the use of HFCs would be phased out and eventually stopped, initially by rich countries in 2019, which has now been achieved, followed by low-wage countries in 2024 and 2028. The US Secretary of State at the time, John Kerry, called this agreement "the best thing we can do in one go (for the climate agreement)", as scientists estimate that this agreement could reduce projected global warming by almost half a degree Celsius.[7]

We now know that the demand for air conditioners is only going to increase and the "phasing out of harmful refrigerants" by all countries in the world and not only the initial 170 is far from being achieved. The total amount will only increase for now before all countries ban them. Indeed, the International Energy Agency (IEA) expects global air-conditioning use to triple by 2050.[8] That means there will be ten new air conditioners every second until then, and is the reason why Paul Hawken, author of the book

Drawdown, puts forward the regulation of harmful refrigerants as the best solution to combat climate change. And that is precisely the dry-to-cool technology that Ton, Vincent and Arthur can now realise on a large scale, thanks in part to the help of sustainability entrepreneur Maurits Groen.

Meanwhile, the company Dutch Climate Systems (DCS) has reached the point where they have installed their ICECUBE in every possible type of building, such as schools, healthcare facilities, restaurants, offices, hotels and commercial buildings. Other countries, too, have now discovered DCS and delegations have visited from countries such as Indonesia, China, South Africa and Brazil.

Good example leads to good practice

It is often the small acts that inspire hope, something that I know from past experience. For example, in the years before the Taliban retook Afghanistan in 2021, I received somewhat promising reports about developments in the country. The Afghan National Environmental Protection Agency agreed to work with the Ministry of Religious Affairs to persuade spiritual leaders in rural and urban areas to raise environmental and climate issues during prayers.[9] This is bearing fruit. Afghan spiritual leaders have since been regularly advising adults and children during prayers to plant trees. They plant trees themselves too. They also educate people on how to treat their environment better. They ask people to be careful with the use of plastic, for instance. "Recycle as much as you can and don't burn plastic waste", they advise. "God created nature and the Prophet Muhammad told us to take good care of it", said mullah Qary Samiullah in an interview.[10]

During that same period, I heard about people in Afghanistan being helped by international organisations to plant trees and build underground canals to transport water from a water source or aquifer to their lands for irrigation and other uses. Organisations such as the Christian World Vision Afghanistan organisation carry out that work, paying Afghans to build or repair an underground canal. That is what is happening in the village of Naizabeha, for example, providing 450 households and several surrounding villages with drinking water. Not only that: they can also use the water to grow crops and plant trees. So people can once again harvest crops, sell produce and sustain themselves.

Underground canals like these are the motivation for some Afghans at the time to return from exile. Like Mohammad Amin, who tells the organisation World Vision Afghanistan a year before the Taliban seized power, "When I came back, the land was green and the area was much cooler than before."[11] He highlights how planting trees and greening the area helps reduce dust and make the air fresher. It also protects children from respiratory diseases and heat exhaustion. In the same interview, Amin said that he himself had now planted and irrigated 150 tree seedlings. He plans to plant many more.

I remember thinking at the time: so it can be done. People can do a lot themselves. Ultimately, things will only change if local people bring about change themselves, partly through small initiatives. After all, just one such project shows how people can literally gain the prospect of a better future, one in which they can raise their children. They do that themselves and that gives hope, even though it sometimes feels like a drop in the ocean. It is cruel to think that all these efforts to adapt have been undone by the evolving security situation in Afghanistan. At the same time, it also shows the connection between adaptation and security and that things can always be done differently. And that is precisely why we should always keep the security situation in mind in our adaptation plans.

Greening

Greening and the large-scale restoration of nature are crucial. Trees, for example, not only provide food for people, but in many cases in symbiosis with micro-organisms and fungi, also provide shade and prunings for cooking. Tree leaves serve as fodder and fertilizer, and trees have roots that improve the water balance of the soil and also fix nitrogen from the air. The government of Bangladesh is therefore reforesting parts of its coastal zone with mangroves. This tempers the destructive force of hurricanes and cyclones and creates spawning grounds for fish, which is important for local fishermen. Even in parts of Spain, trees are now being enthusiastically planted in the bone-dry earth, making a small contribution to the pledge made by more than 130 countries at the Glasgow Climate Summit to stop deforestation and land degradation by 2030.

Whether that will really make a difference remains to be seen. Spanish scientists have shown in *Science* magazine that in 80 years' time, 18% of the earth will be arid, beyond the currently existing desert areas. For Spain, the figure is as high as 75% of its territory.[12] This means that Spain, as well as Italy and other countries in the region, will eventually become part of a new, northern Sahel. Besides limiting global CO_2 emissions, there is therefore a huge amount of work to be done when it comes to greening.

Digging holes

The importance of greening is also the reason why I invited the non-profit organisation Justdiggit to the Future Force Conference organised by Defence in 2017. Justdiggit comes to places where the top layer of soil has become so hard that rainwater can no longer properly soak into the ground. As a result, the water evaporates or causes erosion and flooding, which washes away the remaining fertile soil. To prevent this, the organisation works with local people in their project areas in Kenya and Tanzania to dig tens of thousands of holes, known as *bunds*, in the ground. To do so, they use innovations co-developed by Wageningen University, drawing on centuries-old techniques.

These *bunds* trap rainwater, giving it time to sink into the soil. This allows the seeds still in the ground to germinate. And so natural vegetation returns. The fact that so many areas have now dried up does not mean they are now infertile. There are still many seeds and nutrients in the soil, and by digging *bunds*, water can get to them. Moreover, anyone who helps with the digging receives financial support from the organisation, which they can use, for example, to send their children to school.

Justdiggit is also restoring trees that were cut down in the past. Many trees used to grow in Sub-Saharan Africa. These have been cut down over the years for charcoal and firewood production and to make way for agriculture. Restoring these trees will improve biodiversity and habitability for the local community. Since 40% of all rainfall comes from evaporation through vegetation, restoring them also restores the water cycle. "So a little more greenery creates even more greenery", as the people at Justdiggit like to say. After all, the greener the earth is, the cooler it is. That is why it is fantastic to see people so committed to making the earth's dry land green again.

The effect of the bunds can be seen after the first rains. It really works. Where at first all that can be seen on photos is a barren plain, you soon see vegetation returning. Eventually, all this should lead to a hydrological corridor, an ever-expanding and self-multiplying fertile area, where an organisation like Justdiggit will then no longer be needed. In short, with a shovel, smart innovations and collaboration, the power of nature fully used and enhanced, farmers will once again be able to graze their herds and cultivate their land, and there will be more drinking water.[13]

The desert in bloom

Ecological agriculture also provides an answer to the global problem of food and water shortages and famine in desert areas. The Sekem community in Egypt is a good example of this. In Egypt, the Sekem – the name refers to the power of the sun – has turned 700 hectares of desert land into fertile farmland in the space of 40 years by greening desert land into biodynamic farmland. This is mainly due to the work of Dr Ibrahim Abouleish, a pharmacologist and chemist in Egypt, who was awarded the Right Livelihood Award, the "Alternative Nobel Prize", for this project in 2003. His story is in many ways a dream come true.

In 1977, Abouleish bought a piece of barren desert near Belbes, sixty kilometres northeast of Cairo. He had a well dug there to water the soil and make the desert sand suitable for biodynamic farming. No one would have thought that possible at the time. At the same time, he was building a community and working on the personal development of everyone in it. Factories for processing agricultural produce were set up. Bedouins in the desert were given jobs in the community. Nursery, primary, secondary and vocational schools were also opened. After a while, more than two thousand people were studying sustainable development at Heliopolis University. Abouleish writes in his book *Sekem*: "When young people internalise the idea of sustainable development and work for the development of nature and society, there is hope for a better and more equitable future."[14]

I also discover that a disability group and a children's nursery have been set up in this community. And there is a project for underprivileged children who are victims of child labour – a widespread problem in Egypt. For these children, there is the "Chamomile Children" programme, which gets its name from the chamomile harvest. In the Sekem community, they can earn a full day's wage for half a day's work; the other half of the day they can go to school free of charge. There is also a medical centre on site that treats some 40,000 patients a year, and the farm near Belbes is home to several businesses that sell tea, juice, foodstuffs, herbal medicines, organic cotton children's clothing and herbs that develop a stronger aroma due to lack of water.

Because Sekem organises its own processing and trading, this community can realise greater added value. Of this, 10% goes to the Sekem Development Foundation, which funds new developments in health, education, arts, sustainability and social projects. For instance, health education and a refuse collection service have been set up in the 13 villages in the region, which is home to about 30,000 people. Small entrepreneurs can also apply for a loan through a micro-credit programme and receive guidance on making a business plan.

Sekem is located in the middle of the desert. It employs 1,300 people and now looks almost idyllic. Sekem has become a thriving oasis with ornamental shrubs around the buildings, mixed flowers along the paths and blooming fields with many different trees, such as yoyo bush, casuarina tree and date palm, which add to the biodiversity, and which also suit the desert conditions because they can survive with a limited amount of water.

The trees provide shade for a long row of hives with native bees. The systems to irrigate desert land are now solar-powered and highly reliable. Water wastage is thus kept to a minimum. A prime example of how a community can make a huge difference in the very dry areas of the world.

Set good examples elsewhere

How wonderful and effective it will be if we can irrigate dozens of hectares of date palms in other places too, plant fast-growing trees that provide shade and break sandstorms, supply compost and use pumps powered by solar panels, with people also producing food and benefiting from health care, public information and education. Not only can poverty then be fought more effectively, but the quality of food will also increase, as will the biodiversity of plants, insects, birds and other animals. Last but not least, people will once again have prospects and young people will be more likely to choose to become farmers instead of jihadists.

So besides working on security in dry and unstable areas, such as the Sahara and the Sahel, we should also choose to work on a mix of investments at the same time. Investments aimed at restoring agriculture and ecosystems, but also investments in the necessary human capital.

Afghanistan shows how the lack of a secure environment blocks this kind of investment. My French counterpart CDS at the time and good friend Pierre de Villiers often uses a quote by Aristotle: "It is not enough to win a war; it is more important to organize the peace." Security and investments to improve local resilience to climate change go hand in hand. This requires a broader, integrated deployment of economic, technological and security-related efforts; in other words, a climate-centric 3D approach. We also need to be open to entirely new concepts and ideas to combat erosion and keep the earth habitable. This is only possible if we give the incredible power and knowledge of individuals a chance and help them to scale up. As an Afghan proverb says: many little drops make a river.

Notes

1-2-3. Kumar-Rao, A. (2020, 16 June), "One way to fight climate change: make your own glaciers", *National Geographic*, https://www.nationalgeographic.com/magazine/article/one-way-to-fight-climate-change-make-your-own-glaciers-perpetual-feature

4-5-6. Rodriguez, S. (2020, 2 March), "As glaciers shrink, Peruvian sisters build 'sacred' reservoirs for city water", Reuters, https://www.reuters.com/article/climate-change-peru-water-idAFL8N2AB8BK

7. Davenport, C. (2016, 15 October). Nations, fighting powerful refrigerant that warms planet, reach landmark deal. *The New York Times*, https://www.nytimes.com/2016/10/15/world/africa/kigali-deal-hfc-air-conditioners.html

8. IEA (2018). The Future of Cooling, IEA, Paris, https://www.iea.org/futureofcooling/

9. Khan Saif, S. (2020, March19), "As climate impacts grow, Afghan clerics offer green guidance in prayers", Reuters, https://www.reuters.com/article/us-afghanistan-climate-change-religion-idUSKBN2160BG

10. Glinski, S. (2020, 12 February), "Why Afghanistan's religious leaders preach about climate change", *The National News*, https://www.thenationalnews.com/world/asia/why-afghanistan-s-religious-leaders-preach-about-climate-change-1.975102

11. World Vision (2020, 1 September), "A fairer fight – one Afghan village tackles the impacts of climate change", World Vision press release, https://www.wvi.org/stories/climate-change/fairer-fight-one-afghan-village-tackles-impacts-climate-change

12. Berdugo, M., Delgado-Baquerizo, M., Soliveres, S., Hernández-Clemente, R., Zhao, Y., Gaitán, J.J., Gross, N., Saiz, H., Maire, V., Lehmann, A., Rillig, M.C., Solé, R.V., Maestre, F.T. (2020), "Global ecosystem thresholds driven by aridity", *Science* 367(6479), p. 787-790, https://doi.org/10.1126/science.aay5958

13. See website, https://www.justdiggit.org/

14. Abouleish, I. (2017), "Sekem: social entrepreneurship brings the desert to fruition", Spark Publishers

Chapter Twenty
Adaptability reduces vulnerability

"The sun is about to set, the 'golden hour' has arrived.
Children are playing in the waves and dogs are running in joyous glee
across the endless sands. Will people still be walking here in a hundred
years?"
Journalist Sanne Bloemink, *De Groene Amsterdammer* 20 October 2021

Climate catastrophe can no longer be prevented but it can still be mitigated. It is already under way. It is therefore vital not only to focus on reducing CO_2 emissions in order to prevent further global catastrophe, but also to adapt to the effects of climate change. On the one hand, to protect cities, islands and coastal regions and, on the other, to enable regions and populations to cope with those effects. Because whether we like it or not, changes on one side of the world can have major consequences for societies and economies on the other. By investing in adaptation elsewhere, we are therefore investing in stability and prosperity at home. Otherwise, we are only as strong as the weakest link.

The Dutch economy and the country's prosperity are, for instance, entirely dependent on our international trading position. Banks, insurers, investment institutions and international companies also see that climate change and security is affecting their business and their future. They realise that they too need to join the energy transition and adapt, especially if people are fleeing their homes or simply moving away due to a lack of prospects.

The instability, crises and migration flows that arise will also indirectly affect the economies and societies of richer countries. Migration flows, for instance, lead to changes and instability in the markets and supply chains for our products. Many component suppliers are located in low-wage countries and these are precisely the countries at increased risk of flooding and instability, which can lead to serious disruptions. Raw materials are also becoming scarcer and more expensive, which impacts directly on product prices.

We are also seeing a change in the values and standards of consumers and employees, as there is an increasing demand for circular and low-emission products, forcing companies and organisations to change. Moreover, we are seeing growing numbers of polluting products being made more expensive or banned altogether. All this is forcing companies and organisations to adapt to the consequences of climate change.

In addition, we must ask ourselves whether it is morally justifiable not to spend money on climate adaptation. It is after all mainly rich countries that are causing all the misery with their emissions, and the people who have not actually contributed to CO_2 emissions are the ones who suffer most. This is also the reason why the rich countries agreed in the Paris agreement to spend some $100 billion a year from 2020 on the Green Climate Fund, the UN climate fund for the most vulnerable countries. But they failed to honour this agreement, which is why critics are now talking about "climate apartheid" and calling for "climate justice".[1]

Meanwhile, the UN environmental agency UNEP has calculated in a report that vulnerable countries will need up to $300 billion a year around 2030 to adapt to such phenomena as increased drought and rising sea levels.[2]

How to adapt

There are, therefore, plenty of reasons to press ahead with adaptation. Let us look at what we need to consider. Earlier in this book, I mentioned the Global Center on Adaptation (GCA), the international centre based in the Netherlands where global plans on climate adaptation are being forged under the leadership of Ban Ki-moon, the former UN secretary-general. This centre has drawn up six focal points for successful adaptation.

First, adaptation should be mainstreamed; an ugly word for a beautiful goal. Policymakers should assess every plan and decision in terms of how it can contribute to improving resilience to climate change. Second, considerably more money is needed for adaptation and new technology, especially in developing countries.

Third, the GCA advocates greater involvement of the private sector as well, because the market is often better than governments at identifying opportunities, although it does on occasion need some extra incentive to actually invest. Fourth, enhanced warning systems are needed to give people enough time to flee storms and floods. A fifth priority is to provide more opportunities to young people.[3] In Africa, for example, 43% of the population is under 15 years old. This generation will have to bear the consequences of climate change, but they are also better educated than their parents. They can start putting adaptation into practice.

Finally, the GCA recommends more active involvement of women. I mentioned earlier how crucial the role of women was within local communities. This is equally true at national level.

So the bigger picture is broader than the natural disaster warning systems discussed previously. It involves very real issues such as cultivating drought-resistant crops, measures for more efficient freshwater management, building natural coastal protection such as mangrove forests, or building climate-proof infrastructure, particularly, in the case of the latter, in urbanised coastal areas and river deltas, where much of the world's population lives.

This is particularly true of the river delta that makes up the Netherlands, much of which is already below sea level. To become climate-proof, we need to consider what sea level rise means for the infrastructure of the home port of our fleet of naval ships in Den Helder, for instance. Perhaps a floating structure that moves with the sea? The US is exploring the possibility of floating bases that are also self-sufficient in their energy supply: separate modules that you can link together and also relocate.[4] It does not take much imagination to see that this could offer a solution for living or working at sea. During my talks with the leading Dutch maritime research institute MARIN, it turned out that they too already have far-reaching ideas about the possibility of larger floating – and self-sufficient – platforms. Here, too, entire new technological concepts can offer solutions, both civil and military.

From scenarios to concrete plans

First and foremost, we need to look ahead and anticipate what we might expect. In my opinion, we still do not do this enough, which is somewhat strange given that on an individual level we usually like to be prepared for what lies ahead. When we go on holiday, for example, we find out about the country's security situation, check our tyre pressure, pack the first-aid kit, charge our phones, make sure we have a working navigation system, check we have enough money in the bank and make sure we have some extra cash in our wallet. We also water the plants one last time, leave a light on at home to deter burglars, lock the door extra securely, take out an insurance policy and, on the day before we leave, go to the garage for a safety check. So we leave little to chance and we take unpleasant and drastic eventualities into account.

To govern is to look ahead, but it is precisely that precautionary stance that has been lacking until now where climate change is concerned. In the Netherlands, for instance, we are still investing in living and working in the lowest and most vulnerable part of the country in terms of the expected sea level rise. The construction of the Eastern Scheldt Barrier, the storm surge barrier protecting our country from high water, was based on a sea level rise of only 40 centimetres.[5] We now know that this is not enough. The Royal Netherlands Meteorological Institute (KNMI) expects that by the year 2100 – in the worst-case scenario – the expected sea level rise will have reached

1.2 metres,[6] and if the Antarctic ice sheets melt faster than expected, a rise of up to 2 metres is possible.

Anyone building new infrastructure in the Netherlands should therefore be looking 10, 20, 50 and even 100 years ahead in terms of sea level rise and potential coastal response. Meanwhile, we could invest in new construction elsewhere in the country, further away from the sea. But drastic and expensive measures are also an option, such as raising the height of dykes, simultaneously spraying large quantities of sand on the beach to counter erosion of the shoreline and to fortify the dunes. Or creating new Wadden Islands off the Dutch coast, which would then be linked to new flood defences.

Another radical and almost unimaginable option is to build a dam across the northern part of the North Sea, a dam similar to the Dutch *Afsluitdijk*, which would cost us 250 to 500 billion euros every year for 20 years. That is a lot of money, but it amounts to just 0.1% of the gross domestic product (GDP) of all the countries protected by such a dam.[7] It is certainly a radical solution, as it would involve a dam of some 476 kilometres between the north of Scotland and the west of Norway, which could then protect more than 25 million Europeans from the effects of the expected sea level rise. There should then be another 161-kilometre dam in the south between the western tip of France and the south-west of England.[8] The scientist presenting this solution is Sjoerd Groeskamp, oceanographer at the Royal Netherlands Institute for Sea Research. He says he is proposing this to make everyone aware of the consequences of sea level rise. Groeskamp: "If we do nothing, this extreme dam might well be the only solution."[9]

Range of measures

Scientists not only expect that sea levels could rise significantly in the coming decades, but also that in the Netherlands the heaviest summer showers will become more extreme, while at the same time the probability of dry springs and summers will increase.[10] We are thus moving more and more towards the climate of southern Europe, and will also have to deal with heavy rainfall. This again calls for additional measures to protect ourselves.

Scenario analyses can help to identify future vulnerable areas in order to implement targeted protection measures.

For instance, where more rain is going to fall, we need to build major highways in such a way that they remain passable. We can also keep nursing homes, hospitals and prisons accessible by building them at higher elevations. In lower-lying buildings, we should at least place electrical sockets and other critical facilities at a higher point.

Individuals themselves are also an important link when it comes to increasing resilience. This starts with awareness of the risks and of the measures that can be taken at individual level. For example, information campaigns can warn people that more hours of sunshine lead to greater evaporation and thus less moisture in the soil, which means that every cigarette butt thrown from a car window, every burning exhaust in the tall grass, every spark from a braking train, every smouldering campfire or every bottle left behind that can act as a magnifying glass can all trigger devastating wildfires.

Another possibility is a campaign which provides people with information on how they themselves can reduce the flammability of their home or neighbourhood. For example, by removing leaves from gutters, removing dead plants, not putting wood chips close to your house and not having wood piles for the fireplace nearby.[11] It sounds simple, but in the event of a serious wildfire, everyone needs to be well informed in advance to prevent the fire from spreading. In wartime, you would make sure you had a shelter and enough supplies to survive for a few days if the power and public facilities went down. In a climate crisis too, we need to build our defences, right down to the resilience of individual citizens.

Better coordination of emergency aid

The need for climate adaptation also applies to military forces. Looking to the future, it is safe to assume that more frequent and more severe natural disasters will occur and that more emergency assistance will therefore be needed. For the military, thorough preparation is key – for instance, by training with civil parties and by making arrangements for the provision of sufficient emergency supplies, such as water, food, tents, beds and medical equipment.

This was brought home to me when Hurricane Irma swept over Sint Maarten in the Caribbean part of the Dutch Kingdom in 2017. We saw that the relief effort there was mainly effected *via* national channels, whereas it would have been much more effective and efficient to coordinate with other Western countries that have a shared interest in the Caribbean, such as the US, Canada, the UK, France and also the Netherlands. In fact, the island of Sint Maarten is part French and part Dutch, and yet everything was organised *via* national channels. That was a particularly valuable lesson learned.

In order to act as quickly as possible once the hurricane had passed, the Dutch armed forces had already sent military personnel to Sint Maarten before Irma made landfall. This meant that the impact of the disaster was immediately visible and it was easier to determine what emergency assistance was needed. That information arrived at the operations centre in The Hague *via* the Dutch commander in the Caribbean, so *via* the national line. There, a decision was made as to what personnel, equipment and relief supplies needed to be flown in, or rushed aboard a large navy ship to sail to the disaster area.

At the same time, however, the French were making their own plans for emergency assistance to the French part of Sint Maarten. The British did the same for other affected islands in the region. The International Red Cross was also considering relief measures. And so we all did this separately, from our own sphere of responsibility: despite the best of intentions, largely at cross purposes. We obviously tried to coordinate our efforts, but the possibilities are limited without prior planning and in a situation where every second counts. For example, the Dutch naval supply ship, HNLMS *Karel Doorman*, took relief supplies from the Netherlands, France and England. Everyone did their best, but there was just too much improvisation. We cannot prevent hurricanes, but if we work together, we can prepare ourselves better to minimise their impact.

Further professionalisation and greater collaboration

A changing climate with more extreme effects will result in other disaster scenarios with greater frequency and more severe impact. As a result, different demands will be placed on disaster response support from emergency services, including the Defence organisation.

Civil capabilities, such as police and fire services, are by definition overstretched in large-scale disasters, and military capabilities then become necessary, as we saw in the recent flood disaster in Limburg in 2021. Rapid assistance is therefore key and good preparation is half the battle.

Knowing that we will have to face this kind of disaster more often, and that the Ministry of Defence will always be called upon to provide assistance, it is important that we professionalise this task and make the necessary arrangements for collaboration.

In cases where civil authorities reach capacity, the military must be able to step in quickly. Joint scenario analyses with local civil authorities, local emergency services and armed forces are then crucial to be able to define the necessary collaboration and translate it into binding agreements. You will then know what to expect from each other and will not have to figure it all out during the crisis. Logistics arrangements can be made in advance and a regional centre could be set up where efforts can be coordinated and activities allocated. International agreements can also be made for the allocation of tasks. For instance, one country could refurbish a port and another an airport, and Britain, France and the Netherlands could jointly set up a logistics supply route for relief goods from Europe.

It is also worth considering arrangements for locally available relief items at different locations in a potential (disaster) area, so that these items do not have to be purchased first, nor do they have to be brought in from Europe. In the case of Hurricane Irma, the procurement and supply of emergency relief items in particular proved to be a delaying factor, because it all had to be arranged after the disaster had already occurred. Ideally, everything should be on site beforehand: camp beds, medical supplies, emergency lighting, sleeping bags, blankets, tents, psychosocial support, drinking water and food.

Planning alone is not enough, however. Professionalisation also means rehearsing those contingency plans together. Only then will you be on the same wavelength, even under time pressure, and get to know each other. Only then will you learn to speak the same language, ensure that communication systems and reporting are aligned, and be sure who has what mandate. You cannot play a champions league match without being trained as a team. Joint exercises and training for contingency plans boosts collaboration and prevents panic football. That saves time and saves lives, and saves money too.

Coordination mechanisms

International regional coordination is essential here. The example of Hurricane Irma makes that clear. Regional coordination mechanisms are actually necessary in many parts of the world that are vulnerable to natural disasters, such as the Caribbean, Southeast Asia and South America. The US already has Regional Commands such as AFRICOM for Africa and SOUTHCOM for Central and South America. These focus mainly on building a picture of the local security situation and shaping US partnership programmes with countries from that region. These centres are also responsible for the international coordination of all military efforts in the region on behalf of the US and they direct regional implementation programmes and operations. It would be beneficial to create similar multinational coordination centres in regions where climate change and its impacts are most likely to occur so that we can work together to increase resilience to those effects. And also, of course, to be able to function as a regional coordination mechanism in a joint disaster response when a disaster has occurred.

Water diplomacy

Global water scarcity also requires adaptation at the diplomatic level. The UN's 2023 Water Conference laid a foundation for a substantial change in the understanding, appreciation and management of water. The UN secretary-general concluded that water was something that affected everyone and deserved a place at the heart of political decision-making. The conference also adopted a Water Action Agenda with over 800 voluntary commitments, specific actions and initiatives.

One example is the Global Commission on the Economics of Water convened by the Netherlands in 2022. An initial report on the importance of water for the economy, society and the environment was presented at the conference.[12] The report underlines that the limits of freshwater use have been exceeded globally and that the water cycle has been disrupted.

The report makes it clear that the causes and impact of water problems can be global as well as local. Countries are much more water-dependent on each other than is generally known; not only because of rivers flowing from one country to another, but also because of the atmosphere, which transports even larger amounts of water between countries. However, those quantities are changing due to climate change and deforestation. International coordination and agreements are needed to designate stability of the water cycle as a global common good.

The Netherlands has announced funds to improve the ability to cope with water-related disasters in East Africa and make the most vulnerable populations more resilient. There is also a commitment to improve weather and climate data, strengthen early warning systems and increase disaster preparedness. The aim is to take action at an early stage and for people to be mobilised in time in the event of an imminent disaster.

The Netherlands is also involved in a major programme entitled "Water as Leverage for Resilient Cities" in Asia and South America. Partly because of this programme, dozens of projects have now been completed in major cities in India, Bangladesh, Indonesia and Colombia and, with the help of the World Bank and the Netherlands Enterprise Agency (RVO), the Water as Leverage programme is working to scale up in other parts of the world.

These projects are designed to provide solutions for converting urban ecosystems to more natural ones: capturing and retaining water, making cities greener, raising groundwater levels and cleaning up the groundwater itself. At the same time, investments are being made in housing construction, renewable energy and waste recycling, thus creating jobs and maintenance work in the long term.[13] The overall aim is to increase and consolidate capability, knowledge and understanding, as well as "ownership" among people and local communities and collaboration with partners to ensure that everything you do endures and retains support. Here in the Netherlands, the motto is "Invest in water, and you invest in everyone".[14]

It would be beneficial if diplomats and experts were to start applying this kind of diplomacy in many more places with a view to future developments, so that they are not only able to transfer knowledge to the most vulnerable people, but can also enable them to take control in adapting to the effects of climate change.

Education and equal rights

It may be less obvious, but investment in education for women and girls is extremely important in increasing the resilience of fragile states. For example, I remember from my time in Afghanistan that anyone who sent two daughters to school, so that they could later teach in a primary school, would ensure that the two daughters could together earn about 4,000 euros a year. That was the same amount that the father of the two daughters earned in agriculture before the great drought in 2018. So those who sent their daughters to school were better off financially.

Research shows that educating girls also helps to reduce climate impact. More highly educated women have been found to have fewer children. According to global research by the Brookings Institute, the difference between an uneducated woman and a woman with 12 years of education is four to five children.[15] Also, it is often women in low-wage countries who are responsible for providing and managing food, soil, trees and water. If all these women were better educated, they would also be better able to cope with the challenges of the changing climate.

It is safe to assume that some of the girls who attend school will go on to become decision-makers who support or encourage investment in and reform of their communities.[16] Or, as the Brookings Institute puts it: "For every extra year of a girl's education, a country is better prepared for climate disasters and also better able to recover after drought and floods."[17] If women then share their own experiences, they can influence future generations better than anyone else. So every girl getting an education, in Afghanistan or any other country, offers hope. What would it mean if women did not lose everything due to natural disasters or did not have to walk miles every day in the heat to find some murky drinking water? If they *could* go to school and have the chance to earn an income? Great strides could then be made in climate adaptation.

In addition, women worldwide are responsible for more than half of the world's food production, that is of edible food crops rather than cash crops.[18] But in most cases, women do not have the same rights as men. Now what if all those women were given as much financial support from governments as men, and greater access to information, assistance, credit and land rights? They would then be able to invest in things like irrigation, crop diversification or windbreaks that could make their land more resilient to the effects of climate change.

Those who also ensure that women are legally allowed to own or inherit land independently, have the right to be members of agricultural cooperatives, may purchase resources for marketing and sales, have access to technological information, and can borrow money that allows them to buy fertilisers, tools, water, seeds, and so on, have acted wisely. The UN Food and Agriculture Organisation (FAO) reports that women farmers increase their crop yields by 20-30% if they have the same access as men to agricultural production resources, participation mechanisms and support services.[19]

Indeed, when women have more income, they reinvest 90% of the money they earn in education, healthcare and food for their families – for men, the figure is 30-40%. In Nepal, for instance, there is a direct link between improving women's land rights and the health of their children.[20] And women are also able to come up with smart, sustainable and affordable solutions that are often overlooked. In many Pacific islands, for instance, it is mainly women who harvest the "taro" in particular. The cultivation of this 2-metre-tall plant with edible corm is threatened by climate change. Any attempt to address the food shortage in a region like this therefore needs to involve women, who use their traditional knowledge and expertise to come up with a solution.

In short, it is clear that the fight for girls' and women's rights and the fight against climate change are closely linked. If we want to mitigate the impacts of climate change, it is crucial that we invest in equal rights for women – including education for girls and women. Although women are often the victims of climate change, they also have the ability to do something about the impact. Failure to take advantage of that is sheer stupidity.

Sustainability education and awareness

Finally, I would like to mention education in our schools as another important tool to increase adaptivity. In many cases, change begins with awareness. Only if you are aware of how climate change is going to affect your future will you feel the need to do something about it. That is one reason why, as chairman of the IMCCS, I spend most of my time explaining and demonstrating the security implications of climate change. Every week, I give talks and guest lectures on the subject. Without that awareness, I will remain a lone voice in the wilderness and nothing will change. Climate change is about the future security of our children, of the generations to come.

This is also why at one point I was approached by Marte Visser, who was involved in political lobbying work for sustainability education with the foundation she was with at the time, the Time is Now Foundation. She believed that a "crowbar project" was needed to ensure that sustainability education would be fully secured in the statutory curriculum. The political lobbying had set some wheels in motion, but not enough.

The crowbar project she approached me about was Think Now; a think tank consisting of 32 secondary school students from different school levels and different socio-economic and cultural backgrounds. Together, students will devise and try out solutions – large and small – to climate and environmental issues for three months. During the 3-day think-tank, they will discuss and refine all their experiences and solutions with each other. The results will be processed into a smart manuscript that will then be presented to (inter) national policymakers in the EU, the UN, the House of Representatives and to celebrities such as Arnold Schwarzenegger. A documentary will be made of the entire project for everyone to see that sustainability education is not only important, but also enormously inspiring.

It was not a small project that Marte approached me about, but she got me thinking. Not only did the project itself really appeal to me, but also its aim. Just as the defence organisation should not make the classic mistake of basing its preparations on the last war, the same applies to education. Climate change is one of this century's biggest issues that future generations will have to deal with. So it is our responsibility to prepare them properly for it. Not by adding a separate subject of climate to the already overcrowded curriculum, but by integrating it into all existing subjects.

That is why I immediately said "yes" when I was asked to act as an ambassador for Think Now and to assist the students in the subfield "climate and safety" during the think tank sessions. I was only too happy to help, because I believe that every pupil can do their bit for a cleaner and healthier planet, regardless of their school level or interests. Sustainability education will give pupils a better understanding of what lies ahead and thus give them greater control of their future. I firmly believe in this way of empowering young people.

Young people themselves need this. Various organisations, including Youth for Climate, conducted a survey in March 2021 of Dutch secondary school students' views on sustainable education. That survey showed that 37% of students say they learn nothing at all about climate change, its impact or sustainable development. But young people themselves do see the importance: 87% of the pupils surveyed want to learn more about climate change and sustainable development. An overwhelming majority of young people therefore think they should learn more about these topics at school.

Young people also want to learn more skills so that they can help to solve climate issues, and they say they want to learn more about the social repercussions of climate change and the impact of the individual on global warming. They want to learn more about these issues throughout the school year and in different subjects.[21] This survey shows, therefore, that young people want to be properly prepared for their future in which the changing climate will clearly play an important role. Knowledge is essential for that.

So why not focus the Dutch curriculum on a world in which fighting the climate crisis is a priority? I once heard about Bas de Bruijn, an inspired chemistry teacher from Huizen, who had his students investigate how expensive a shower was. They discovered (at a time when gas prices were much lower) that showering for about 12 minutes used around 100 litres of water; as much as "a hundred cartons of milk", was how they pictured it. That water also has to be heated by gas, Bas explains to the students. "Go and work out how much gas you burn for the water you use and how much it costs." The pupils worked out that it was about 32 cents per shower. They quickly calculated that, if four people live in a house, they will spend €1.20 on showering. If they multiply that by 365 days a year, they arrive at about €500 a year. That's €500 that parents were spending to heat the water for the shower. And that did not include any cooking or heating for the house. So after all the calculations, Bas said: "If you shower less often now or turn the thermostat down a degree, your mum and dad will save €200 a year, and you can say at Christmas dinner: well, Dad, I saved you money. Now I'd like some more pocket money." And with that, says the teacher with a wink, he has won his pupils over.

It is clear that people like Bas make a difference, but ideally every student in the Netherlands (and beyond) should get this kind of teaching – and more. In maths, pupils should do arithmetic related to sustainability, or discuss the "rights of nature" in social studies, asking questions such as: should ecocide be an offence?

Let young people do projects on one of the UN sustainability goals, or debate one of these goals in Dutch classes. If you are talking about Europe, you can look at what different countries are doing for the climate, and in history, discuss the 1953 flood disaster and the construction of the Delta Works and see what the consequences were for the Netherlands. There are so many possibilities. But then there has to be a curriculum that does justice to the major issues of our time and which define the future in which today's young people will become adults. Because only with awareness can change begin.

So all in all, there are still plenty of steps we can all take. And how wonderful it would be to do so on an international level. That is precisely why I seized the moment to ask Arnold Schwarzenegger, the famous film star and former "Green Governor" of California, to join forces on this issue. I sat with him on a panel at the Austrian World Summit in May 2023 to talk about climate and security. It provided a great opportunity to ask him later by letter if it would be possible to have some students from our think tank present the best ideas at the Schwarzenegger Climate Initiative in June 2024. "Perhaps we could even arrange a meeting between the students and your guests to talk about the importance of sustainability education in secondary schools", I wrote. "That would not only generate huge attention for this topic but it would also be an enormous boost to students around the world and hopefully provide a springboard to launch this initiative worldwide."

Line of defence

In this chapter, I have offered a multitude of suggestions for adapting to climate change, solutions that are important for our security and our way of life. It is clear that everyone needs to adapt: governments, institutions, businesses, organisations, individuals, and certainly military forces. For all the adaptation measures mentioned, humanity still has time to make plans and implement them. Groningen professor and director of the Global Center on Adaptation (GCA), Patrick Verkooijen, once put it aptly in an interview with daily newspaper Het Parool: "Adaptation is not a defeat, it is a line of defence."[22] So in addition to reducing CO_2 emissions, let us now fully commit to building resilience, physically and socially.

Notes

1. BBC News (2019, 25 June), "'Climate apartheid' between rich and poor looms, UN expert warns", *BBC News,* https://www.bbc.com/news/world-48755154

2. UNEP (2021). Adaptation gap report 2020. UNEP, Nairobi, https://www.unep.org/resources/adaptation-gap-report-2020

3. Global Center on Adaptation (2021). State and trends in adaptation report 2021: Africa. GCA, Rotterdam.

4. Naval News Staff (2021, 3 December). Construction begins on US Navy's fifth expeditionary sea base. *Naval News,* https://www.navalnews.com/naval-news/2021/12/construction-begins-on-us-navys-fifth-expeditionary-sea-base/

5. NOS (2021, 4 October). "Nature is changing as Eastern Scheldt barrier closes more often", NOS, https://nos.nl/artikel/2400358-natuur-verandert-als-oosterscheldekering-vaker-dicht-gaat

6. KNMI (2021). Climate signal '21. KNMI, *De Bilt.* https://www.knmi.nl/kennis-en-datacentrum/achtergrond/knmi-klimaatsignaal-21

7-8. Groeskamp C., Kjellsson, J. (2020), "The Northern European Enclosure Dam for if climate change mitigation fails", *Bull Am Meteorol Soc.,* https://doi.org/10.1175/bams-d-19-0145.1; https://journals.ametsoc.org/doi/pdf/10.1175/BAMS-D-19-0145.1.

9. NIOZ (2020, 31 January), "A dam across the North Sea: climate change warning scenario", Press release Royal Netherlands Institute for Sea Research, https://www.nioz.nl/en/news/een-dam-dwars-door-de-noordzee-waarschuwscenario-voor-klimaatverandering

10. KNMI (2021). Climate signal '21. KNMI, *De Bilt.* https://www.knmi.nl/kennis-en-datacentrum/achtergrond/knmi-klimaatsignaal-21

11. According to Cathelijne Stoof of Wageningen University in the radio programme *Met het Oog op Morgen* (2020, 20 July). Can be heard at https://www.nporadio1.nl/fragmenten/nieuws-en-co/ba188cd1-e00a-4af3-aa9e-ca671d9f5160/2020-07-20-is-nederland-klaar-voor-toename-bosbranden

12. The Global Commission on the Economics of Water, "Turning the Tide: a Call to Collective Action" (2023), https://turningthetide.watercommission.org

13. More information on this project can be found at https://www.worldwateratlas.org/curated/water-as-leverage

14. Interview with climate envoy Henk Ovink on BNR, https://www.bnr.nl/player/audio/10157237/10412821

15. Winthrop, R. & Kharas, H. (2016, 3 March), "Want to save the planet? Invest in girls' education". *Brookings Opinion,* https://www.brookings.edu/opinions/want-to-save-the-planet-invest-in-girls-education/

16. "In Rural Afghanistan some Taliban gingerly welcome girls schools", 4 May 2020, *Foreign policy,* https://foreignpolicy.com/2020/05/04/afghanistan-taliban-girls-schools/

17. Brookings Institute, "Climate change, fertility and girls' education", 16 February 2016, https://www.brookings.edu/blog/future-development/2016/02/16/climate-change-fertility-and-girls-education/

18. FAO (2011), "The role of women in agriculture", ESA Working Paper No 11-02, World Food and Agriculture Organisation, Rome, https://www.fao.org/NEWS/1998/980305-e.htm

19. Report FAO conference held in Washington on 19 November 2020, see https://www.fao.org/north-america/news/detail/en/c/1334901/

20. "Drawdown: the most comprehensive plan ever to reverse climate disruption", compiled by Paul Hawken, p. 77

21. Climate in the Classroom (2021). Survey of secondary school students' opinions on sustainability in education. Available at https://drive.google.com/file/d/1EiMMLEqhLn1n35w5ZdVGaWfVes9ZO8_o/view

22. Zoelen, B. (2021, 22 January). "Trillions of dollars for Covid-19. What about the climate?" *Het Parool*

Chapter Twenty-One
Towards a sustainable peace mission

"Use military bases as 'food' for the next generation."
Architect and urban designer Floris Alkemade at the Future Force Conference 2017

It is May 2016. I have been asked to open the Dutch pavilion "Blue" at the Venice Biennale of Architecture, by Israeli-Dutch architect Malkit Shoshan. For 10 years, she has been researching peace operations carried out by the UN worldwide and she had previously presented her findings at the UN headquarters in New York. In her report, she calls for UN missions to be made more effective, and in particular the UN mission in Mali, MINUSMA. At the time, it is the largest mission. The Netherlands is part of that mission, which is also why I was asked to open the exhibition.

Malkit calls her design "Design for Legacy", suggesting the addition of a fourth "D" to the familiar 3D protocol (defence, development, diplomacy). If the UN pays attention to what they build, erect and leave behind, and then take into account the local conditions and needs of the population, she believes we can thus help to fight the root causes of conflict and offer new prospects to the population.

It does feel a little strange walking around in Venice in my uniform, amidst lovers of art and architecture. When I arrive, I am pleasantly surprised. The Dutch pavilion is a soft shade of blue from the camouflage netting that filters the incoming sunlight. Apparently, the architect borrowed them from the navy. The colour symbolises peace. It is, of course, the colour of the UN peace missions, but also somewhat resembles the indigo blue colour of the Tuareg's clothing in Mali.

Malkit shows me around the pavilion. She shows me her ideal UN camp, which she has built on rectangular white tables above which spotlights hang. She tells me that while the priority of UN missions is security, the question in the long term is what the UN leaves behind when the mission ends and the military leave. "Ultimately, it is the people themselves who have to rebuild their country. They are not involved now", she says. That is why she has designed a communal space for UN camps: an open space where soldiers and locals can meet. But also a place where knowledge can be shared and support can be generated for long-term solutions; in other words, addressing the root causes of tensions. "The UN military hardly ever have any contact with the local population at the moment", Malkit explains. "The compounds are built as impenetrable islands shielded by barbed wire. That remoteness poses problems, for example for the acceptance of the large UN mission by the people of Mali." This is an important point, because it is especially important for the Dutch personnel in the mission to have contact with local people in order to find out what is going on and thus be able to determine what is needed to help make the country more stable and secure.

The architect says she knows that in the Dutch camp in Mali, Camp Castor, the water drainage system is highly advanced and innovative, while the neighbouring UN super camp, as well as the city of Gao, sometimes experience flooding and damage due to extreme rainfall. She has therefore developed four steps to address these flooding problems, as well as four steps to improve the safety of children in the vicinity of the UN camp and their education.

"Primary education for children in Gao is too expensive for local families", Malkit explains. "People cannot afford to send their children to school, which is why many children roam the streets of Gao. At the same time, parents worry that jihadist groups will recruit their children. So why not let the children play in a secure area on the outskirts of the UN camp?" she asks. "Then they can have lessons there too."

Positive impact

I immediately agree that security is a pressing issue to which we need to find an answer, both for the military in the area, and of course also for the local population, especially around the camps. After all, a military base can also be a target for attacks. There have been missile attacks on our base in Mali, for example, fortunately without casualties. In early 2016, there was an attack on the UN base in Kidal, another city in Mali. Unidentified militants there fired more than 30 missiles at UN soldiers, killing three people and wounding many more. A brutal reminder of how terrorists want to make their presence felt everywhere, and how they sometimes seek only one confrontation, solely to kill. So for a military engineer, security is the most important consideration when building a camp.

But as I try to come up with an answer for Malkit, I am aware of the importance of local development, the importance of local solutions and local ownership. If we as an international community want to help bring stability, then security efforts must go hand in hand with programmes of sustainable regional development. Otherwise, we are just treating the symptoms.

This starts with the ecological footprint of our presence, which has a negative impact on the local community when what we are trying to do is help. We can do that by, on the one hand, focusing much more attention on avoiding that ecological impact in the design of missions and, on the other, by considering how the base could actually have a positive impact; the latter, for instance, by applying the technologies we use for energy or water to help the local population too in the form of quick-impact development projects. This also increases support for the mission among the local population, especially if you provide space for facilities and activities under the safe umbrella of the camp that you, as an international force, can hand over to the population after departure.

This does require a thorough analysis during the preparation and planning of a mission. It also needs to be underpinned by social science research, along with knowledge and expertise from anthropologists and economists, as well as local knowledge from the communities, for instance from teachers and spiritual leaders, to understand what underlies the tensions and what the needs are. These are all different actors who can work together in a local security ecosystem from the point of view of their own objectives and interests.

Sustainable ecosystems around peace missions

Malkit is nodding happily while I'm saying all this, but I also say straight away that we still have a long way to go here for peace missions to be successful in the long run. First and foremost, we are directly dependent on the local security situation. Within that security context, we can look for possible courses of action that address not only the symptoms of conflict, but also the root causes. A good idea like Malkit's that contributes to this does not become a reality overnight.

When I leave Venice the next day, I cannot get the idea of a different kind of sustainable peace mission out of my head. Could we not explore with various experts whether we could use our sites more for the benefit of local people? For example, by creating a safe environment for children to play and have lessons? That means creating a kind of ecosystem – a partnership – around peace missions, in which various experts with different backgrounds work within their own discipline and mandate towards the same goal: making unstable regions and countries stable again. In Afghanistan, I saw how the city of Tarin Kowt expanded towards our camp and how people sought its protection.

But there are other opportunities to improve peace missions, both for the sake of the mission and for the local population. Consider, for example, fuel consumption. That consumption is not only an operational risk if you have to keep hauling large quantities by road through dangerous territory, but it is also harmful to the environment. Moreover, it can push up local fuel prices. Today, a military unit is still very dependent on fossil fuels such as kerosene and diesel for its operations and for diesel generators that power the camps. This dependence on fossil fuels also requires a huge and very expensive logistical effort, and it makes our people vulnerable. What if fuel supplies suddenly stop, or the fuel runs out and you are stuck somewhere? Also, military personnel are regularly killed or injured in attacks on fuel trucks; they therefore need to be heavily protected, which in turn takes a great deal of capacity.

At the Fieldlab Smart Base referred to earlier, the Ministry of Defence is therefore investigating how military camps can become more self-sufficient. The use of renewable energy sources such as solar, wind and hydrogen play an important role here. Greater independence in energy supply reduces the logistic and ecological footprint of deployed units and increases people's security. The expertise and possibly even the installations for this self-sufficiency can be transferred after the mission ends.

Reusing water at a UN camp is another example. At the moment, when the UN (and the countries participating in UN missions) arrive somewhere in the world and build a camp for often hundreds or even thousands of military personnel, they drill wells in the ground to get water. That water is used for activities like cooking and showering. However, this lowers the groundwater level in the area and may cause the wells of nearby villages to run dry. As a result, local people have even less water, when there is often already a severe water shortage. And we know that a water shortage is a potential source of conflict and can further exacerbate existing tensions and conflicts.

This is the reason why, on deployment in Mali, the Dutch military tries to reuse as much water as possible at their camp by collecting the used water and filtering and purifying it. With the right equipment, it can even be reused as clean drinking water. In the end, this allows us to reuse more than half of the used water. This is in contrast to the neighbouring UN super camp, where almost all used water is lost. It makes a huge difference to the population in the vicinity of the camps if the missions do not adversely affect the groundwater level and thus the water supply. And it also makes a huge difference if countless plastic water bottles are not being constantly flown or trucked in.

Buying locally

Another way to help local populations while reducing the ecological footprint of UN missions is to ensure that more goods and services are sourced regionally and locally, thereby avoiding the need to import environmentally unfriendly goods or products *via* a long supply line. In Mali, for example, we used locally hired construction equipment, but that depended on local market availability. The UN has a fairly rigid logistics system in which it works worldwide with framework contracts that involve large sums of money. As a result, relatively little use is made of the local market. That is a shame. Local procurement should always be a starting point when building UN camps.

I believe the procurement rules should therefore be changed. Make sure you can buy and acquire more items locally, and set sustainability requirements for their use, whether they are building materials, furniture or consumables. This would avoid the need to bring in metal containers from China for the living and working areas at the base in Mali. Production of these containers is not environmentally friendly; they also have to be moved over huge distances and they are taken away again when the mission is over. Partly because they get too hot, and partly because the UN has a "leave no trace" rule. So why not just buy bricks in the area with which to build houses at the camp? Then there is no mess left behind when you leave; as in the case of local purchasing and acquisition, you not only stimulate local industry and economy, but local people can also use the buildings afterwards, to live in, for example, or as shops, schools, storage or community spaces. And if they are built by local contractors, you prevent the use of materials and equipment that cannot be locally maintained or repaired. The Germans did this in Afghanistan, in

Kunduz, where they set up the military camp with stone buildings, using local contractors, with the aim of eventually handing this infrastructure over to the local community. Care must obviously be taken to avoid driving up prices on the local market, because otherwise the local population will still have little to gain.

It is also important to be mindful of local needs and potential areas of tension in terms of building style, functionality and choice of location. Many development projects fail in terms of acceptance by the local population because their interests and customs have not been sufficiently taken into account.

Working on resilience

Earlier, I referred to the great importance of data analyses as a tool to be able to see what climate risks lie ahead and to be able to identify them in time. These analyses should allow us to anticipate events and start highly targeted adaptation programmes in identified risk areas. In other words, not reacting after the event, but preventing it from happening in the first place. The importance of data analysis does not stop there, however. Also in the preparation and implementation of these adaptation programmes, it is particularly important to gain a local insight into the security effects of the changing climate.

In the planning of adaptation programmes, intelligence agencies could, for example, ensure an integrated climate security assessment to better understand the relationship between climate change and the local security situation. The UN could contribute by strengthening cooperation with regional climate centres and national meteorological and hydrological agencies to monitor climate change and collect data. That information would help the countries and UN agencies concerned to better understand climate-related security risks and to come up with solutions to mitigate them.

A coherent approach like this, based on a good picture of the root causes of tension and conflict, requires military intelligence services to look at problems from a climate point of view and broaden their focus. This means that, just as these services now invest in cyber specialists, for example, they must also start investing in climate analysts: people who not only analyse the effects of climate change but can also link them to national security.

This will facilitate a coherent approach to problems in fragile states, where security and development go hand in hand, based on the understanding that one cannot exist without the other. In this way, we can also focus UN missions more on the root causes of security problems and thus help to take the sting out of local tensions. The military component of such a mission can then set up a "green" line of operations aimed at enabling other civil efforts and making fragile countries more resilient to the effects of climate change. This does require broader involvement of and collaboration with other parties, such as NGOs, business, banks and philanthropists, not to mention local leaders.

Let me give an example. If the analyses show that migration problems and breeding grounds for terrorism are the result of growing discontent among the population due to soil erosion and increasing infertility of the land, this calls for a plan in which security efforts go hand in hand with local programmes to improve water management and to plant trees. This may involve the use of UN military personnel for security or logistic support, for example. Or, if the conclusion is that people need to be relocated to somewhere they can grow crops in safety and build a new livelihood, then it is important to carefully consider the impact of that relocation: is it really necessary, are there any alternatives, what locations are suitable, how do we prevent potential new tensions there? All these are questions that require comprehensive answers. The knowledge and expertise for such considerations should therefore be an integral part of the UN organisation and the military units deployed.

Adaptive UN peace missions

UN peace missions could also be a tool in development efforts to help local people when it comes to clean water, food and a smaller carbon footprint. Consider, for example, helping to build infrastructure to provide people with safe access to clean water and good sanitation in order to prevent the outbreak of disease and ensure that people do not lose their livelihoods and their dignity.

People also need to be prevented from illegally tapping water at the expense of other users, which leads to further violence. Along rivers, military personnel could therefore provide security during crop irrigation, and support civil training efforts. Or they could help to distribute seeds for crops that are more drought-resistant, or to restore ravaged grazing lands by building earthen dykes on the contour lines so that rainwater can be retained for longer.

Assistance in enforcing fishing quotas could also help; or assistance with well management by pastoralists, so that grazing land around the wells is kept from overgrazing. In the context of this assistance, consider local conflict management too, so that farmers do not deprive each other of access to fertile land. Military personnel could alert people to the importance of surveillance in villages at night to prevent the theft of timber. But they could also install panels on the roofs of houses for cheap solar energy, or give away small portable devices that work on solar energy so that smoky oil lamps are replaced by electric lamps to provide light for children to do their homework. It may all sound basic and a little like charity, but these are the activities that can quickly make a big difference in boosting local resilience with relatively little effort. By guiding and training local security forces in this respect, they can develop as a force for good.

On a somewhat larger scale, support from the international community can be used to plant trees that can survive in extreme heat and dry conditions. After all, greening is an ideal cure for desertification. This is not a direct task for the military, but security is often a prerequisite here; military personnel could provide the impetus.

I realise that this does not sound very military and may give the impression that I have become some kind of tree-hugger, but virtually all peace missions now take place in fragile states where climate change is a driver of instability and conflict. The link between climate change and peace and security is a reality, and the international community's security efforts are an important part of the response to this complex security issue. Whether we are talking about changes in groundwater levels, desertification or migration flows, military personnel increasingly find themselves on the front lines of climate-related crises.

The international community needs to set a good example and take the lead here. It is unacceptable for a UN camp to draw groundwater in the area, causing wells to run dry, and for the UN to be the biggest fossil fuel consumer in the regions where they operate. Good example leads to good practice, especially if we help it along a little.

For that to happen, however, things need to change. All too often, efforts in fragile countries still run *via* separate civil and military programmes. As a result, we work at cross purposes with each other, even get in each other's way, and we do not always understand each other. Whether we like it or not, security and development go hand in hand. One is not possible without the other. Again, a safe environment is a prerequisite for doing what is necessary if you want to offer local people decent prospects. For that, a change of mindset is needed.

I am well aware that in today's world, many are sceptical of such an approach. In a number of fragile countries, resistance to Western interference is growing and Russia and China are wading in to fill that vacuum. Fragile countries therefore risk becoming the battleground of mounting global competition for influence and access to resources. This polarisation is also affecting the ability of multilateral institutions to come up with sustainable solutions and it reduces the chances of decent prospects for the most vulnerable, particularly given that it is precisely these vulnerable people who will be hit hardest by the effects of climate change.

The solution lies in bridging those contradictions. We all have a common interest in stability in fragile regions. Climate change is a common global enemy and, despite the clash of national interests, it is the ideal issue on which we could and should pool our international resources. For this, we need the multilateral mechanisms that are now under so much pressure.

Chapter Twenty-Two
From partnerships to ecosystems

"For, in the final analysis, our most basic common link is that we all inhabit this planet. We all breathe the same air. We all cherish our children's future. And we are all mortal."

President John F. Kennedy, American University speech

Ever since my visit to the Venice Biennale of Architecture, where I first saw Malkit's design for UN missions, the idea of an ecosystem approach to security has been on my mind. It is why, six months later, I change the theme of the Future Force Conference completely. While everyone is expecting a security conference pur sang, that is, a conference where military people meet with knowledge institutes and people from the industry, we surprise visitors with an alternative format. We invite people from different backgrounds and with different areas of expertise. They look at security and sustainable development from an angle very different from that of the military.

It works quite well, I would say with some modesty. Some 1,200 people descend on The Hague from far and wide. Anthropologists, diplomats, entrepreneurs, architects, CEOs, cyber specialists, big data analysts, local activists, virtual reality creators, journalists, terrorism experts, gender specialists, religious leaders, administrators, politicians, aid workers, economists, teachers, game developers, ethical hackers, students and even deradicalized youths and a former child soldier.

Of the 1,200 participants, therefore, only a small number are military. The oldest participant is 84 years old and the youngest 19, and there are participants from every continent. The World Forum in The Hague, which is hosting the conference, lives up to its name. It is buzzing with ideas and the desire to work together. All the organisations we approached personally are participating free of charge. Not only because they see opportunities for a variety of projects, but also because they want to contribute to a safer, more stable and sustainable world in which there are opportunities and prospects for everyone. Because that is the whole idea behind the ecosystem approach. Everyone has a heartfelt self-interest, and that is served by the overarching interest for everyone: a secure world.

Special partnerships

The director of War Child, an organisation dedicated to children growing up amid war and violence, gets to work on organising an interactive session for all participants during this unique conference. The aim is to see how resources can be pooled. The same goes for the women's network, WO=MEN, the World Resources Institute (WRI) that researches sustainable management of natural resources, the UN University and the think tank FAST, a project by the architect Malkit whom I met in Venice. These are just a few examples of organisations working voluntarily to make something amazing out of that joint conference in 2017.

No long speeches by series of experts, but a variety of stimulating and surprising plenary presentations by people with diverse experiences, interspersed with about 20 sessions in separate rooms on various topics. Ultimately, these breakout sessions cover an array of topics that are important in the ecosystem concept. All those present are in search of solutions in areas such as cyber threats, migration, future military bases, child development, new disruptive technologies, the use of big data, logistic challenges for peace missions, leadership, smart and resilient cities, and opportunities to shape the organisation of an ecosystem.

Innovations are also presented and demonstrated during the conference. In the main hall, for example, visitors see an electric bicycle, the Trefecta, designed for special forces. Similar to a mountain bike, it allows personnel with full packs to reach a top speed of more than 70 kilometres per hour. The range of the bike itself is about 100 kilometres. Our deployed soldiers in Mali are currently testing the bike in the field. It is a useful invention that seems to offer many operational advantages. Most importantly, the bike makes you independent of fossil fuels, allows you to move quickly through difficult terrain, and makes you very sustainable.

Concrete results

Besides the innovations and the many interesting conversations that take place, the conference also leads to some concrete results. To cite a few examples of collaboration created by the conference: the WRI and HCSS agree to link their databases on resources and social and political instability. This makes it possible to predict instability and water scarcity, or the scarcity of rare earth metals, in the future. It is the seed for the subsequent Water, Peace and Security partnership I wrote about earlier.

During the conference, colleagues from the Dutch air force met the director of the NGO Save the Children, as well as some enthusiastic creative minds from the international consultancy Capgemini, which eventually – a year later – resulted in the creation of a "Whiteflag Protocol". Intended for the International Red Cross and NGOs, amongst others, the protocol provides for the digitisation of international humanitarian law using what is known as blockchain technology. This is a reliable technology that can be used to capture data from all participants on a variety of issues of interest to everyone in the area. With this new initiative, aid workers, journalists and other parties in conflict situations can digitally "fly a white flag", making it impossible for warring parties to claim they did not know about this surrender, as it is demonstrably and immutably recorded in a blockchain; in other words, a register or database with up-to-date information that is highly reliable and extremely difficult or impossible to hack.

The same technology can be used to see where humanitarian aid will potentially be needed due to famine, drought or migration; where danger areas such as minefields are located; where NGOs are working and where vital infrastructure, such as energy facilities, is located. For people in conflict zones, such as humanitarian workers, this information is crucial.

Getting inspired

Besides the specific new partnerships, I also see how people are inspired by the conference, because they are meeting completely different people from those they would normally meet at conferences. For example, I remember clearly how moved a Dutch general is by his exchange with the former child soldier from Africa. He meets the boy during the breakout session "Children are the future", organised by War Child. During that session, the boy tells the Dutch officer how, at the age of 11, he and 33 of his peers were forced to kill people with an AK47. "I will never forget his story", my colleague says afterwards, full of emotion.

Another colleague, a military adviser on gender, meets someone at the conference who works in the field of child protection for PLAN International, an NGO that advocates for children's rights and a dignified existence for girls worldwide. Together, after a good discussion, they plan to explore the possibility of collaboration so that they can better support children in the future. I also remember how an ethical hacker from service provider Deloitte is affected by the documentary we show in a cinema room on the effects of climate change. This documentary, *Age of Consequences*, is a first in Europe at the time. The young hacker reveals that he had not realised before that there was a link between climate change and terrorism. It really makes him think.

In another part of the building, a Canadian officer and Colombian Ana Saldarriaga meet. Ana is a powerful young woman who has experienced a great deal of violence in her country. She is committed to AIESEC, an NGO that mobilises young leaders around the world. She is therefore one of the speakers at the conference. The Canadian officer immediately walks up to her when he sees her, saying that her speech earlier that day reminded him why he does what he does. He had tears in his eyes. "That touched me so deeply, I can't even put it into words", Ana says later. All these small examples show how entirely new initiatives can come about by bringing together people from different backgrounds and with overlapping interests. Cross-fertilisation such as this is crucial in the quest for innovative concepts and partnerships. It also helps to dispel preconceptions and identify how we can strengthen each other, knowing that none of us can face the issues alone.

The value of virtual reality

Prior to the conference, I ask a team of young brilliant minds to create a base of the future in virtual reality (VR). Unfortunately, I can't give them the money they deserve for this extraordinary work, but I do promise them plenty of enthusiastic responses and thus exposure for their company. Luckily, that is what they get. In fact, everyone who gets to put on their VR headset in the main hall can hardly believe their eyes. Even all the high-ranking generals from abroad. With the VR headset, they see themselves right in the middle of a modern, or rather futuristic military camp somewhere in the desert, where different groups of people are working to rebuild a country. In addition to military personnel, the professionals include medical specialists, diplomats, teachers and agricultural experts. "It's so inspiring", I hear someone say after one such virtual visit. "You're actually walking around a base from the future, where different people are working on security." That is partly why the VR company is quickly offered a contract by the British Ministry of Defence.

More important, however, is the frame of mind that is awakened when the headset is on. The idea of the Fieldlab Smart Base is a good example. The idea is that any innovations created there will later be more widely applicable. Not only for the Defence organisation, but also for aid organisations that need to quickly set up a temporary safe location where large groups of people gather; humanitarian camps, for example, as well as locations for major events. In my view, therefore, the Fieldlab Smart Base is a great example of an ecosystem approach in which universities, tech companies, the Ministry of

Defence and others can pool their resources to come up with new integrated concepts and applications around the central theme of a self-sufficient base.

Philanthropists

There is no doubt that this was an incredibly successful conference, and I think more people share that view. This is evident from the number of enthusiastic reactions that appear on social media afterwards and from the delightful thank-you letters from participating organisations and countries. We should really aim to do this on a more regular basis. The format of this conference can be seen as a best practice to bring together scientists, companies and implementing agencies to come up with new concepts and new partnerships for the express purpose of problem-solving. It is also important to ensure support and supervision for compliance with the agreements that are made.

We could also invite philanthropists next time, because it is always a good idea to link benefactors – who have a lot of money to spend – with people with good innovative ideas. My personal invitation to Bill Gates, for example, in the vain hope that he might be tempted to come to the Netherlands, was ready to be sent prior to the Future Force Conference in 2017. Unfortunately, that was a step too far for some at the ministry.

I am still being approached by people asking whether there will be a follow-up to the conference and whether the Ministry of Defence will organise it again. Unfortunately – not least because of the coronavirus pandemic – it has been a long time now and Defence seems to be opting for a more conventional security conference with existing security partners after all. As far as I know, no-one else has yet taken up the ecosystem approach to a security conference elsewhere.

I hope, therefore, that through this book, I can instil in other people the same enthusiasm about this integrated approach as shown by the people who participated in the conference at the time. In the end, you have to work with new partners, towards a shared vision of the future. Everyone can then contribute from their own background and benefit from it. All contributions are mutually beneficial. The coronavirus crisis has shown how important it is to work together, to consider not only the medical side of the crisis, but also the social and economic side, and to seek collaboration to make it work.

Teamwork

It is clear that coherence and collaboration are key to the ecosystem approach. It is not the easiest path, but it is the only way to reach solutions to the immense and complex issue of climate change. Different players with diverse backgrounds working together have a much greater chance of achieving success. By being open-minded, sharing knowledge, ideas and experiences to reach new insights, sustainable results can be achieved.

As people become more aware of the way things are connected, they discover interdependencies, and they also see where activities overlap and where they can complement each other. An ecosystem approach also stimulates new thinking and innovation, because by revealing interconnections and through the process of cross-pollination, people are inspired and come up with ideas. Innovation can be encouraged and practical solutions emerge more quickly. Those who can actually put an integrated approach like this into practice will see that it leads to success.

I believe that this approach is therefore crucial to addressing the climate and biodiversity crisis in which we find ourselves. Only through a bold and coherent approach will we create sustainable solutions to the huge and complex climate problems facing us all. That coherent approach consists of actions and measures at every level, from individuals to major world leaders. Think big and just start somewhere – anyone can make a difference at their own level through the ecosystem approach.

For me, the 2017 Future Force Conference was a demonstration of best practice in how platforms can be created to bring a wide range of people together on an issue such as climate and security. A platform like this can help to take a complex issue out of the political frenzy of the day and discuss it on a more professional and substantive level. It can thus serve a bridging function, with or without a political angle, especially in times of polarisation and mounting political tensions. It can help to unite us in our approach to the challenges we all face.

Conclusion

"Twenty-five years ago people could be excused for not knowing much, or doing much, about climate change. Today we have no excuses."

Desmond Tutu, in *The Guardian*, 10 April 2014

In 2015, former California governor, ex-film star and bodybuilder, Arnold Schwarzenegger, wrote a message on his Facebook page that included a question he said required a bit of "imagination". "There are two doors," Schwarzenegger wrote. "Behind door number 1 is a completely sealed room, with a regular, gasolene-fueled car. Behind door number 2 is an identical, completely sealed room, with an electric car. Both engines are running full blast. I want you to pick a door to open, and enter the room and shut the door behind you. You have to stay in the room you choose for one hour. You cannot turn off the engine. You do not get a gas mask. I'm guessing you chose door number 2, with the electric car, right? Door number 1 is a fatal choice – who would ever want to breathe those fumes? This is the choice the world is making right now."[1]

A powerful analogy from this man who, for years, has been trying to convince world leaders and people worldwide to join him in a smarter, cleaner, healthier and more profitable energy future. If you read his entire speech, it is hard to say that global warming is not that bad and that we do not need to change our way of life. Like 'Arnie', I believe climate change is a major crisis. Indeed, apart from the possibility of a nuclear war, it is probably the most defining development for global security.

That is because we are emitting so many greenhouse gases into our atmosphere that the climate is warming dangerously, resulting in much more frequent extreme weather events such as drought, flooding and severe storms. Many people on our planet are now affected by natural disasters and can barely survive in coastal and arid areas. Nearly every day, there are alarming reports of natural disasters, melting polar ice and growing desertification. Climate change is thus affecting our security at global, regional and local level.

Global impact

At the global level, we see that the most vulnerable countries are being particularly hard hit by climate change. Parts of those countries are now at risk of becoming uninhabitable due to temperatures of up to 50 degrees Celsius or increasing frequency of drought and flooding. This has huge humanitarian repercussions and widens the gap between rich and poor. In addition, climate change is making raw materials in vulnerable countries increasingly scarce and the countries themselves are at risk of becoming a battleground for large, affluent countries competing for those resources.

Melting polar ice also has major global implications. For Russia, for example, the faster the ice melts, the better, as it opens up new ocean routes that Russia has always dreamed of. Russia's grain supplies have also given it a position of power over a commodity that African countries desperately need because of drought and the conflict in Ukraine. And what about the natural resources that are now becoming accessible because of the melting ice? That is something China has on its radar too. All in all, climate change is creating a need for geopolitical and strategic reorientation.

Vulnerable countries

At regional level, climate change acts primarily as a catalyst – a risk multiplier – for security risks of all kinds. More and more people on our planet are affected by natural disasters, increasing desertification and flooding, and can barely survive in their native areas. This makes people desperate and causes major internal tensions that can soon escalate into local conflicts.

In Niger, for example, about half of young people are under the age of 15. In situations where people, especially youngsters, have no prospects, they are susceptible to hateful ideologies and criminal alternatives that appear to offer a way out and hope for a better future. Climate-sensitive areas are thus breeding grounds for extremists, local power brokers and organised crime.

For criminals and extremists, this makes climate change a fantastic tool, a weapon in fact, to make more money, recruit more people and gain more power. We are now also seeing what is being called a "water mafia" emerging in many places, such as Pakistan and India. These are people who buy up water sources for their own gain and sell bottles of water at over-inflated prices to people fleeing the effects of climate change.

Iraq and Syria – like Somalia and Afghanistan – are examples of countries where a toxic cocktail of vulnerabilities already existed and where drought, and the ensuing water shortage, have just reinforced the negative spiral. The result was widespread misery, not only for the local population, but also for the international community, which was faced with refugee flows, attacks and the recruitment of fighters among its people.

Higher temperatures, drought-stricken farmland and extreme weather are driving food prices up even further. Farmers and pastoralists are forced to seek refuge elsewhere. Such desperation and lack of prospects are expected to trigger an unprecedented wave of migration, especially from Africa. The World Bank predicted a few years ago that by 2050, less than 30 years from now, the world will have more than 216 million 'climate refugees' in six regions of the world.[2] In other words, people moving to cities and fleeing to other countries, all looking for a place to survive.

Young people and women in the most vulnerable countries are hardest hit. For example, UNICEF pointed out that the aftermath of the floods in Pakistan in the summer of 2022 was more deadly than the flooding itself. In Pakistan, four million children were still living near stagnant and polluted water months after the flood, with many of them suffering from respiratory infections, a leading cause of child mortality. Nearly 10 million children in Pakistan needed urgent help to survive the winter.[3]

Climate change not only threatens many human lives, but it also undermines local economic growth and stability, which has direct implications for our own stability and security too. There is actually a direct and growing relationship between climate security in vulnerable regions and our own security. So we cannot tell ourselves we are safe behind dykes and national borders. If we do not do all we can to counter the disruptive effects of climate change and make vulnerable countries more resilient, we will be overwhelmed by the effects eventually.

It is understandable, therefore, that institutions such as the World Bank and IMF are under growing pressure to provide more funds for climate adaptation.[4] It is in our own interest to help the vulnerable regions around us increase their resilience to the impact of climate change. Waiting just leads to more symptom relief and there will be a much higher price to pay.

Crippling conflicts

The Russian invasion of Ukraine is also generating many climate-related effects. For instance, it led to an unprecedented energy crisis in Europe, major disruptions in global food chains and significant local environmental damage. Water dams and power plants became Russian targets in order to break the economy and resistance in Ukraine. The massive destruction of all that infrastructure has resulted in unprecedented environmental damage. Indeed, agricultural land has been rendered useless by pollution and minefields, the supply of drinking water for parts of the population is at risk, and a huge cash-guzzling reconstruction operation will be needed after the conflict ends, putting enormous additional pressure on European economies as well.

In Europe, polluting coal-fired power plants had to be restarted, albeit temporarily, but we also saw how the energy transition moved up a gear to reduce our dependency on fossil fuel supplies; solar panels, wind turbines and heat pumps have suddenly become matters of national security. Calls for European and national autonomy are growing louder, as war is showing us that dependencies on countries like Russia and China can also be used against us as a vulnerability. This in turn fuels geopolitical competition for access to resources.

This is creating a new geopolitical situation in which major powers are shuffling the cards and we find ourselves in a world of sharp contrasts and rival blocs. It is a disunity that simultaneously has a paralysing effect on, for instance, the work of multilateral UN institutions that can only take decisions by consensus, precisely at a time when it is vital to be able to reach international agreements on global problems that individual countries alone cannot solve.

To govern is to foresee

Clearly, the West – like resource giant China that appears to be doing so well – needs to think and act strategically, in terms of a hundred years or more. Then we need to acknowledge that greater independence is of strategic value, but that everything in the world is interconnected and no country can completely isolate itself from the rest of the world. There is a huge political dilemma between competing harder with each other to increase our own autonomy and the need to arrive at common global solutions.

We also need to realise that we are heading towards a dead end. There is a finite availability of scarce raw materials and fiercer competition will not solve that. We will have to reduce our dependence on raw materials to avoid further crises. This can only be done by transforming our current consumer economy into a circular economy. Currently, only 9% of the many billions of tons of raw materials are reused. The vast majority of all products we use today end up being discarded, creating polluting emissions and waste.[5] So let us come up with creative solutions for circularity and for reducing the use of scarce raw materials. Only then can we make our economies more self-sufficient and reduce our fragile dependencies.

We must also accept that it cannot be left to one ministry or a single organisation to slow down global warming and deal with the effects of climate change. It is a broad issue that affects not only all countries and ministries, but also the business sector and every society. Just as war is too important to "leave to the generals", as French statesman Georges Clemenceau once so aptly said, we cannot leave the impact of climate change to a climate minister. We will need to establish this global challenge internationally as a central and common goal and pool our resources accordingly.

Far-reaching forms of collaboration

In the fight against the effects of climate change, military forces worldwide are indispensable partners for world leaders. While climate change is not a military problem, it does lead to increased human suffering and insecurity, and is therefore also a matter of national and international security. Military forces can contribute in many ways, as I describe in the second part of this book. For instance, they can help increase predictive capability through analyses by security services. In other words, where will climate change lead to a greater likelihood of conflict, migration flows or extremism? That information will enhance governments' anticipatory capabilities.

Furthermore, military forces can make a significant contribution towards reducing CO_2 emissions and resource consumption. In almost all countries, military forces are the biggest polluters. Sustainability and climate security should therefore become an integral part of the strategy, doctrines and organisational development of military forces and the configuration of operational missions. This should obviously not be at the expense of the deployability of those military forces or their ability to ensure our security.

It is important that armed forces see sustainability not as a cost, but as an opportunity to innovate. New green technologies in areas such as energy supply, water production and 3D printing of spare parts enable operational units to become more self-sufficient and reduce their footprint, thereby offering huge operational benefits. The Defence organisation could be a kind of innovation platform to work with industry and knowledge institutes to develop new, more self-sufficient concepts that not only have added value in military terms, but are also more widely applicable.

Military forces will also need to further professionalise civil-military cooperation in disaster response in both national and international contexts. This is necessary to deal effectively with the impact of natural disasters and other consequences of a changing climate. An integrated disaster response requires integrated preparation and the ability to pool resources quickly. Also in the wider adaptation efforts in the fragile regions around us, military forces can help to reduce any tensions.

All these transitions require us to invest in and provide space for new initiatives and experiments, even though we cannot always be sure in advance whether they will really work, or what the precise effects will be. Ground-breaking innovations are almost always a result of trial and error, of courage and perseverance, of thinking big and starting small, and of working with unknown partners.

Work for the best, prepare for the worst

We all have a piece of the solution in our hands. The trick is to put the right pieces together in new and effective solutions. This is only possible if you are willing to think outside the box and seek collaboration. In fact, it is the ultimate test of leadership: will world leaders succeed in putting the health of future generations ahead of short-term interests?

World leaders should, in fact, wage a real war. I do not mean a battle between peoples or countries in the original sense of the word, nor a mobilisation in which the economy is transformed into a wartime economy aimed at producing military materiel, ammunition and equipment for the umpteen thousands of military personnel called up for duty. By war I mean the battle that we are fighting together against the degradation of the earth. A radical change in the global economy and the way we live, in which a rapid reduction in global CO_2 emissions is a crucial first step to prevent the situation from getting any worse. Drawing on my military experience, my aim in this book is to show that climate change is much more than an ecological problem;

that it is also a source and driver of conflict. And that countering climate change also contributes to our security. It does not paint an optimistic picture, but I am convinced that together we can win the war on climate change. Together, we can stop the negative spiral of the changing climate and be more resilient to its worsening adverse effects.

I have great faith in our ability to survive and innovate, but we should not wait until it is too late. This means we need to look ahead, rise above the issues of the day, invest in our children's future and, above all, be willing to bridge divides and reach out to each other in the fight against this common enemy.

We can and should all contribute to this in our own environment as the inspiring examples in this book show; after all, many little drops make a river.

It is simply no longer an option to sit back and wait. Not for any country. That would be like jumping out of a plane without a parachute, hoping someone will catch you on the way. We are facing a state of emergency. All of us. And if we do not reduce our emissions of CO_2 quickly and drastically while the earth continues to warm, we will saddle our children and grandchildren with a much bigger problem and with less time and opportunity to repair the damage we have caused. We must therefore take all the signs seriously now, join forces, increase our knowledge and work on big and small solutions. Under the motto: work for the best, prepare for the worst.

Notes

1. Arnold Schwarzenegger (2015, December 7). I don't give a **** if we agree about climate change. Facebook, https://www.facebook.com/notes/10158687852561760/

2. Clement, V., Kanta Kumari, R., de Sherbinin, A., Jones, B., Adamo, S., Schewe, J., Sadiq, N., Shabahat, E. (2021), 'Groundswell Part 2: Acting on Internal Climate Migration', World Bank, Washington DC, https://openknowledge.worldbank.org/handle/10986/36248

3. UNICEF (2023, 9 January), 'Up to 4 million children in Pakistan still living next to stagnant and contaminated floodwater', https://www.unicef.org/press-releases/4-million-children-pakistan-still-living-next-stagnant-and-contaminated-floodwater

4. Beunderman, M. (2023, 16 April), 'IMF and World Bank walking on eggshells due to political tensions and climate threat', NRC, https://www.nrc.nl/nieuws/2023/04/16/imf-en-wereldbank-lopen-op-eieren-door-politieke-spanningen-en-klimaatdreiging-a4162195

5. Kunzig, R. (2022, 19 April). 'Is a world without waste possible?' *National Geographic*, https://www.nationalgeographic.nl/natuur-leefomgeving/2020/05/is-een-wereld-zonder-afval-mogelijk

Abbreviations

3D	Defence, Diplomacy and Development
ACLED	Armed Conflict Location and Event Database
AFRICOM	African Command
ASLCG	Australian Security Leaders Climate Group
AU	African Union
CAR	Central African Republic
CDS	Chief of Defence
CILSS	Comité permanent inter-Etat de lutte contre la sécheresse au Sahel [Permanent Interstate Committee for drought control in the Sahel]
ECB	European Central Bank
eFP	enhanced Forward Presence
EJF	Environmental Justice Foundation
EU	European Union
FAO	Food and Agriculture Organization (UN)
FFC	Future Force Conference
GCA	Global Center on Adaptation
HCSS	The Hague Centre for Strategic Studies
HDV	Advanced Defence Studies
HMV	Advanced Military Studies (later replaced by the HDV)
ICG	International Crisis Group
IEA	International Energy Agency
IHE Delft	IHE Delft Institute for Water Education (formerly IHE/UNESCO)
IMAU	Institute for Marine and Atmospheric Research
IMCCS	International Military Council on Climate and Security
IPCC	Intergovernmental Panel on Climate Change
IS	Islamic State (also called ISIL, ISIS or Da'esh); read ISIS
ISAF	International Security Assistance Force
ISIS	Islamic State of Iraq and Syria; also called IS, ISIL or Da'esh;
IUCN	International Union for the Conservation of Nature
KNMI	Royal Netherlands Meteorological Institute

KMA	Royal Military Academy
MARIN	Maritime Research Institute of the Netherlands
MINUSMA	Multidimensional Integrated Stabilisation Mission in Mali (UN)
NATO	North Atlantic Treaty Organisation
NCAR	National Center for Atmospheric Research
NGO	Non-governmental organisation
OPCW	Organisation for the Prohibition of Chemical Weapons
OSCE	Organisation for Security and Cooperation in Europe
PBL	Netherlands Environmental Assessment Agency
PIK	Potsdam Institute for Climate Impact Research
PLAN International	formerly Foster Parents Plan
RVO	Netherlands Enterprise Agency
SIPRI	Stockholm International Peace Research Institute
SOP	Standard Operating Procedure
UNDRR	United Nations Office for Disaster Risk Reduction
UNHCR	United Nations High Commissioner for Refugees
UNEP	United Nations Environment Programme
UNODC	United Nations Office on Drugs and Crime
UNSCEAR	United Nations Scientific Committee on the Effects of Atomic Radiation
UN	United Nations
US	United States
WEF	World Economic Forum
WFP	World Food Programme
WMO	World Meteorological Organization (UN)
WPS	Water, Peace and Security Initiative
WRI	World Resources Institute
WWF	World Wide Fund for Nature

About the authors

General **Tom Middendorp** has broad operational experience with extensive international components. He was deployed to Afghanistan in 2006-2007 as deputy ambassador to NATO, then in 2009 as commander of the Netherlands/Australian Task Force Uruzgan. As a Director of Operations, he was involved in more than 20 international missions before becoming Chief of Defence in 2017. He studied in the US Command and General Staff College, and was closely involved in the international strategy development for the fight against ISIS. He initiated close cooperation programs within the Benelux and between the Netherlands and Germany, leading to the integration of binational operational tactical units. Together with France, he worked on countering piracy in Somalia, operations in Libya and Mali, humanitarian operations in Ivory Coast, and disaster relief operations in the Caribbean. He received several international decorations including the French « commandeur de la Légion d'Honneur ».

After his military career, he dedicated himself to the issue of climate and security, working with the Clingendael Institute and The Hague Centre for Strategic Studies (HCSS). Since 2019, he has been the chairman of the International Military Council on Climate and Security (IMCCS), developing this network together with the former US Assistant Deputy Undersecretary of Defense, Mrs Sherri Goodman. The IMCCS is supported by a consortium of four research institutes in the US, France and The Netherlands, with 16 other research institutions from different continents affiliated.

He is a speaker at numerous international conferences, such as the Munich Security Forum, Berlin Defence and Security Conference, Austrian World Summit, NATO's Responsible Innovation Conference, World Defense Show *et cetera*.

Antonie van Campen is the former speechwriter of Tom Middendorp. They have known each other for many years. She wrote many of his speeches, her strength lying in storytelling. Together with his personal advisor, she helped to build his profile at home and abroad. Currently, she is a freelance speechwriter, and her writing talent is sought after by various ministers, companies, and organisations. Antonie was an important sounding board for Tom and a voice of the younger generation. She encouraged him to speak out in Halifax about the relationship between climate and security, and she wrote his speech for the Planetary Security Initiative at the Peace Palace, which earned him the nickname "climate general".

That lecture caused quite a stir, but she continued to support Tom in his commitment to this theme, even after he ended his position as Commander of the Armed Forces. When Tom was approached to write a book on this subject, he did not hesitate and asked Antonie to collaborate, as she knew his experience in and perspectives on the issue like no other.

This book, originally published in Dutch, in 2022, has been revised and updated for this edition, published simultaneously in French and English.

What to do with this book once you don't want it anymore?

1. Give it a second life

Extend the life span of this book by giving it to someone or to a charity or by reselling it. A book with little damage can still be useful before being thrown away.

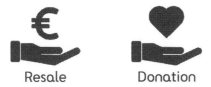

Resale   Donation

2. Recycle it well

If it has to be thrown away, put it in the recycling bin so that the paper it is made of can be reused. But be careful, it is important to remove recycling disruptors first:

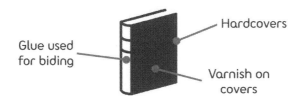

Hardcovers

Glue used for biding

Varnish on covers

To do this, simply remove its cover and put it in the bin for packagings and all the pages left in the waste paper bin.

Legal deposit: December 2023